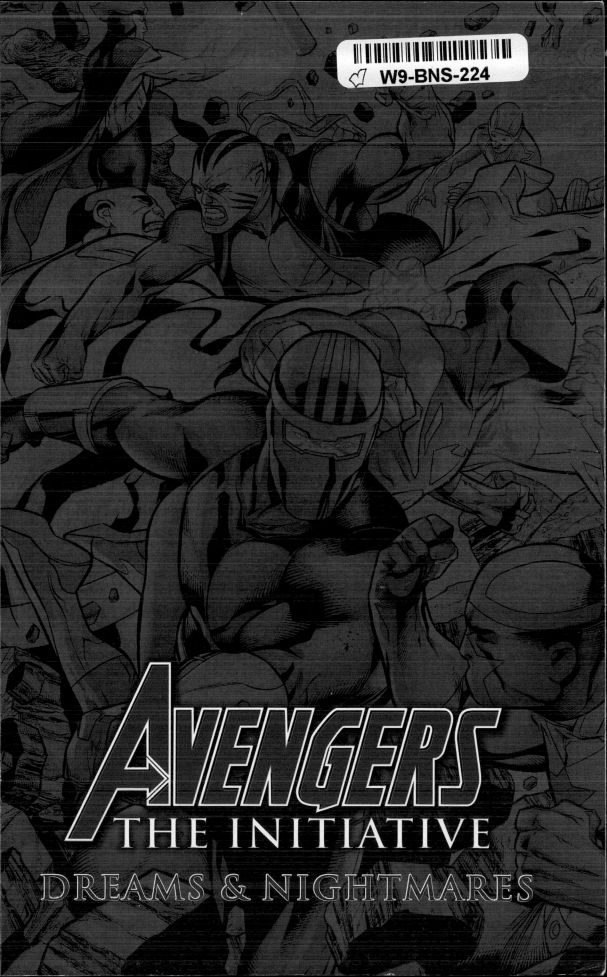

AVENGERS
THE INITIATIVE
DREAMS & NIGHTMARES

AVENGERS
THE INITIATIVE
DREAMS & NIGHTMARES

WRITER: CHRISTOS N. GAGE
PENCILERS: RAFA SANDOVAL
& JORGE MOLINA (ISSUES #29-30)
INKERS: ROGER BONET & VICTOR OLAZABA (ISSUES #29-30)
WITH ANDREW HENNESSY (ISSUE #30)
COLORISTS: EDGAR DELGADO
WITH BIT (ISSUE #30)
LETTERER: VIRTUAL CALLIGRAPHY'S JOE CARAMAGNA
COVER ART: MATTEO DE LONGIS & RAFA SANDOVAL (ISSUE #30)

ASSISTANT EDITORS: MICHAEL HORWITZ & RACHEL PINNELAS
EDITORS: BILL ROSEMANN WITH JEANINE SCHAEFER
EXECUTIVE EDITOR: TOM BREVOORT

COLLECTION EDITOR: JENNIFER GRÜNWALD
ASSISTANT EDITOR: ALEX STARBUCK
ASSOCIATE EDITOR: JOHN DENNING
EDITOR, SPECIAL PROJECTS: MARK D. BEAZLEY
SENIOR EDITOR, SPECIAL PROJECTS: JEFF YOUNGQUIST
SENIOR VICE PRESIDENT OF SALES: DAVID GABRIEL

EDITOR IN CHIEF: JOE QUESADA
PUBLISHER: DAN BUCKLEY
EXECUTIVE PRODUCER: ALAN FINE

AVENGERS: THE INITIATIVE — DREAMS & NIGHTMARES. Contains material originally published in magazine form as AVENGERS: THE INITIATIVE #26-30. First printing 2010. Hardcover ISBN# 978-0-7851-3904
Softcover ISBN# 978-0-7851-3905-8. Published by MARVEL WORLDWIDE, INC., a subsidiary of MARVEL ENTERTAINMENT, LLC. OFFICE OF PUBLICATION: 417 5th Avenue, New York, NY 10016. Copyright © 2009 and
2010 Marvel Characters, Inc. All rights reserved. Hardcover: $19.99 per copy in the U.S. (GST #R127032852). Softcover: $14.99 per copy in the U.S. (GST #R127032852). Canadian Agreement #40668537. All charact
featured in this issue and the distinctive names and likenesses thereof, and all related indicia are trademarks of Marvel Characters, Inc. No similarity between any of the names, characters, persons, and/or institutio
in this magazine with those of any living or dead person or institution is intended, and any such similarity which may exist is purely coincidental. Printed in the U.S.A. ALAN FINE, EVP - Office of the President, Mar
Worldwide, Inc. and EVP & CMO Marvel Characters B.V.; DAN BUCKLEY, Chief Executive Officer and Publisher - Print, Animation & Digital Media; JIM SOKOLOWSKI, Chief Operating Officer; DAVID GABRIEL, SVP of Publishi
Sales & Circulation; DAVID BOGART, SVP of Business Affairs & Talent Management; MICHAEL PASCIULLO, VP Merchandising & Communications; JIM O'KEEFE, VP of Operations & Logistics; DAN CARR, Executive Direc
of Publishing Technology; JUSTIN F. GABRIE, Director of Publishing & Editorial Operations; SUSAN CRESPI, Editorial Operations Manager; ALEX MORALES, Publishing Operations Manager; STAN LEE, Chairman Emerit
For information regarding advertising in Marvel Comics or on Marvel.com, please contact Ron Stern, VP of Business Development, at rstern@marvel.com. For Marvel subscription inquiries, please call 800-217-91
Manufactured between 2/8/2010 and 3/10/2010 (hardcover), and 2/8/2010 and 9/8/2010 (softcover), by R.R. DONNELLEY, INC., SALEM, VA, USA.

10 9 8 7 6 5 4 3 2 1

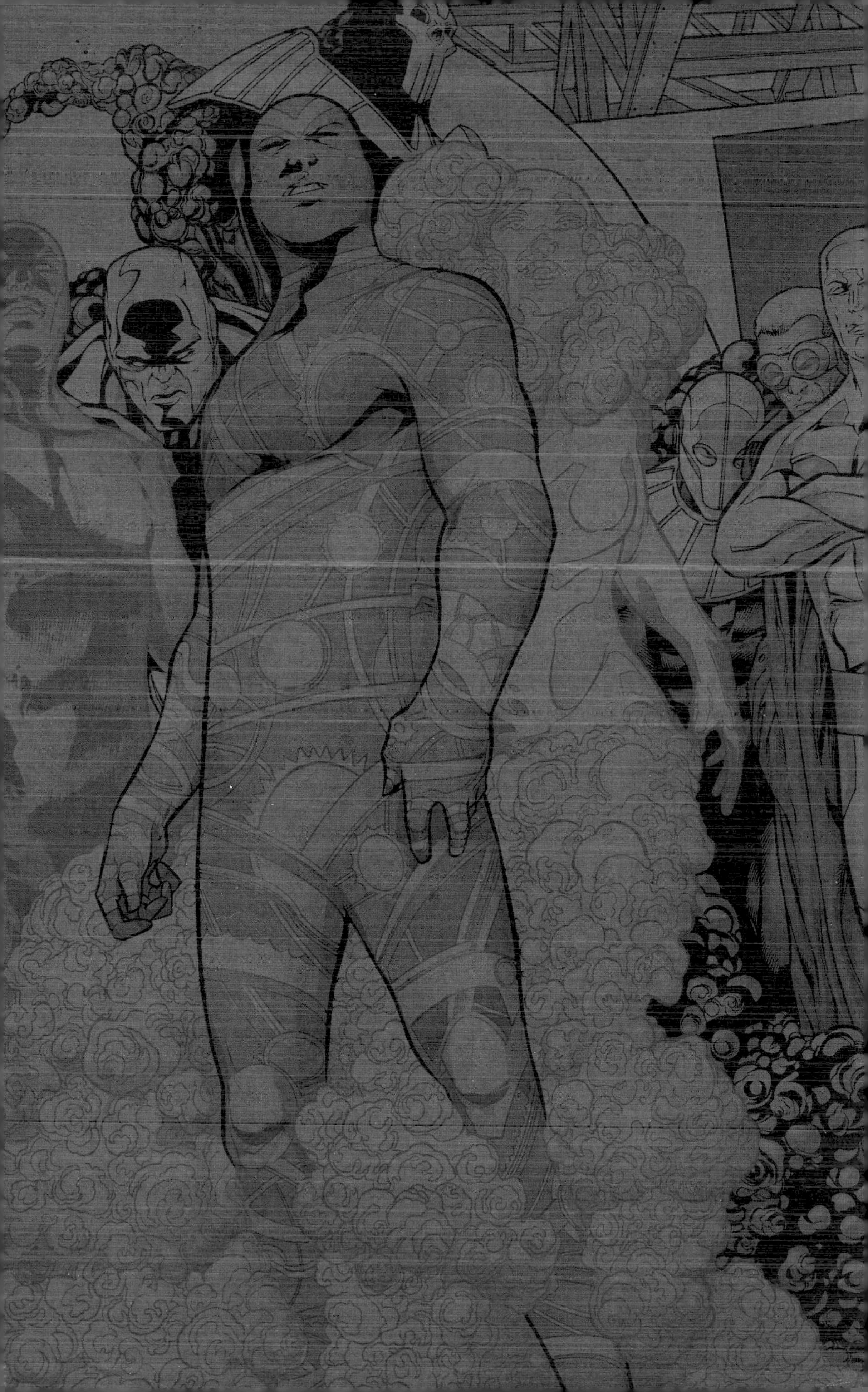

AVENGERS THE INITIATIVE

AFTER STAMFORD, CONNECTICUT WAS DESTROYED DURING A TELEVISED FIGHT BETWEEN THE NEW WARRIORS AND A GROUP OF DANGEROUS VILLAINS, A FEDERAL SUPERHUMAN REGISTRATION ACT WAS PASSED. ALL INDIVIDUALS POSSESSING PARANORMAL ABILITIES MUST NOW REGISTER WITH THE GOVERNMENT. TONY STARK, A.K.A. IRON MAN, HAS BEEN APPOINTED DIRECTOR OF S.H.I.E.L.D., THE INTERNATIONAL PEACEKEEPING FORCE. HE HAS SET IN MOTION THE INITIATIVE, A PLAN FOR TRAINING AND POLICING SUPER HEROES IN THIS BRAVE NEW WORLD, INTENDED TO POSITION A LOCAL SUPER HERO TEAM IN EACH OF AMERICA S FIFTY STATES.

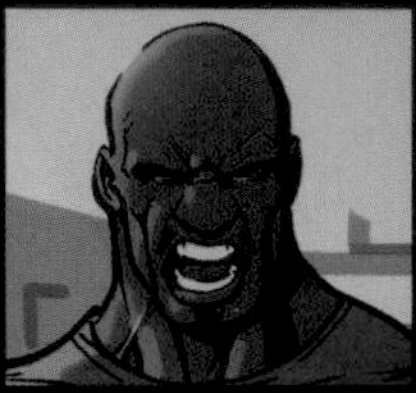

GAUNTLET

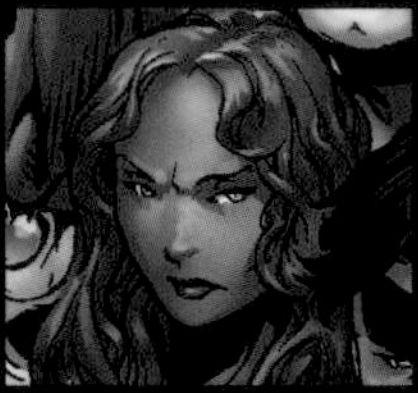

TIGRA

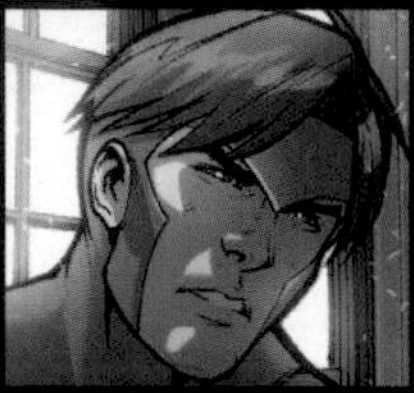

JUSTICE

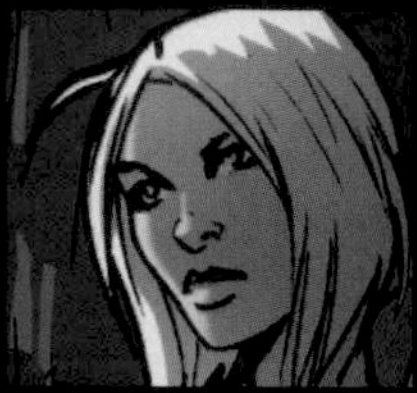

ULTRAGIRL

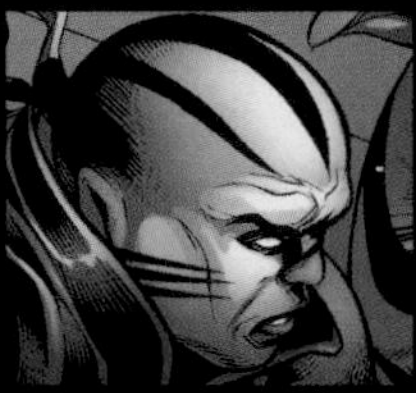

RAGE

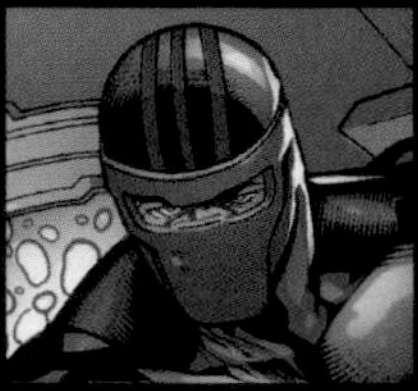

NIGHT THRASHER

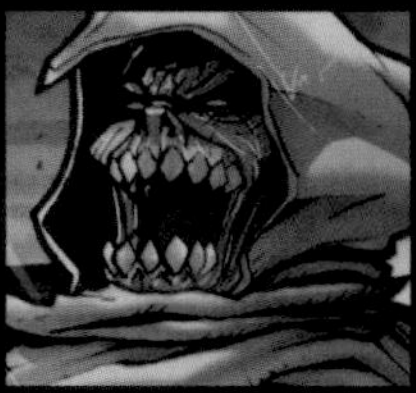

TASKMASTER

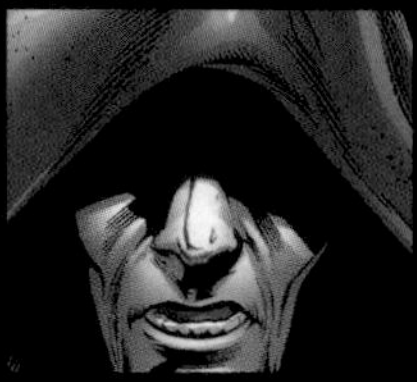

THE HOOD

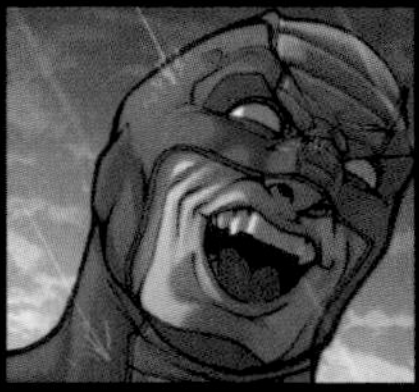

CONSTRICTOR

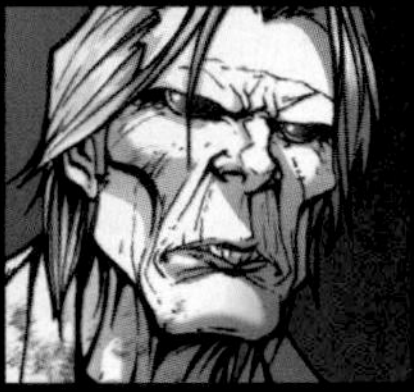

BARON VON BLITZSCHLAG

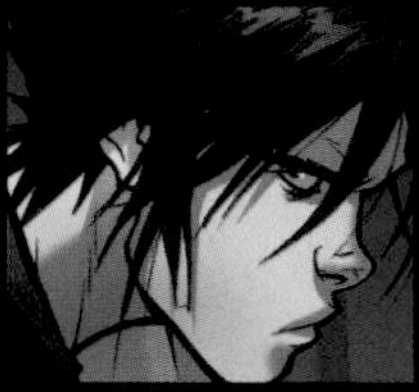

TRAUMA

In the aftermath of the Skrull invasion, Tony Stark, the father of the Initiative, has been removed from his position as Director of S.H.I.E.L.D. and replaced by Norman Osborn, formerly the villainous Green Goblin. Osborn immediately dissolved S.H.I.E.L.D., replacing it with his own taskforce, H.A.M.M.E.R., and shut down the Initiative as we know it!

Its members aren t faring so well, either: After Osborn threatened the life of Tigra s unborn baby and Gauntlet was told he would have to have his arm surgically removed, they re both on the run. Good thing the New Warriors are also on the lam, because they arrived just in time to stop the Hood s gang, on loan to Norman, from catching them!

They ve formed an underground alliance, and they re going to get the Initiative back from Norman no matter what it takes!

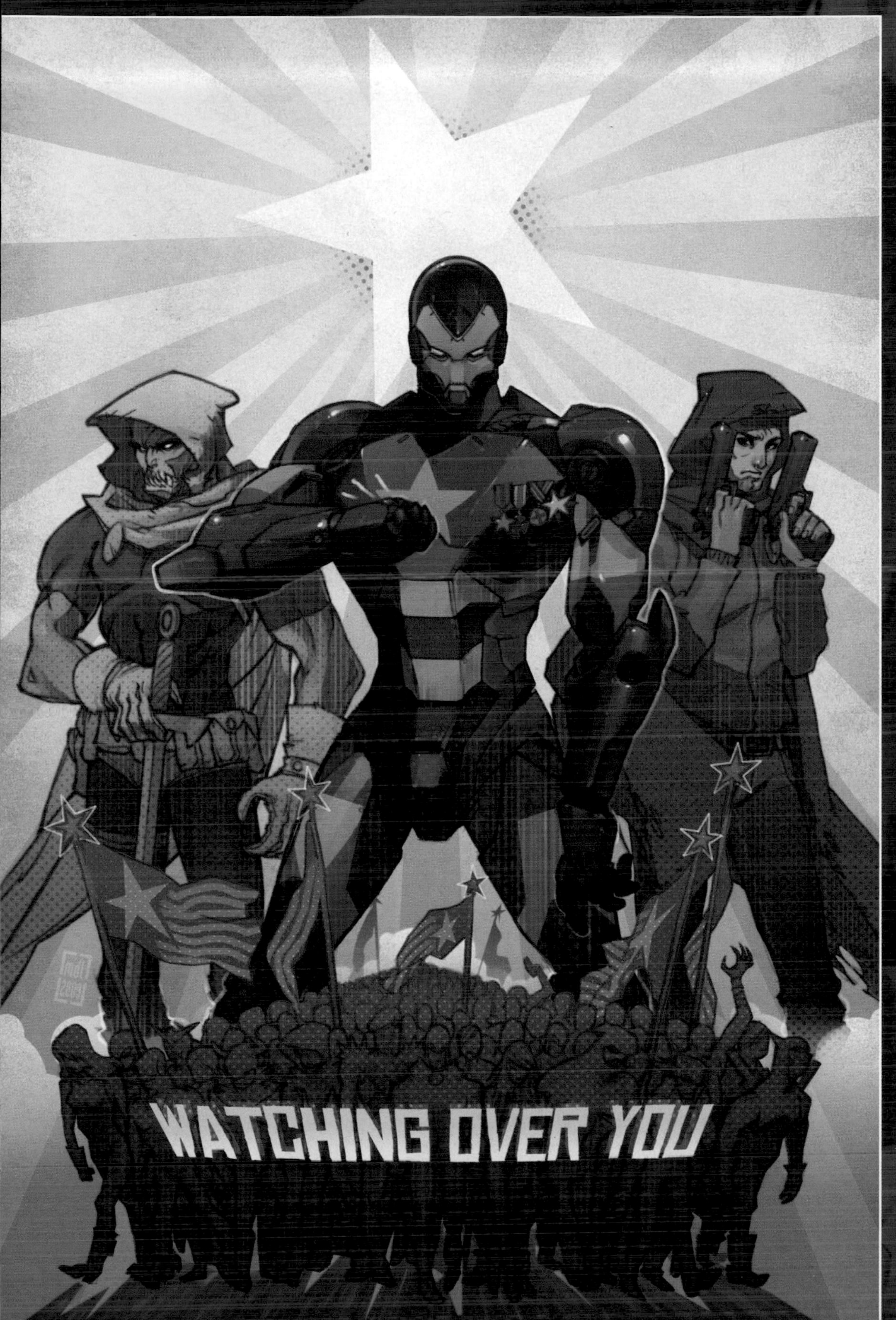
WATCHING OVER YOU

#26

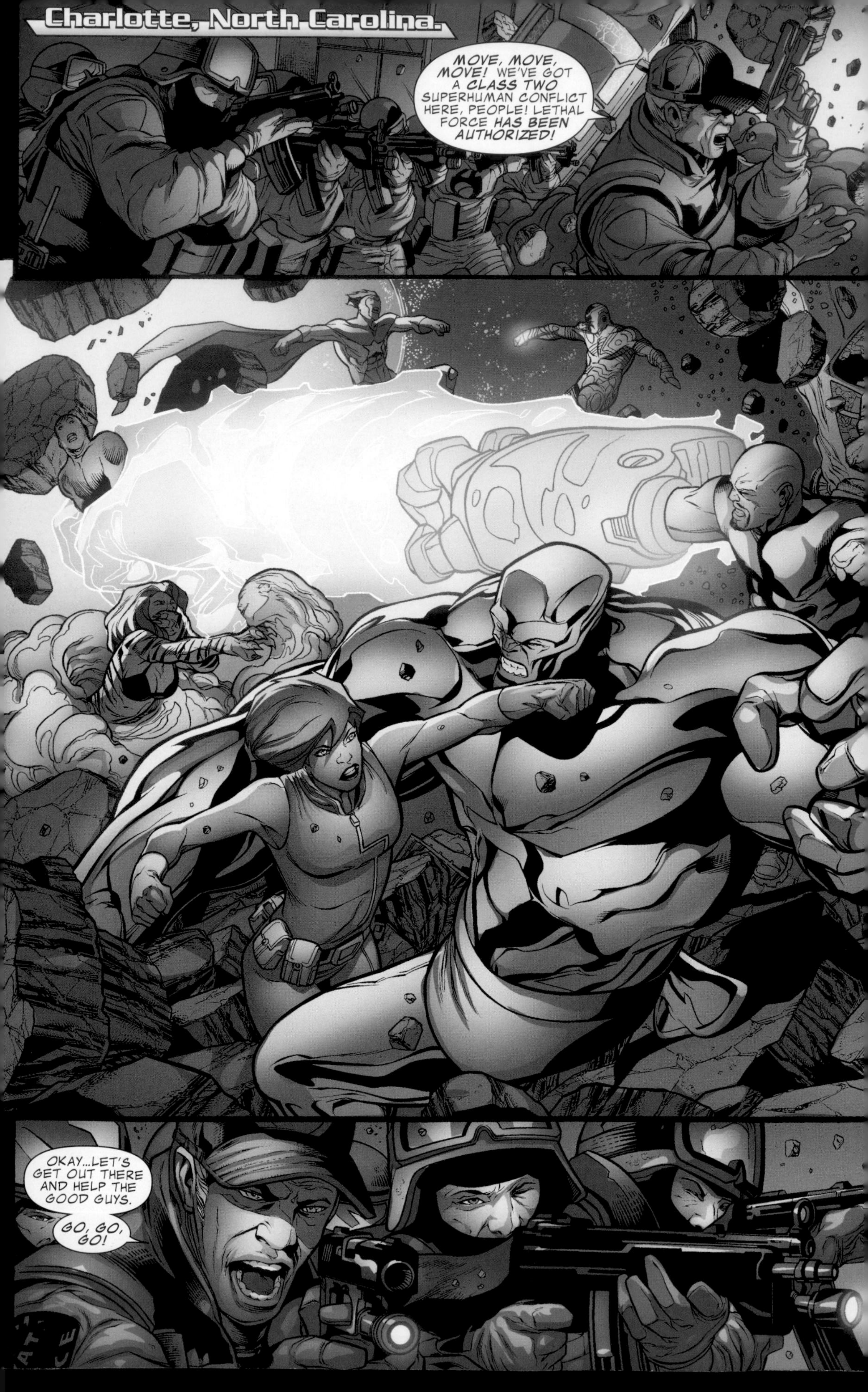
Charlotte, North Carolina.
MOVE, MOVE, MOVE! WE'VE GOT A CLASS TWO SUPERHUMAN CONFLICT HERE, PEOPLE! LETHAL FORCE HAS BEEN AUTHORIZED!
OKAY...LET'S GET OUT THERE AND HELP THE GOOD GUYS.
GO, GO, GO!

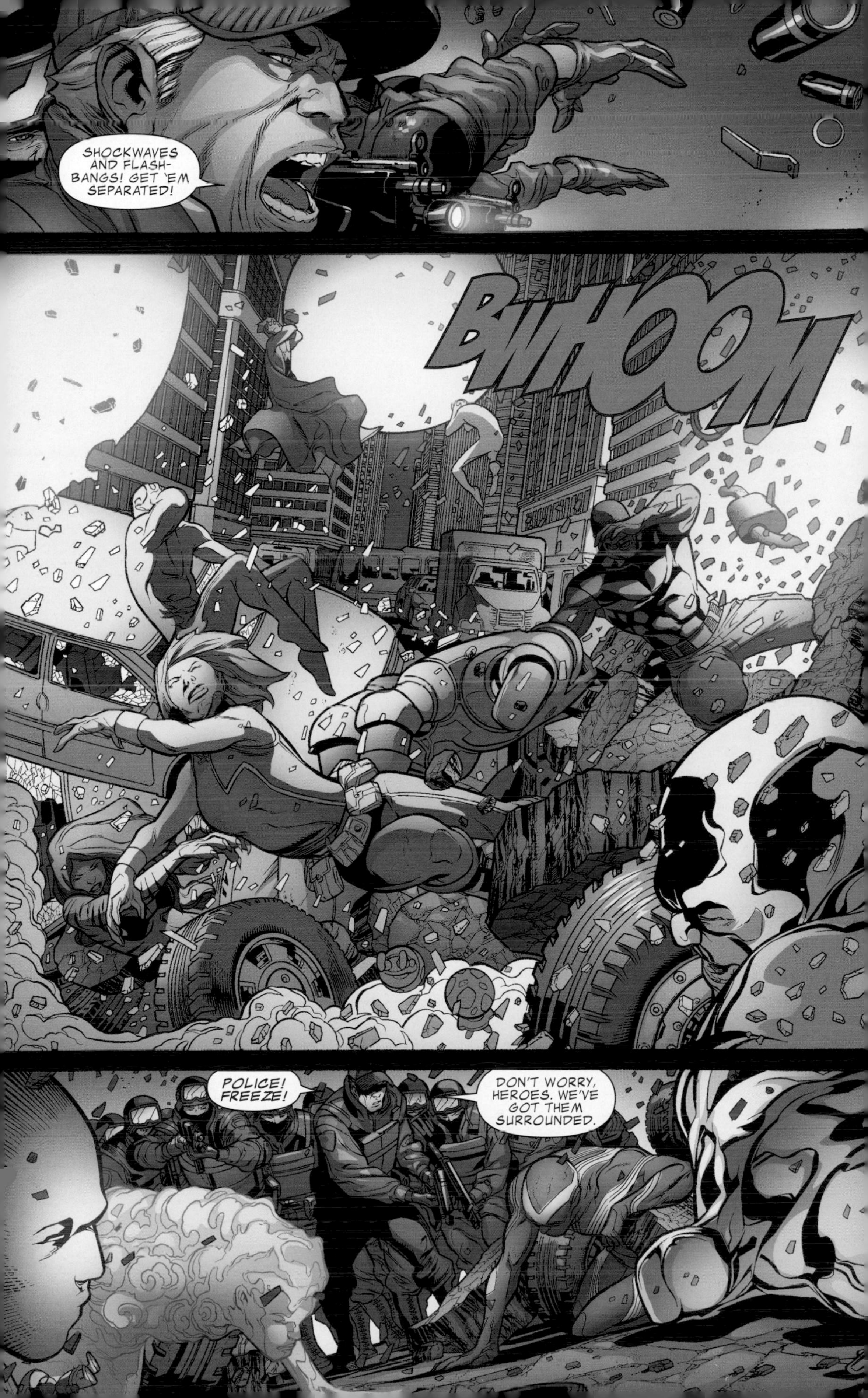
SHOCKWAVES AND FLASH-BANGS! GET 'EM SEPARATED!
BWHOOM
POLICE! FREEZE!
DON'T WORRY, HEROES. WE'VE GOT THEM SURROUNDED.

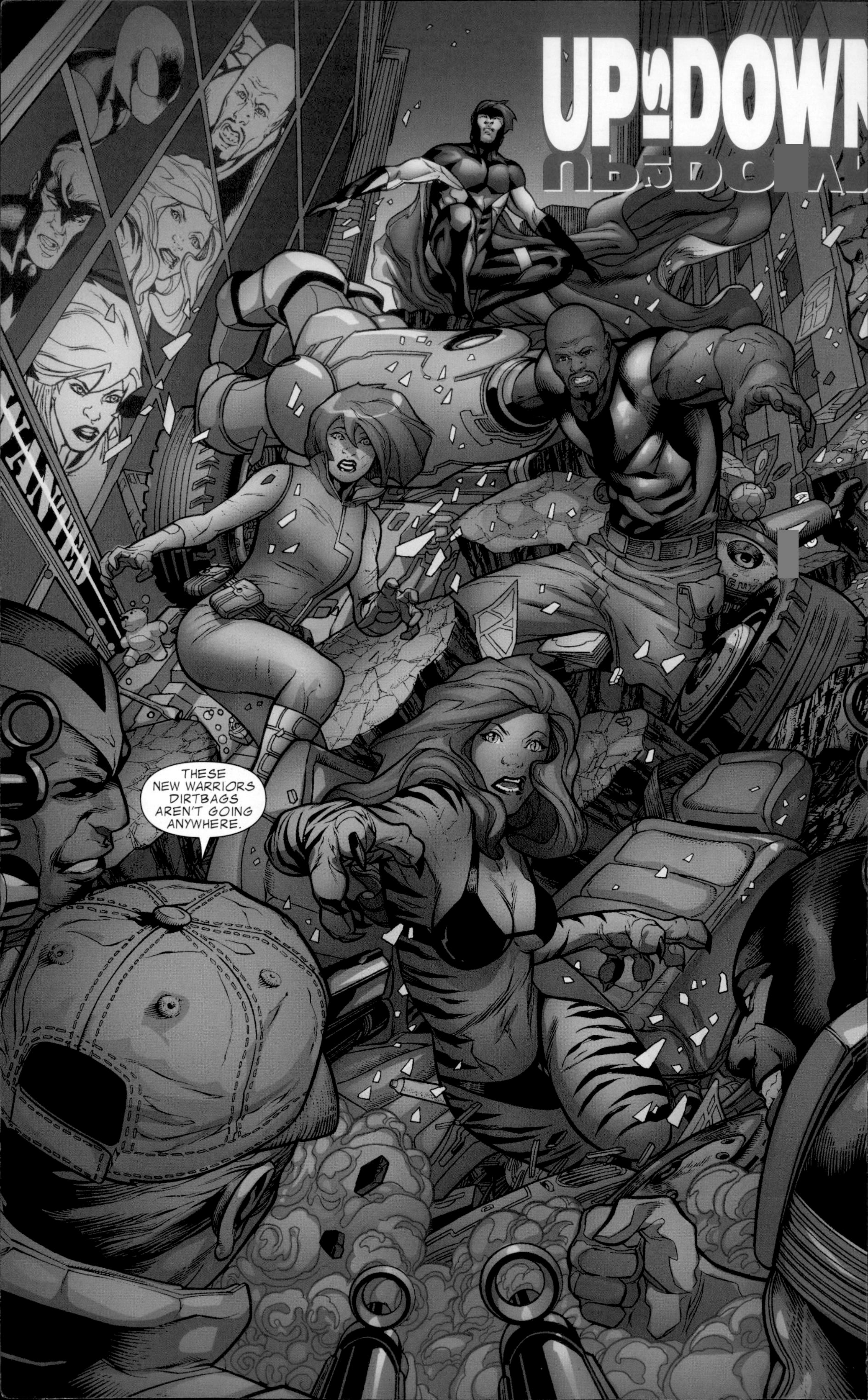
UP IS DOWN
THESE NEW WARRIORS DIRTBAGS AREN'T GOING ANYWHERE.

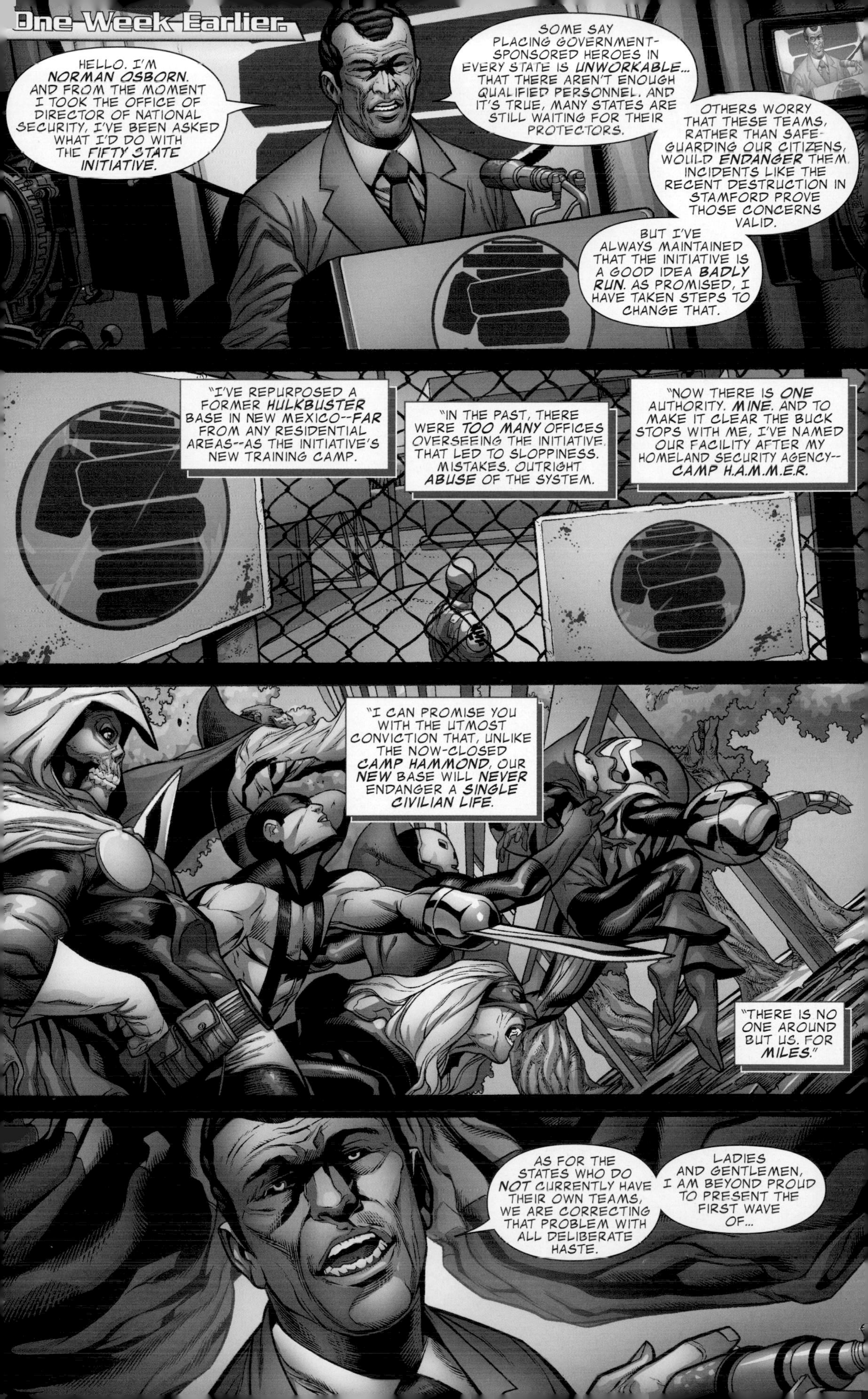

One Week Earlier.
HELLO. I'M NORMAN OSBORN. AND FROM THE MOMENT I TOOK THE OFFICE OF DIRECTOR OF NATIONAL SECURITY, I'VE BEEN ASKED WHAT I'D DO WITH THE FIFTY STATE INITIATIVE.
SOME SAY PLACING GOVERNMENT-SPONSORED HEROES IN EVERY STATE IS UNWORKABLE... THAT THERE AREN'T ENOUGH QUALIFIED PERSONNEL. AND IT'S TRUE, MANY STATES ARE STILL WAITING FOR THEIR PROTECTORS.
OTHERS WORRY THAT THESE TEAMS, RATHER THAN SAFE-GUARDING OUR CITIZENS, WOULD ENDANGER THEM. INCIDENTS LIKE THE RECENT DESTRUCTION IN STAMFORD PROVE THOSE CONCERNS VALID.
BUT I'VE ALWAYS MAINTAINED THAT THE INITIATIVE IS A GOOD IDEA BADLY RUN. AS PROMISED, I HAVE TAKEN STEPS TO CHANGE THAT.
"I'VE REPURPOSED A FORMER HULKBUSTER BASE IN NEW MEXICO--FAR FROM ANY RESIDENTIAL AREAS--AS THE INITIATIVE'S NEW TRAINING CAMP.
"IN THE PAST, THERE WERE TOO MANY OFFICES OVERSEEING THE INITIATIVE. THAT LED TO SLOPPINESS. MISTAKES. OUTRIGHT ABUSE OF THE SYSTEM.
"NOW THERE IS ONE AUTHORITY. MINE. AND TO MAKE IT CLEAR THE BUCK STOPS WITH ME, I'VE NAMED OUR FACILITY AFTER MY HOMELAND SECURITY AGENCY--CAMP H.A.M.M.E.R.
"I CAN PROMISE YOU WITH THE UTMOST CONVICTION THAT, UNLIKE THE NOW-CLOSED CAMP HAMMOND, OUR NEW BASE WILL NEVER ENDANGER A SINGLE CIVILIAN LIFE.
"THERE IS NO ONE AROUND BUT US. FOR MILES."
AS FOR THE STATES WHO DO NOT CURRENTLY HAVE THEIR OWN TEAMS, WE ARE CORRECTING THAT PROBLEM WITH ALL DELIBERATE HASTE.
LADIES AND GENTLEMEN, I AM BEYOND PROUD TO PRESENT THE FIRST WAVE OF...

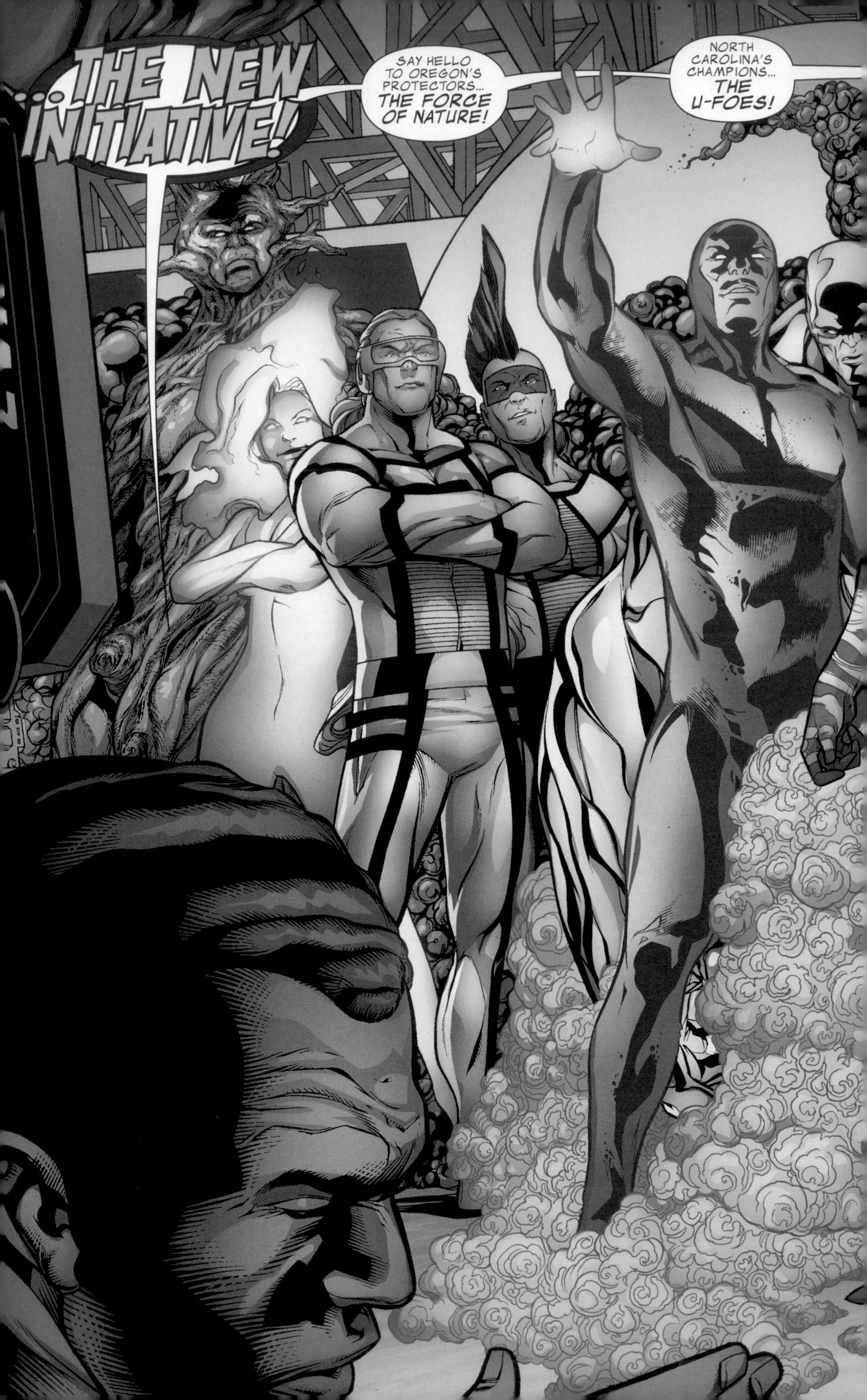
...THE NEW INITIATIVE!
SAY HELLO TO OREGON'S PROTECTORS... THE FORCE OF NATURE!
NORTH CAROLINA'S CHAMPIONS... THE U-FOES!

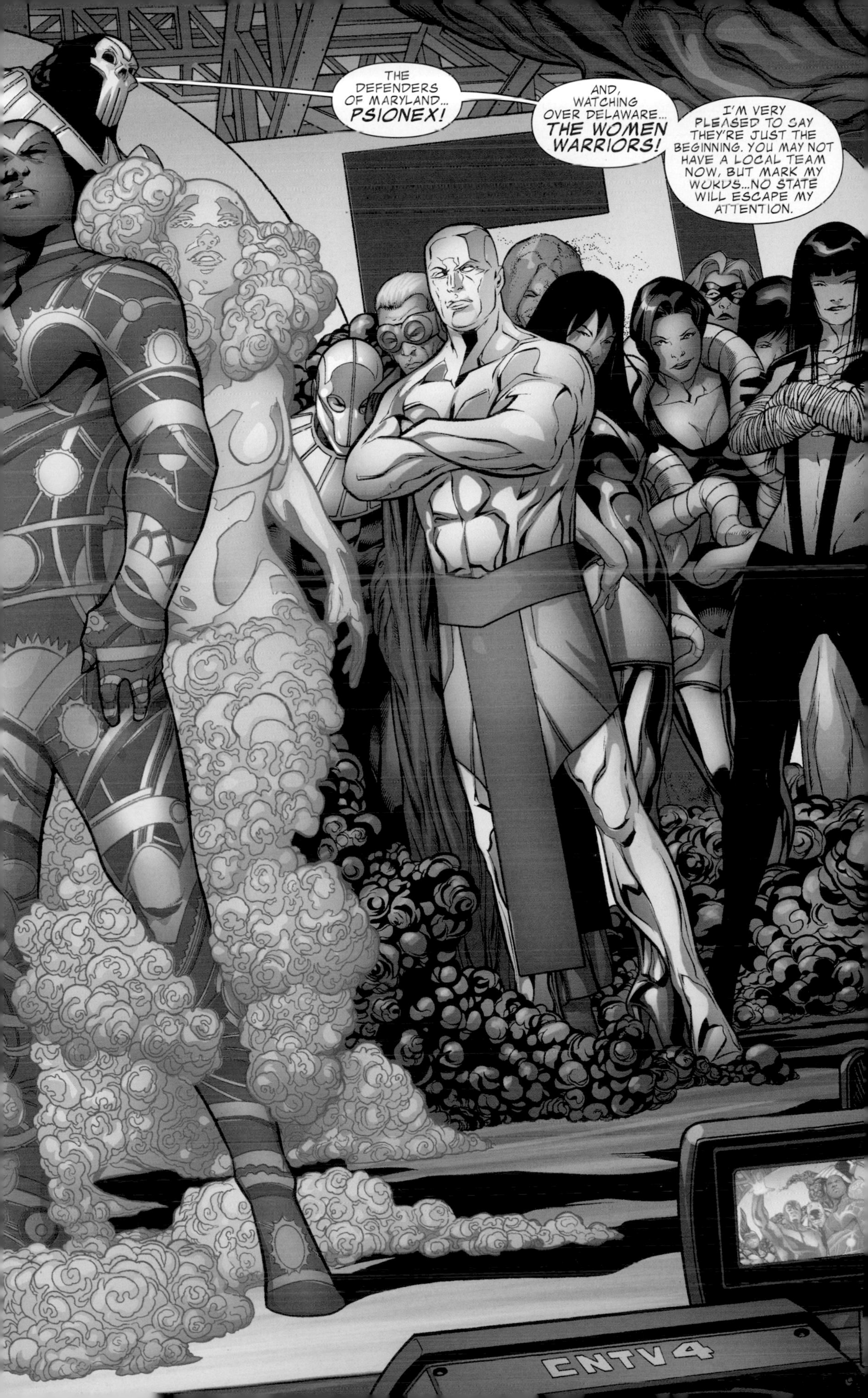
THE DEFENDERS OF MARYLAND... PSIONEX!
AND, WATCHING OVER DELAWARE... THE WOMEN WARRIORS!
I'M VERY PLEASED TO SAY THEY'RE JUST THE BEGINNING. YOU MAY NOT HAVE A LOCAL TEAM NOW, BUT MARK MY WORDS...NO STATE WILL ESCAPE MY ATTENTION.
CNTV4

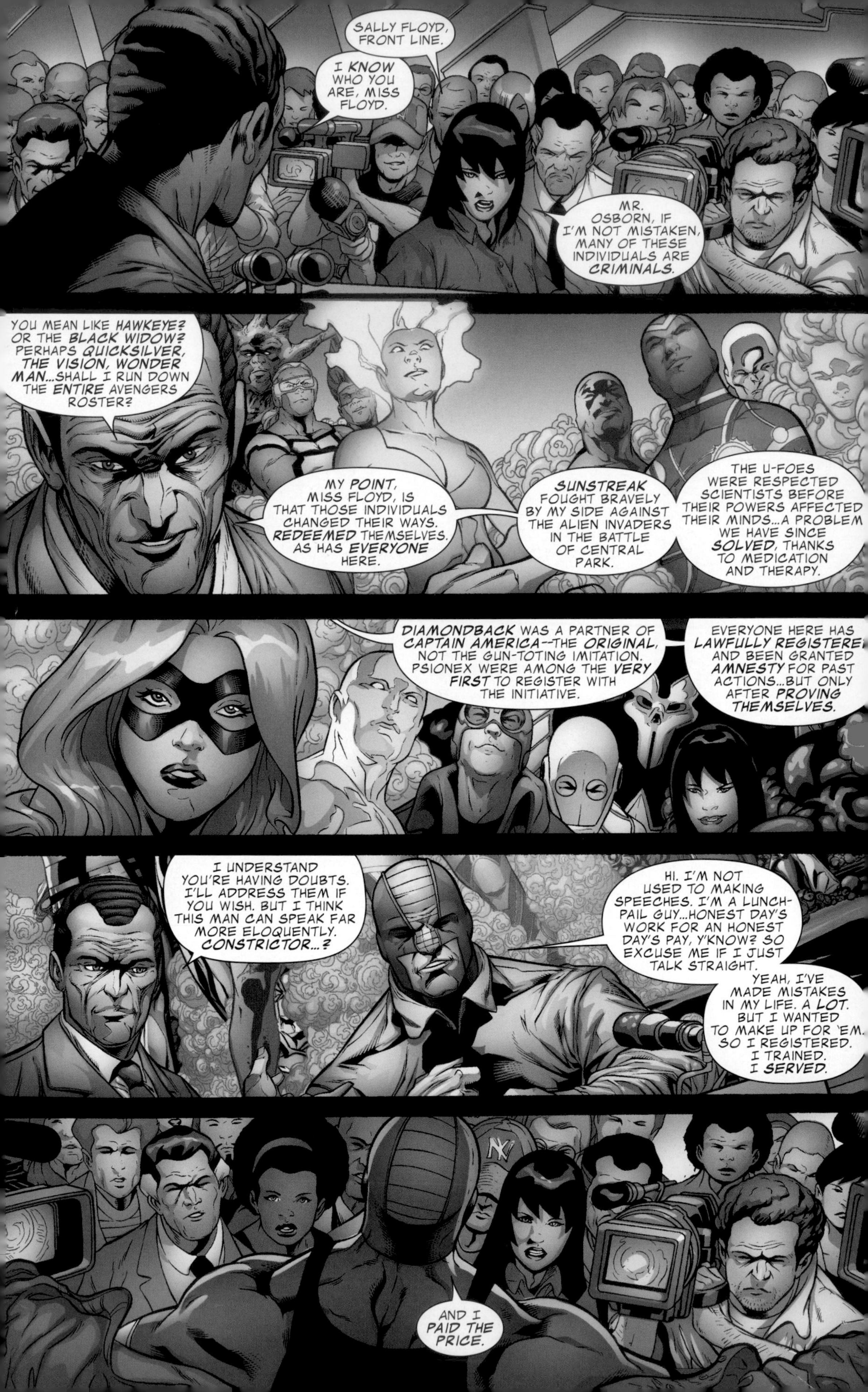
SALLY FLOYD, FRONT LINE.
I KNOW WHO YOU ARE, MISS FLOYD.
MR. OSBORN, IF I'M NOT MISTAKEN, MANY OF THESE INDIVIDUALS ARE CRIMINALS.
YOU MEAN LIKE HAWKEYE? OR THE BLACK WIDOW? PERHAPS QUICKSILVER, THE VISION, WONDER MAN...SHALL I RUN DOWN THE ENTIRE AVENGERS ROSTER?
MY POINT, MISS FLOYD, IS THAT THOSE INDIVIDUALS CHANGED THEIR WAYS. REDEEMED THEMSELVES. AS HAS EVERYONE HERE.
SUNSTREAK FOUGHT BRAVELY BY MY SIDE AGAINST THE ALIEN INVADERS IN THE BATTLE OF CENTRAL PARK.
THE U-FOES WERE RESPECTED SCIENTISTS BEFORE THEIR POWERS AFFECTED THEIR MINDS...A PROBLEM WE HAVE SINCE SOLVED, THANKS TO MEDICATION AND THERAPY.
DIAMONDBACK WAS A PARTNER OF CAPTAIN AMERICA--THE ORIGINAL, NOT THE GUN-TOTING IMITATION. PSIONEX WERE AMONG THE VERY FIRST TO REGISTER WITH THE INITIATIVE.
EVERYONE HERE HAS LAWFULLY REGISTERE AND BEEN GRANTED AMNESTY FOR PAST ACTIONS...BUT ONLY AFTER PROVING THEMSELVES.
I UNDERSTAND YOU'RE HAVING DOUBTS. I'LL ADDRESS THEM IF YOU WISH. BUT I THINK THIS MAN CAN SPEAK FAR MORE ELOQUENTLY. CONSTRICTOR...?
HI. I'M NOT USED TO MAKING SPEECHES. I'M A LUNCH-PAIL GUY...HONEST DAY'S WORK FOR AN HONEST DAY'S PAY, Y'KNOW? SO EXCUSE ME IF I JUST TALK STRAIGHT.
YEAH, I'VE MADE MISTAKES IN MY LIFE. A LOT. BUT I WANTED TO MAKE UP FOR 'EM. SO I REGISTERED. I TRAINED. I SERVED.
AND I PAID THE PRICE.

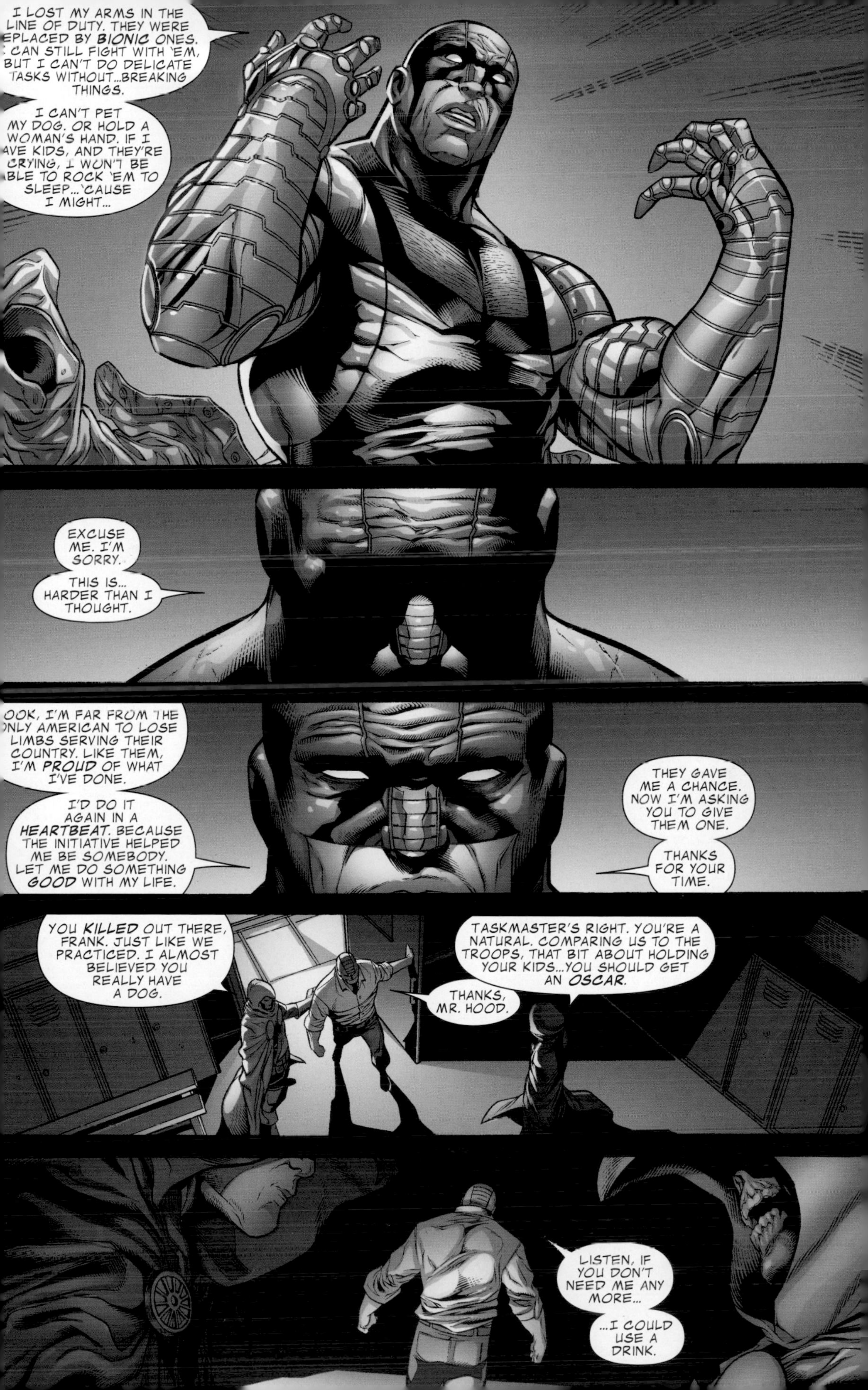

I LOST MY ARMS IN THE LINE OF DUTY. THEY WERE EPLACED BY BIONIC ONES. CAN STILL FIGHT WITH 'EM, BUT I CAN'T DO DELICATE TASKS WITHOUT...BREAKING THINGS.
I CAN'T PET MY DOG. OR HOLD A WOMAN'S HAND. IF I AVE KIDS, AND THEY'RE CRYING, I WON'T BE BLE TO ROCK 'EM TO SLEEP...'CAUSE I MIGHT...
EXCUSE ME. I'M SORRY.
THIS IS... HARDER THAN I THOUGHT.
OOK, I'M FAR FROM THE NLY AMERICAN TO LOSE LIMBS SERVING THEIR COUNTRY. LIKE THEM, I'M PROUD OF WHAT I'VE DONE.
I'D DO IT AGAIN IN A HEARTBEAT. BECAUSE THE INITIATIVE HELPED ME BE SOMEBODY. LET ME DO SOMETHING GOOD WITH MY LIFE.
THEY GAVE ME A CHANCE. NOW I'M ASKING YOU TO GIVE THEM ONE.
THANKS FOR YOUR TIME.
YOU KILLED OUT THERE, FRANK. JUST LIKE WE PRACTICED. I ALMOST BELIEVED YOU REALLY HAVE A DOG.
TASKMASTER'S RIGHT. YOU'RE A NATURAL. COMPARING US TO THE TROOPS, THAT BIT ABOUT HOLDING YOUR KIDS...YOU SHOULD GET AN OSCAR.
THANKS, MR. HOOD.
LISTEN, IF YOU DON'T NEED ME ANY MORE...
...I COULD USE A DRINK.

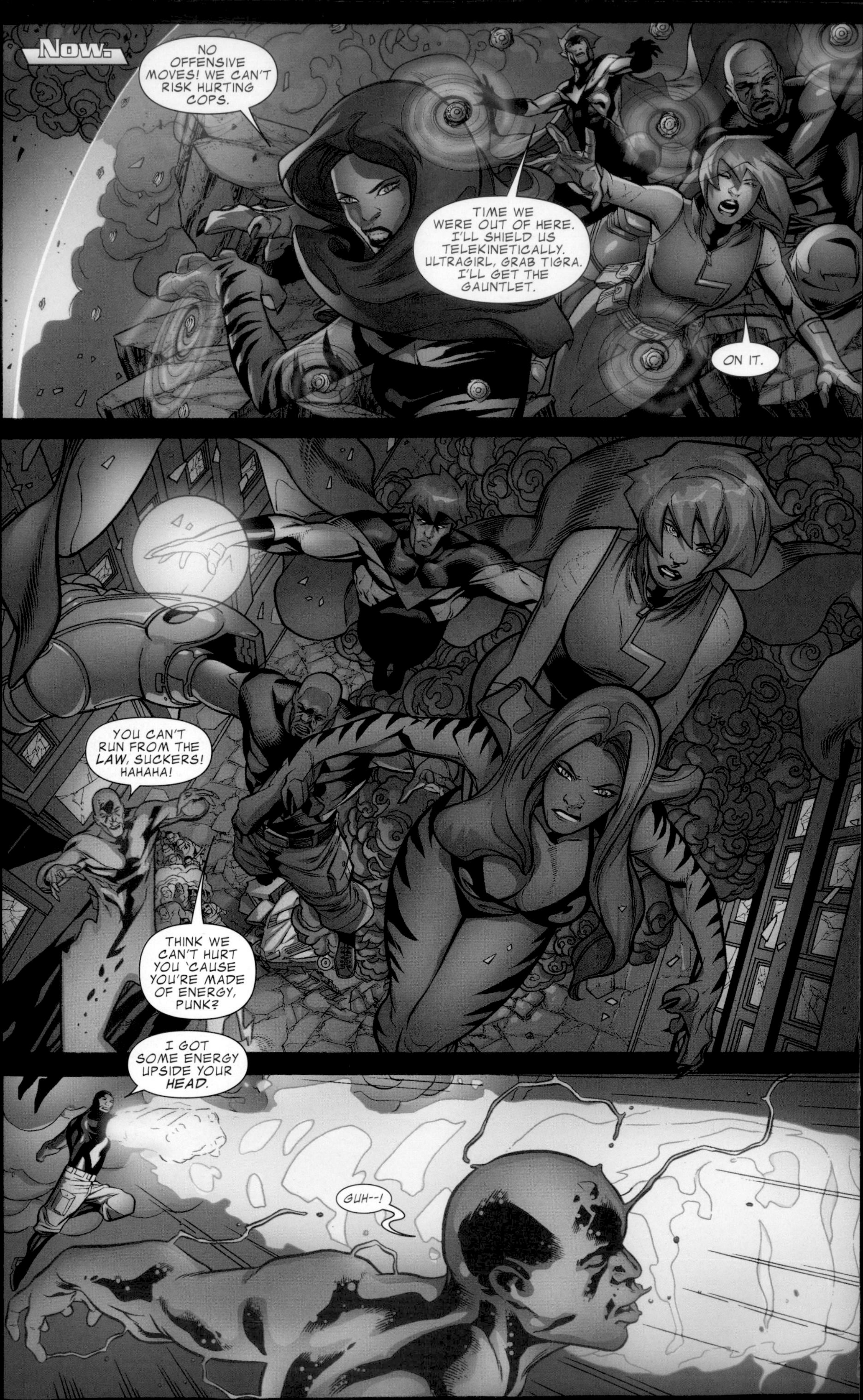
Now.
NO OFFENSIVE MOVES! WE CAN'T RISK HURTING COPS.
TIME WE WERE OUT OF HERE. I'LL SHIELD US TELEKINETICALLY. ULTRAGIRL, GRAB TIGRA. I'LL GET THE GAUNTLET.
ON IT.
YOU CAN'T RUN FROM THE LAW, SUCKERS! HAHAHA!
THINK WE CAN'T HURT YOU 'CAUSE YOU'RE MADE OF ENERGY, PUNK?
I GOT SOME ENERGY UPSIDE YOUR HEAD.
GUH--!

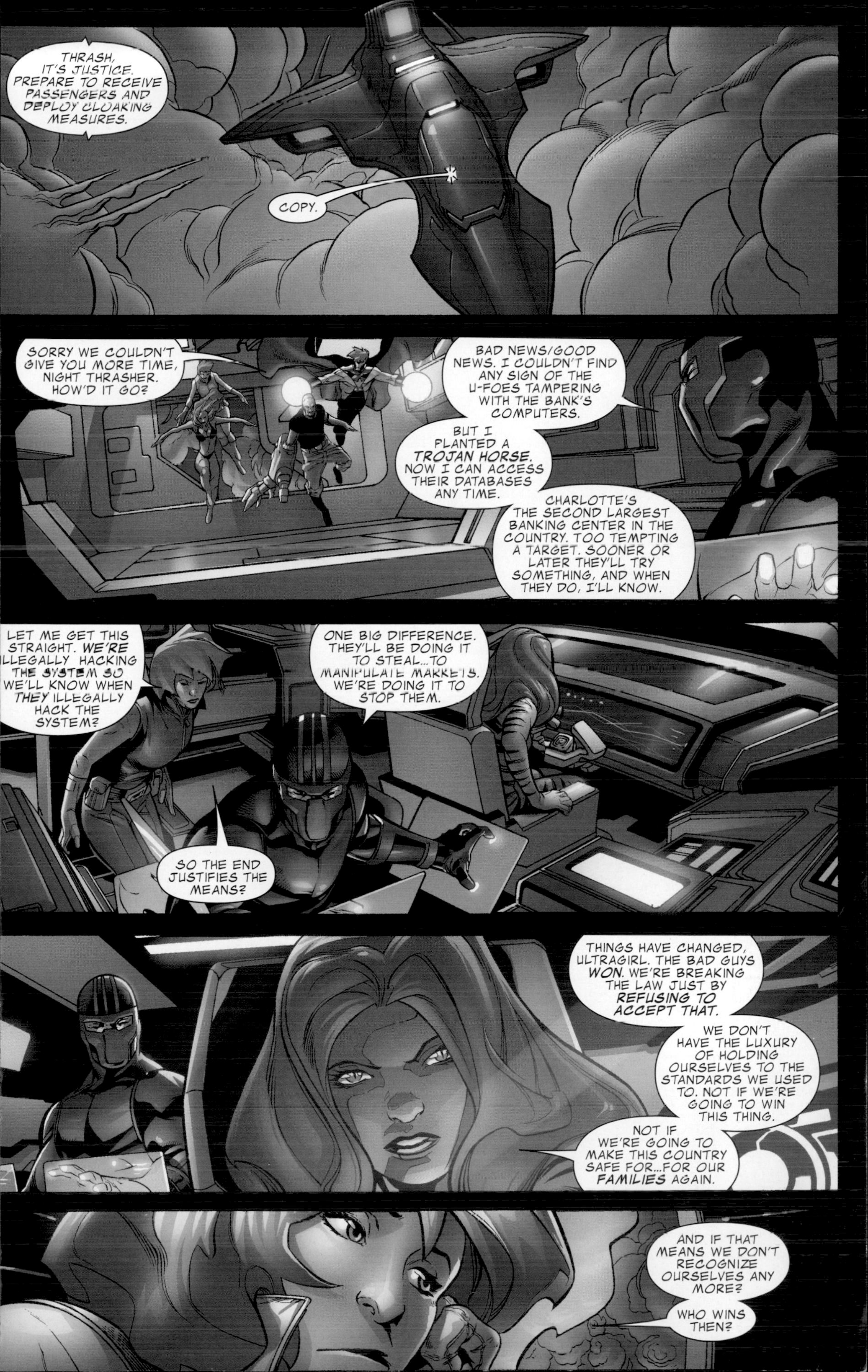
THRASH, IT'S JUSTICE. PREPARE TO RECEIVE PASSENGERS AND DEPLOY CLOAKING MEASURES.
COPY.
SORRY WE COULDN'T GIVE YOU MORE TIME, NIGHT THRASHER. HOW'D IT GO?
BAD NEWS/GOOD NEWS. I COULDN'T FIND ANY SIGN OF THE U-FOES TAMPERING WITH THE BANK'S COMPUTERS.
BUT I PLANTED A TROJAN HORSE. NOW I CAN ACCESS THEIR DATABASES ANY TIME.
CHARLOTTE'S THE SECOND LARGEST BANKING CENTER IN THE COUNTRY. TOO TEMPTING A TARGET. SOONER OR LATER THEY'LL TRY SOMETHING, AND WHEN THEY DO, I'LL KNOW.
LET ME GET THIS STRAIGHT. WE'RE ILLEGALLY HACKING THE SYSTEM SO WE'LL KNOW WHEN THEY ILLEGALLY HACK THE SYSTEM?
ONE BIG DIFFERENCE. THEY'LL BE DOING IT TO STEAL...TO MANIPULATE MARKETS. WE'RE DOING IT TO STOP THEM.
SO THE END JUSTIFIES THE MEANS?
THINGS HAVE CHANGED, ULTRAGIRL. THE BAD GUYS WON. WE'RE BREAKING THE LAW JUST BY REFUSING TO ACCEPT THAT.
WE DON'T HAVE THE LUXURY OF HOLDING OURSELVES TO THE STANDARDS WE USED TO. NOT IF WE'RE GOING TO WIN THIS THING.
NOT IF WE'RE GOING TO MAKE THIS COUNTRY SAFE FOR...FOR OUR FAMILIES AGAIN.
AND IF THAT MEANS WE DON'T RECOGNIZE OURSELVES ANY MORE?
WHO WINS THEN?

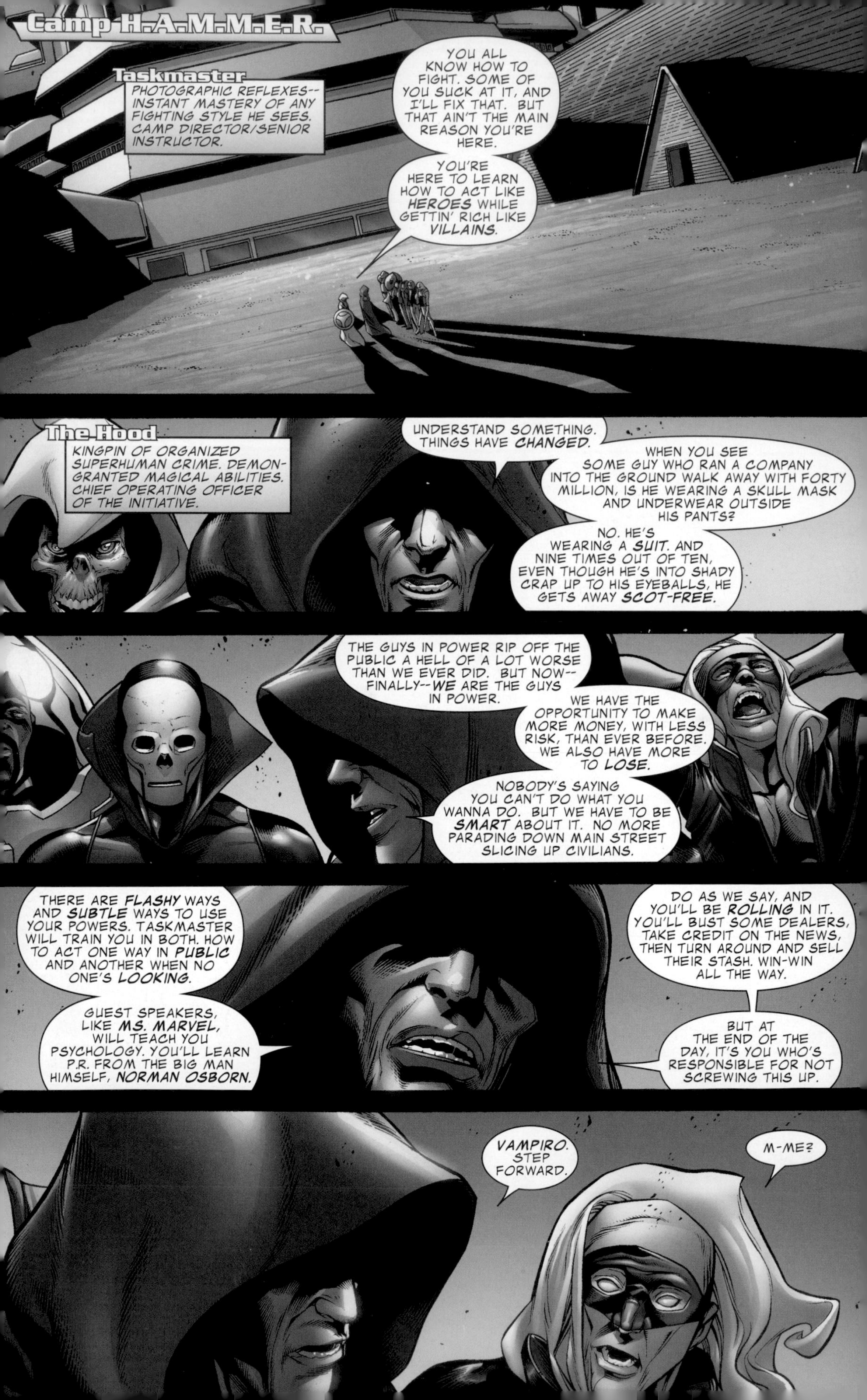
Camp H.A.M.M.E.R.
Taskmaster
PHOTOGRAPHIC REFLEXES--INSTANT MASTERY OF ANY FIGHTING STYLE HE SEES. CAMP DIRECTOR/SENIOR INSTRUCTOR.
YOU ALL KNOW HOW TO FIGHT. SOME OF YOU SUCK AT IT, AND I'LL FIX THAT. BUT THAT AIN'T THE MAIN REASON YOU'RE HERE.
YOU'RE HERE TO LEARN HOW TO ACT LIKE HEROES WHILE GETTIN' RICH LIKE VILLAINS.
The Hood
KINGPIN OF ORGANIZED SUPERHUMAN CRIME. DEMON-GRANTED MAGICAL ABILITIES. CHIEF OPERATING OFFICER OF THE INITIATIVE.
UNDERSTAND SOMETHING. THINGS HAVE CHANGED.
WHEN YOU SEE SOME GUY WHO RAN A COMPANY INTO THE GROUND WALK AWAY WITH FORTY MILLION, IS HE WEARING A SKULL MASK AND UNDERWEAR OUTSIDE HIS PANTS?
NO. HE'S WEARING A SUIT. AND NINE TIMES OUT OF TEN, EVEN THOUGH HE'S INTO SHADY CRAP UP TO HIS EYEBALLS, HE GETS AWAY SCOT-FREE.
THE GUYS IN POWER RIP OFF THE PUBLIC A HELL OF A LOT WORSE THAN WE EVER DID. BUT NOW--FINALLY--WE ARE THE GUYS IN POWER.
WE HAVE THE OPPORTUNITY TO MAKE MORE MONEY, WITH LESS RISK, THAN EVER BEFORE. WE ALSO HAVE MORE TO LOSE.
NOBODY'S SAYING YOU CAN'T DO WHAT YOU WANNA DO. BUT WE HAVE TO BE SMART ABOUT IT. NO MORE PARADING DOWN MAIN STREET SLICING UP CIVILIANS.
THERE ARE FLASHY WAYS AND SUBTLE WAYS TO USE YOUR POWERS. TASKMASTER WILL TRAIN YOU IN BOTH. HOW TO ACT ONE WAY IN PUBLIC AND ANOTHER WHEN NO ONE'S LOOKING.
GUEST SPEAKERS, LIKE MS. MARVEL, WILL TEACH YOU PSYCHOLOGY. YOU'LL LEARN P.R. FROM THE BIG MAN HIMSELF, NORMAN OSBORN.
DO AS WE SAY, AND YOU'LL BE ROLLING IN IT. YOU'LL BUST SOME DEALERS, TAKE CREDIT ON THE NEWS, THEN TURN AROUND AND SELL THEIR STASH. WIN-WIN ALL THE WAY.
BUT AT THE END OF THE DAY, IT'S YOU WHO'S RESPONSIBLE FOR NOT SCREWING THIS UP.
VAMPIRO. STEP FORWARD.
M-ME?

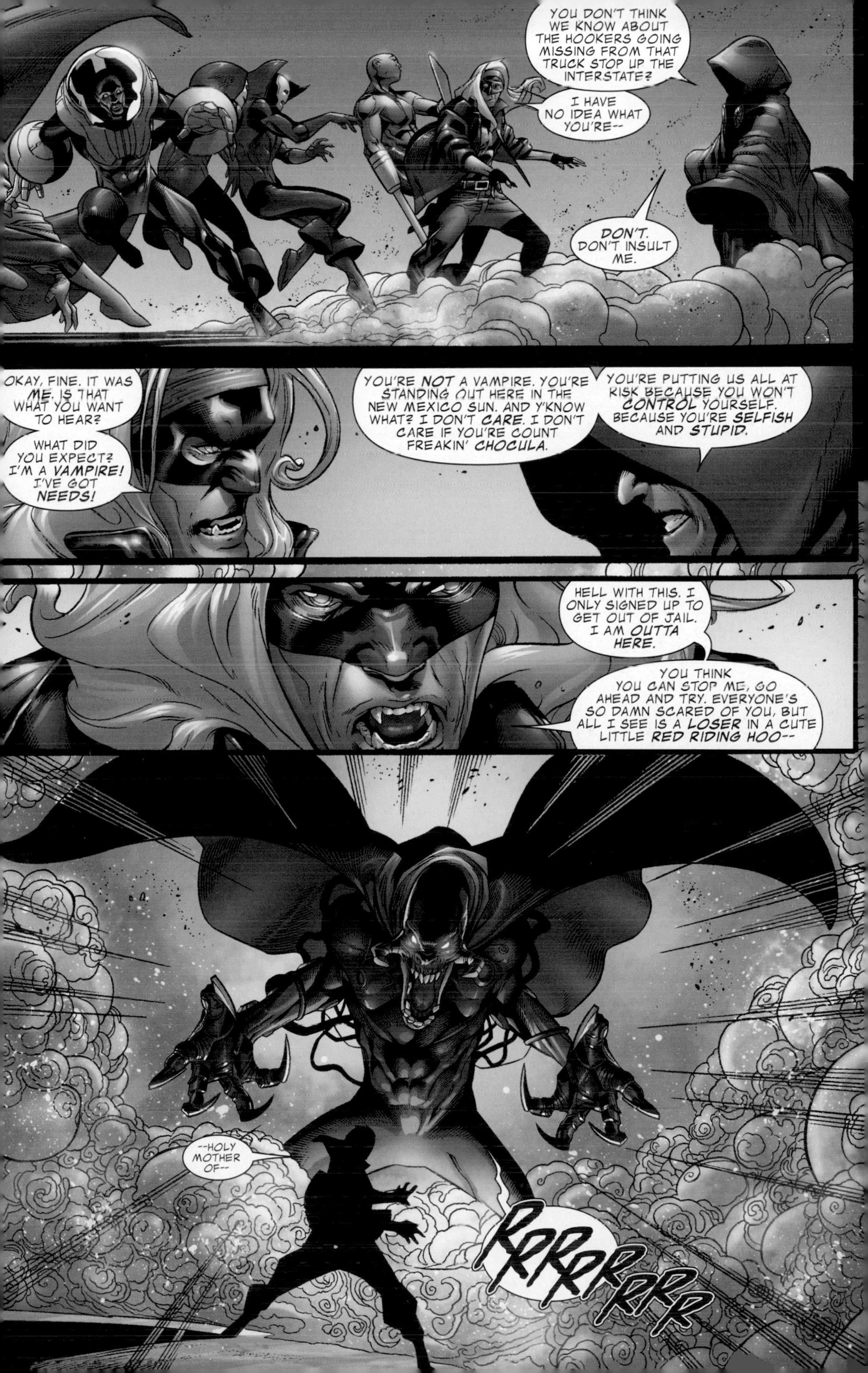
YOU DON'T THINK WE KNOW ABOUT THE HOOKERS GOING MISSING FROM THAT TRUCK STOP UP THE INTERSTATE?
I HAVE NO IDEA WHAT YOU'RE--
DON'T. DON'T INSULT ME.
OKAY, FINE. IT WAS ME. IS THAT WHAT YOU WANT TO HEAR?
WHAT DID YOU EXPECT? I'M A VAMPIRE! I'VE GOT NEEDS!
YOU'RE NOT A VAMPIRE. YOU'RE STANDING OUT HERE IN THE NEW MEXICO SUN. AND Y'KNOW WHAT? I DON'T CARE. I DON'T CARE IF YOU'RE COUNT FREAKIN' CHOCULA.
YOU'RE PUTTING US ALL AT RISK BECAUSE YOU WON'T CONTROL YOURSELF. BECAUSE YOU'RE SELFISH AND STUPID.
HELL WITH THIS. I ONLY SIGNED UP TO GET OUT OF JAIL. I AM OUTTA HERE.
YOU THINK YOU CAN STOP ME, GO AHEAD AND TRY. EVERYONE'S SO DAMN SCARED OF YOU, BUT ALL I SEE IS A LOSER IN A CUTE LITTLE RED RIDING HOO--
--HOLY MOTHER OF--
RRRRRRRRR

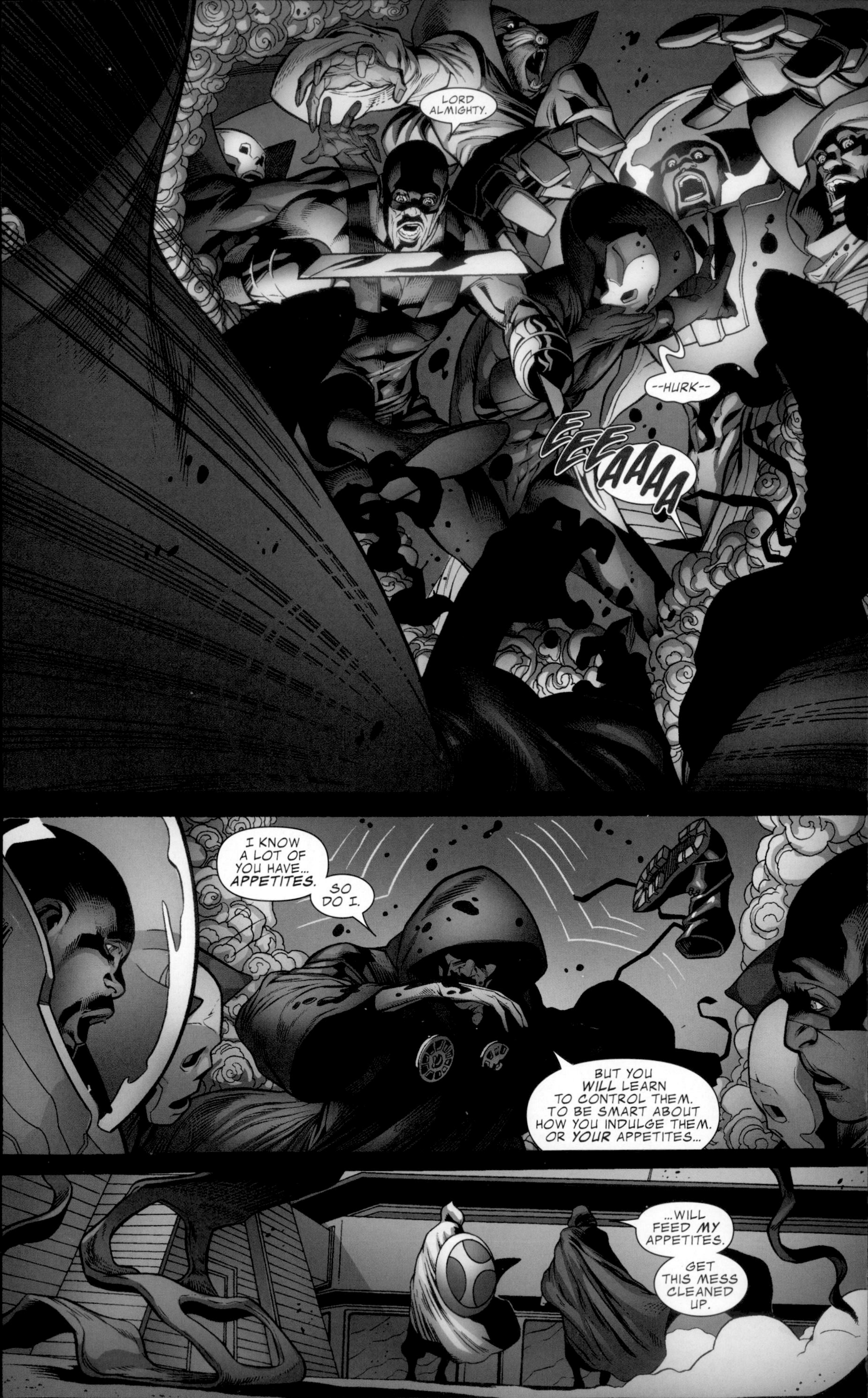
LORD ALMIGHTY.
--HURK--
EEEAAAA
I KNOW A LOT OF YOU HAVE... APPETITES.
SO DO I.
BUT YOU WILL LEARN TO CONTROL THEM. TO BE SMART ABOUT HOW YOU INDULGE THEM. OR YOUR APPETITES...
...WILL FEED MY APPETITES.
GET THIS MESS CLEANED UP.

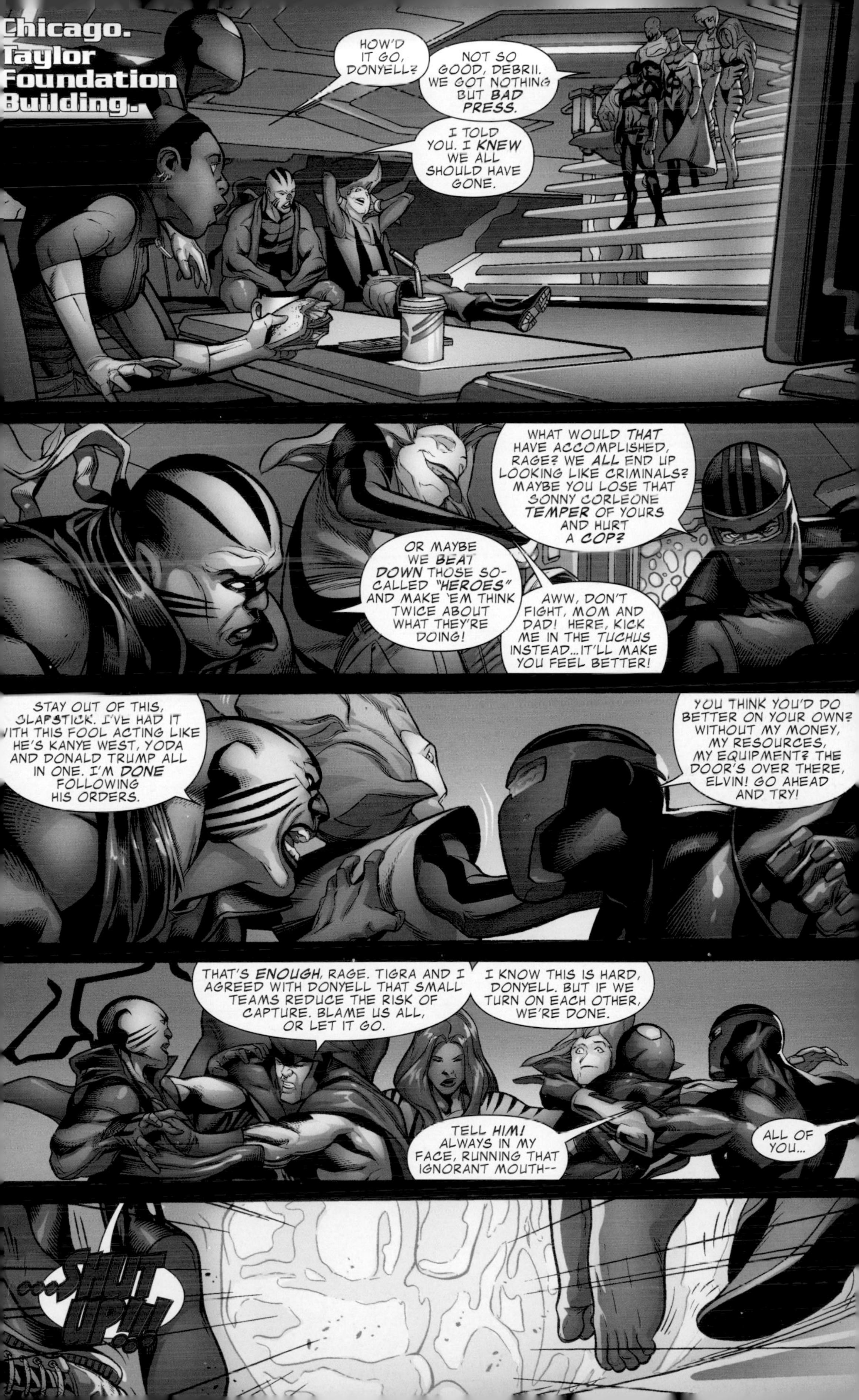
Chicago. Taylor Foundation Building.
HOW'D IT GO, DONYELL?
NOT SO GOOD, DEBRII. WE GOT NOTHING BUT BAD PRESS.
I TOLD YOU. I KNEW WE ALL SHOULD HAVE GONE.
WHAT WOULD THAT HAVE ACCOMPLISHED, RAGE? WE ALL END UP LOOKING LIKE CRIMINALS? MAYBE YOU LOSE THAT SONNY CORLEONE TEMPER OF YOURS AND HURT A COP?
OR MAYBE WE BEAT DOWN THOSE SO-CALLED "HEROES" AND MAKE 'EM THINK TWICE ABOUT WHAT THEY'RE DOING!
AWW, DON'T FIGHT, MOM AND DAD! HERE, KICK ME IN THE TUCHUS INSTEAD...IT'LL MAKE YOU FEEL BETTER!
STAY OUT OF THIS, SLAPSTICK. I'VE HAD IT WITH THIS FOOL ACTING LIKE HE'S KANYE WEST, YODA AND DONALD TRUMP ALL IN ONE. I'M DONE FOLLOWING HIS ORDERS.
YOU THINK YOU'D DO BETTER ON YOUR OWN? WITHOUT MY MONEY, MY RESOURCES, MY EQUIPMENT? THE DOOR'S OVER THERE, ELVIN! GO AHEAD AND TRY!
THAT'S ENOUGH, RAGE. TIGRA AND I AGREED WITH DONYELL THAT SMALL TEAMS REDUCE THE RISK OF CAPTURE. BLAME US ALL, OR LET IT GO.
I KNOW THIS IS HARD, DONYELL. BUT IF WE TURN ON EACH OTHER, WE'RE DONE.
TELL HIM! ALWAYS IN MY FACE, RUNNING THAT IGNORANT MOUTH--
ALL OF YOU...
...SHUT UP!!...

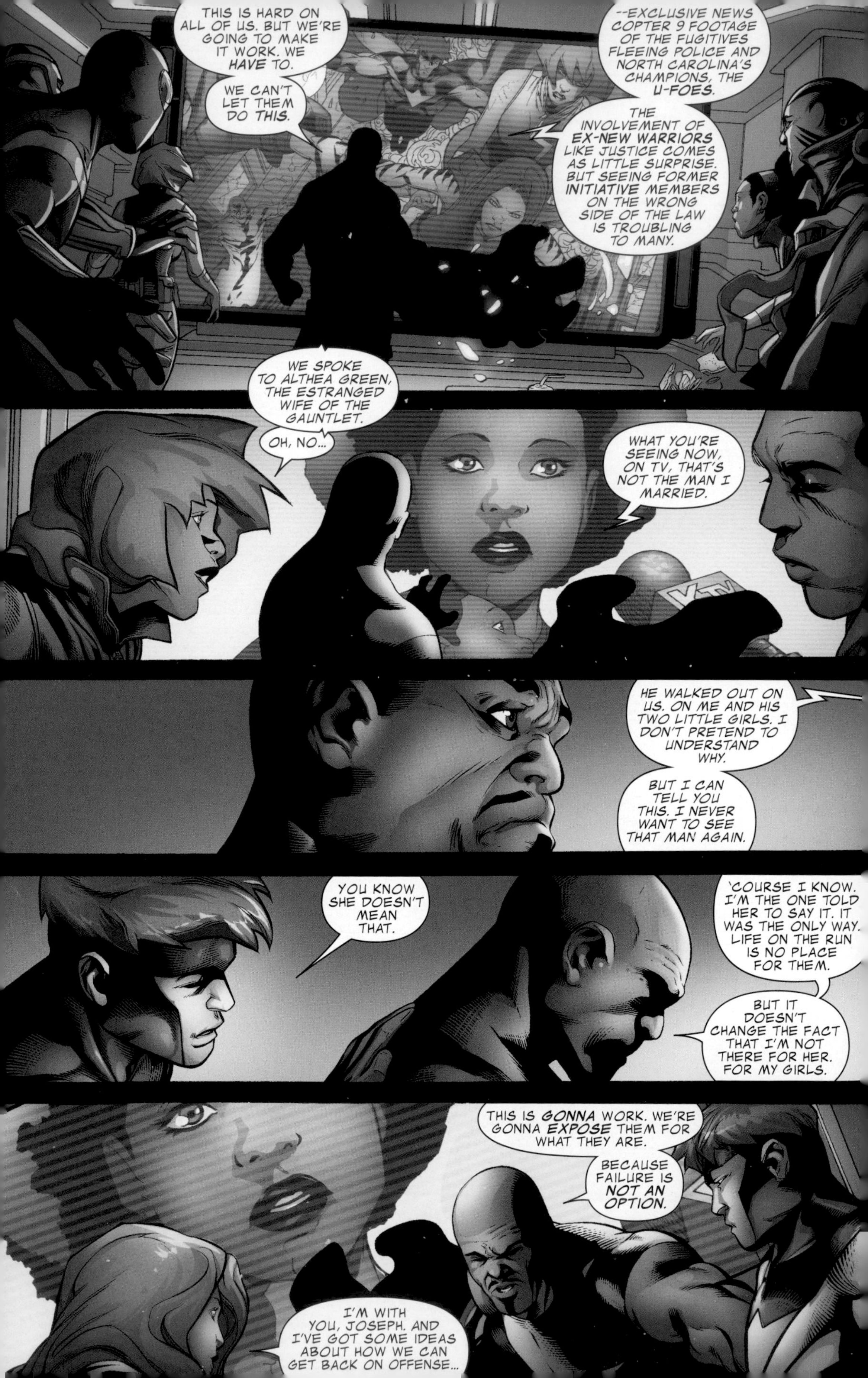
THIS IS HARD ON ALL OF US. BUT WE'RE GOING TO MAKE IT WORK. WE HAVE TO.
WE CAN'T LET THEM DO THIS.
--EXCLUSIVE NEWS COPTER 9 FOOTAGE OF THE FUGITIVES FLEEING POLICE AND NORTH CAROLINA'S CHAMPIONS, THE U-FOES.
THE INVOLVEMENT OF EX-NEW WARRIORS LIKE JUSTICE COMES AS LITTLE SURPRISE. BUT SEEING FORMER INITIATIVE MEMBERS ON THE WRONG SIDE OF THE LAW IS TROUBLING TO MANY.
WE SPOKE TO ALTHEA GREEN, THE ESTRANGED WIFE OF THE GAUNTLET.
OH, NO...
WHAT YOU'RE SEEING NOW, ON TV, THAT'S NOT THE MAN I MARRIED.
HE WALKED OUT ON US. ON ME AND HIS TWO LITTLE GIRLS. I DON'T PRETEND TO UNDERSTAND WHY.
BUT I CAN TELL YOU THIS. I NEVER WANT TO SEE THAT MAN AGAIN.
YOU KNOW SHE DOESN'T MEAN THAT.
'COURSE I KNOW. I'M THE ONE TOLD HER TO SAY IT. IT WAS THE ONLY WAY. LIFE ON THE RUN IS NO PLACE FOR THEM.
BUT IT DOESN'T CHANGE THE FACT THAT I'M NOT THERE FOR HER. FOR MY GIRLS.
THIS IS GONNA WORK. WE'RE GONNA EXPOSE THEM FOR WHAT THEY ARE.
BECAUSE FAILURE IS NOT AN OPTION.
I'M WITH YOU, JOSEPH. AND I'VE GOT SOME IDEAS ABOUT HOW WE CAN GET BACK ON OFFENSE...

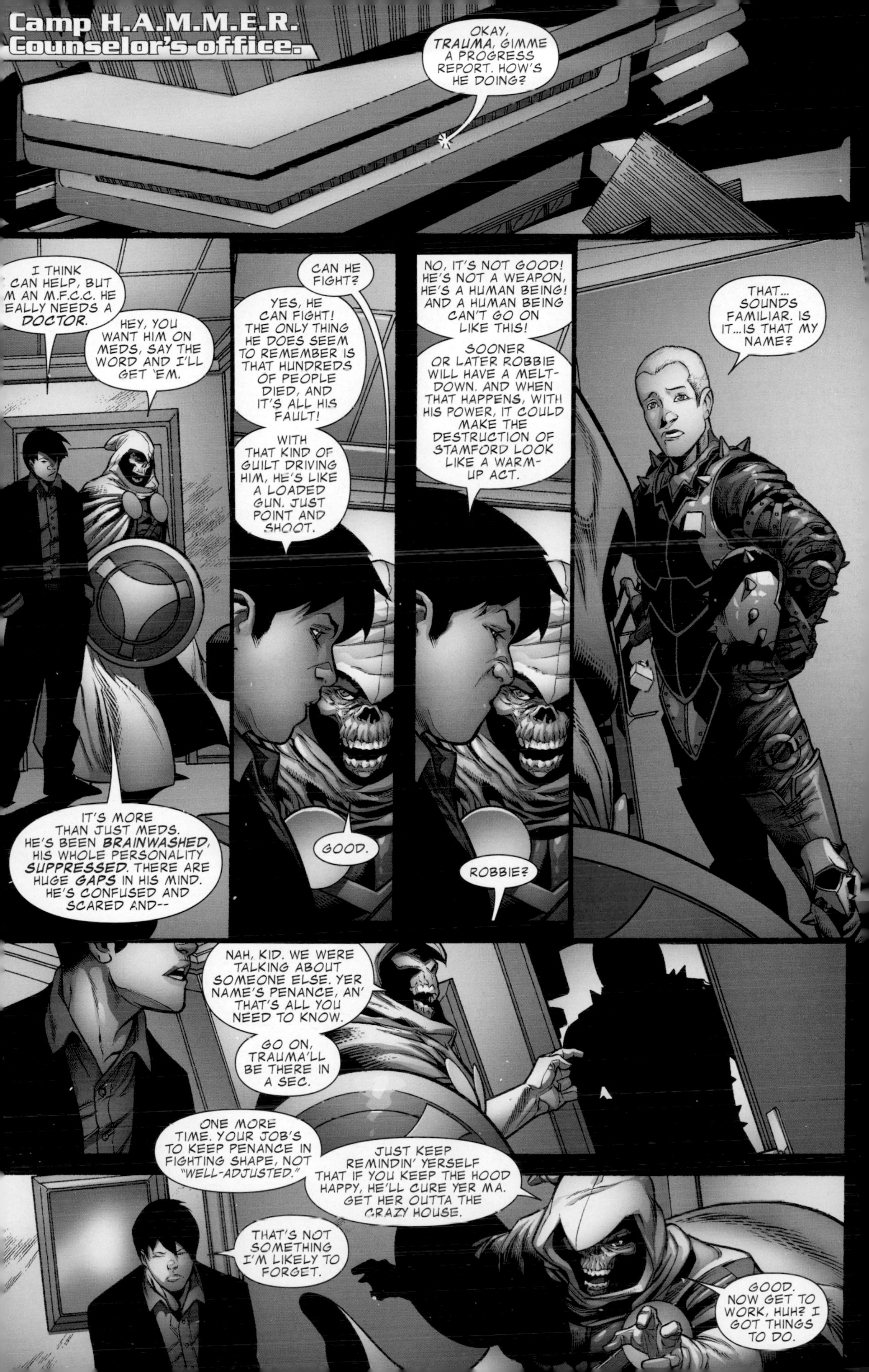

Camp H.A.M.M.E.R. Counselor's office.
OKAY, TRAUMA, GIMME A PROGRESS REPORT. HOW'S HE DOING?
I THINK CAN HELP, BUT M AN M.F.C.C. HE EALLY NEEDS A DOCTOR.
HEY, YOU WANT HIM ON MEDS, SAY THE WORD AND I'LL GET 'EM.
IT'S MORE THAN JUST MEDS. HE'S BEEN BRAINWASHED, HIS WHOLE PERSONALITY SUPPRESSED. THERE ARE HUGE GAPS IN HIS MIND. HE'S CONFUSED AND SCARED AND--
CAN HE FIGHT?
YES, HE CAN FIGHT! THE ONLY THING HE DOES SEEM TO REMEMBER IS THAT HUNDREDS OF PEOPLE DIED, AND IT'S ALL HIS FAULT!
WITH THAT KIND OF GUILT DRIVING HIM, HE'S LIKE A LOADED GUN. JUST POINT AND SHOOT.
GOOD.
NO, IT'S NOT GOOD! HE'S NOT A WEAPON, HE'S A HUMAN BEING! AND A HUMAN BEING CAN'T GO ON LIKE THIS!
SOONER OR LATER ROBBIE WILL HAVE A MELT-DOWN. AND WHEN THAT HAPPENS, WITH HIS POWER, IT COULD MAKE THE DESTRUCTION OF STAMFORD LOOK LIKE A WARM-UP ACT.
ROBBIE?
THAT... SOUNDS FAMILIAR. IS IT...IS THAT MY NAME?
NAH, KID. WE WERE TALKING ABOUT SOMEONE ELSE. YER NAME'S PENANCE, AN' THAT'S ALL YOU NEED TO KNOW.
GO ON, TRAUMA'LL BE THERE IN A SEC.
ONE MORE TIME. YOUR JOB'S TO KEEP PENANCE IN FIGHTING SHAPE, NOT "WELL-ADJUSTED."
JUST KEEP REMINDIN' YERSELF THAT IF YOU KEEP THE HOOD HAPPY, HE'LL CURE YER MA. GET HER OUTTA THE CRAZY HOUSE.
THAT'S NOT SOMETHING I'M LIKELY TO FORGET.
GOOD. NOW GET TO WORK, HUH? I GOT THINGS TO DO.

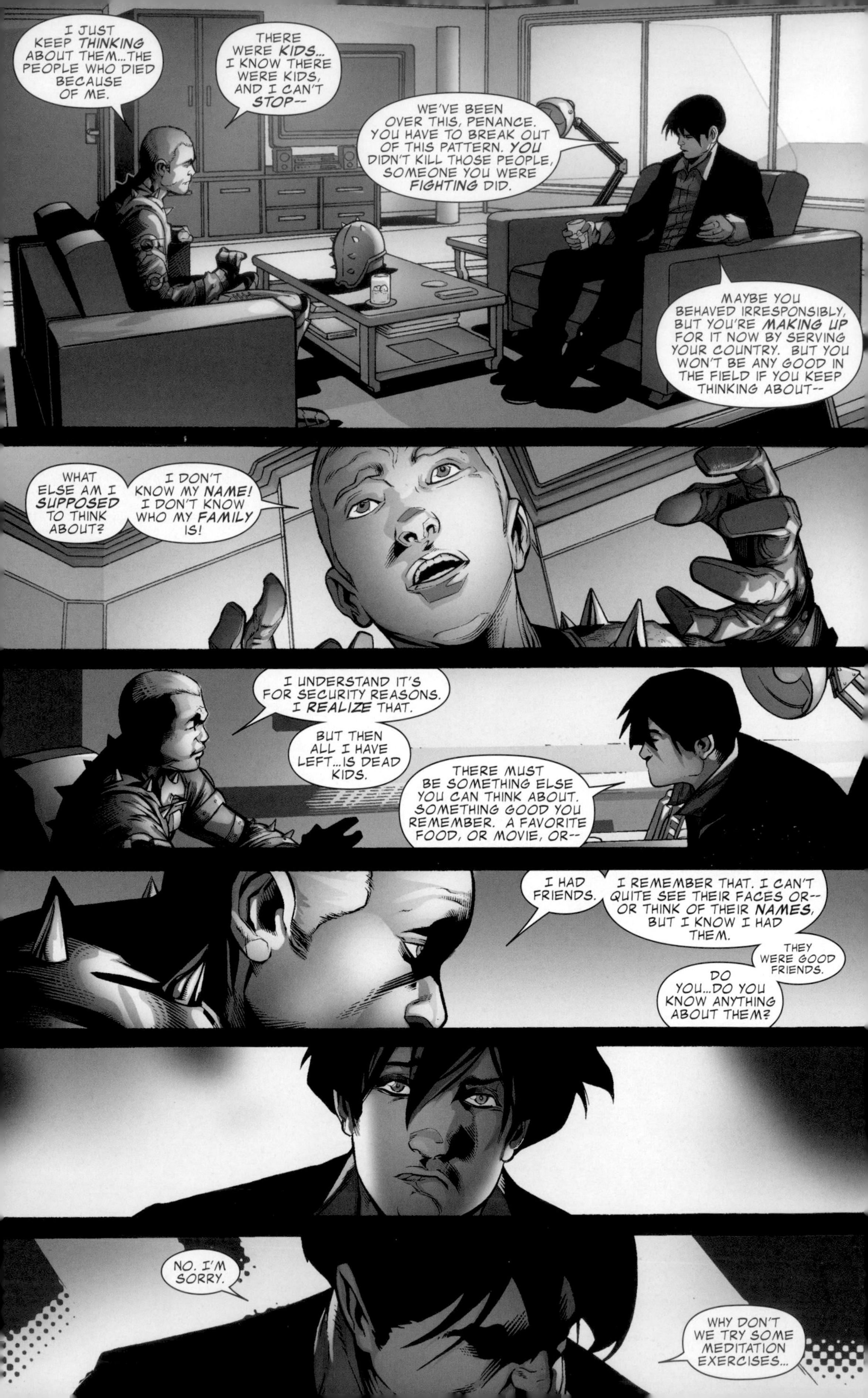

I JUST KEEP THINKING ABOUT THEM...THE PEOPLE WHO DIED BECAUSE OF ME.
THERE WERE KIDS... I KNOW THERE WERE KIDS, AND I CAN'T STOP--
WE'VE BEEN OVER THIS, PENANCE. YOU HAVE TO BREAK OUT OF THIS PATTERN. YOU DIDN'T KILL THOSE PEOPLE, SOMEONE YOU WERE FIGHTING DID.
MAYBE YOU BEHAVED IRRESPONSIBLY, BUT YOU'RE MAKING UP FOR IT NOW BY SERVING YOUR COUNTRY. BUT YOU WON'T BE ANY GOOD IN THE FIELD IF YOU KEEP THINKING ABOUT--
WHAT ELSE AM I SUPPOSED TO THINK ABOUT?
I DON'T KNOW MY NAME! I DON'T KNOW WHO MY FAMILY IS!
I UNDERSTAND IT'S FOR SECURITY REASONS. I REALIZE THAT.
BUT THEN ALL I HAVE LEFT...IS DEAD KIDS.
THERE MUST BE SOMETHING ELSE YOU CAN THINK ABOUT. SOMETHING GOOD YOU REMEMBER. A FAVORITE FOOD, OR MOVIE, OR--
I HAD FRIENDS.
I REMEMBER THAT. I CAN'T QUITE SEE THEIR FACES OR-- OR THINK OF THEIR NAMES, BUT I KNOW I HAD THEM.
THEY WERE GOOD FRIENDS.
DO YOU...DO YOU KNOW ANYTHING ABOUT THEM?
NO. I'M SORRY.
WHY DON'T WE TRY SOME MEDITATION EXERCISES...

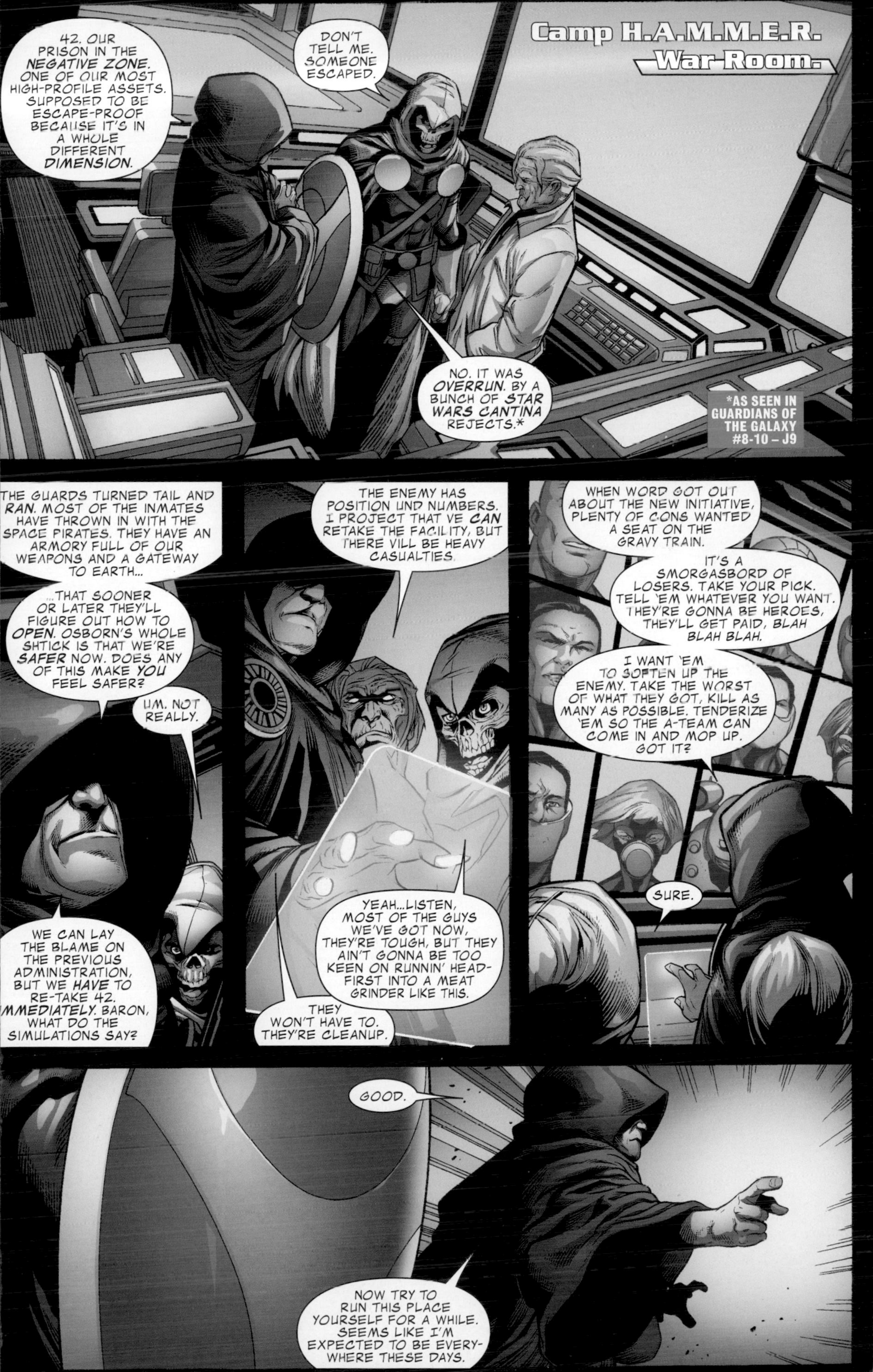
Camp H.A.M.M.E.R.
War-Room.
42. OUR PRISON IN THE NEGATIVE ZONE. ONE OF OUR MOST HIGH-PROFILE ASSETS. SUPPOSED TO BE ESCAPE-PROOF BECAUSE IT'S IN A WHOLE DIFFERENT DIMENSION.
DON'T TELL ME. SOMEONE ESCAPED.
NO. IT WAS OVERRUN. BY A BUNCH OF STAR WARS CANTINA REJECTS.*
*AS SEEN IN GUARDIANS OF THE GALAXY #8-10 – J9
THE GUARDS TURNED TAIL AND RAN. MOST OF THE INMATES HAVE THROWN IN WITH THE SPACE PIRATES. THEY HAVE AN ARMORY FULL OF OUR WEAPONS AND A GATEWAY TO EARTH...
...THAT SOONER OR LATER THEY'LL FIGURE OUT HOW TO OPEN. OSBORN'S WHOLE SHTICK IS THAT WE'RE SAFER NOW. DOES ANY OF THIS MAKE YOU FEEL SAFER?
UM. NOT REALLY.
WE CAN LAY THE BLAME ON THE PREVIOUS ADMINISTRATION, BUT WE HAVE TO RE-TAKE 42. IMMEDIATELY. BARON, WHAT DO THE SIMULATIONS SAY?
THE ENEMY HAS POSITION UND NUMBERS. I PROJECT THAT VE CAN RETAKE THE FACILITY, BUT THERE VILL BE HEAVY CASUALTIES.
YEAH...LISTEN, MOST OF THE GUYS WE'VE GOT NOW, THEY'RE TOUGH, BUT THEY AIN'T GONNA BE TOO KEEN ON RUNNIN' HEAD-FIRST INTO A MEAT GRINDER LIKE THIS.
THEY WON'T HAVE TO. THEY'RE CLEANUP.
WHEN WORD GOT OUT ABOUT THE NEW INITIATIVE, PLENTY OF CONS WANTED A SEAT ON THE GRAVY TRAIN.
IT'S A SMORGASBORD OF LOSERS. TAKE YOUR PICK. TELL 'EM WHATEVER YOU WANT. THEY'RE GONNA BE HEROES, THEY'LL GET PAID, BLAH BLAH BLAH.
I WANT 'EM TO SOFTEN UP THE ENEMY. TAKE THE WORST OF WHAT THEY GOT, KILL AS MANY AS POSSIBLE. TENDERIZE 'EM SO THE A-TEAM CAN COME IN AND MOP UP. GOT IT?
SURE.
GOOD.
NOW TRY TO RUN THIS PLACE YOURSELF FOR A WHILE. SEEMS LIKE I'M EXPECTED TO BE EVERY-WHERE THESE DAYS.

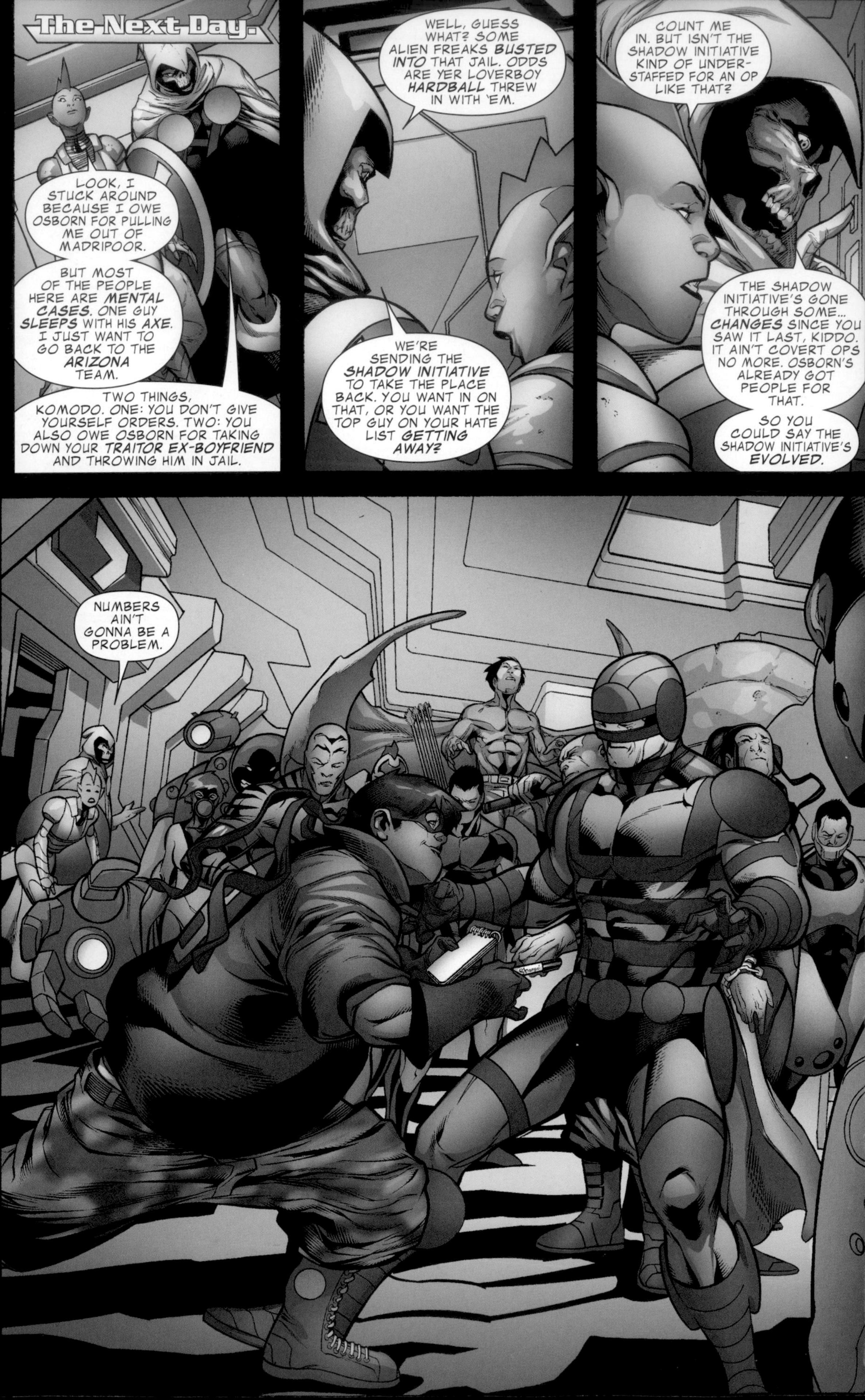
The Next Day.
LOOK, I STUCK AROUND BECAUSE I OWE OSBORN FOR PULLING ME OUT OF MADRIPOOR.
BUT MOST OF THE PEOPLE HERE ARE MENTAL CASES. ONE GUY SLEEPS WITH HIS AXE. I JUST WANT TO GO BACK TO THE ARIZONA TEAM.
TWO THINGS, KOMODO. ONE: YOU DON'T GIVE YOURSELF ORDERS. TWO: YOU ALSO OWE OSBORN FOR TAKING DOWN YOUR TRAITOR EX-BOYFRIEND AND THROWING HIM IN JAIL.
WELL, GUESS WHAT? SOME ALIEN FREAKS BUSTED INTO THAT JAIL. ODDS ARE YER LOVERBOY HARDBALL THREW IN WITH 'EM.
WE'RE SENDING THE SHADOW INITIATIVE TO TAKE THE PLACE BACK. YOU WANT IN ON THAT, OR YOU WANT THE TOP GUY ON YOUR HATE LIST GETTING AWAY?
COUNT ME IN. BUT ISN'T THE SHADOW INITIATIVE KIND OF UNDER-STAFFED FOR AN OP LIKE THAT?
THE SHADOW INITIATIVE'S GONE THROUGH SOME... CHANGES SINCE YOU SAW IT LAST, KIDDO. IT AIN'T COVERT OPS NO MORE. OSBORN'S ALREADY GOT PEOPLE FOR THAT.
SO YOU COULD SAY THE SHADOW INITIATIVE'S EVOLVED.
NUMBERS AIN'T GONNA BE A PROBLEM.

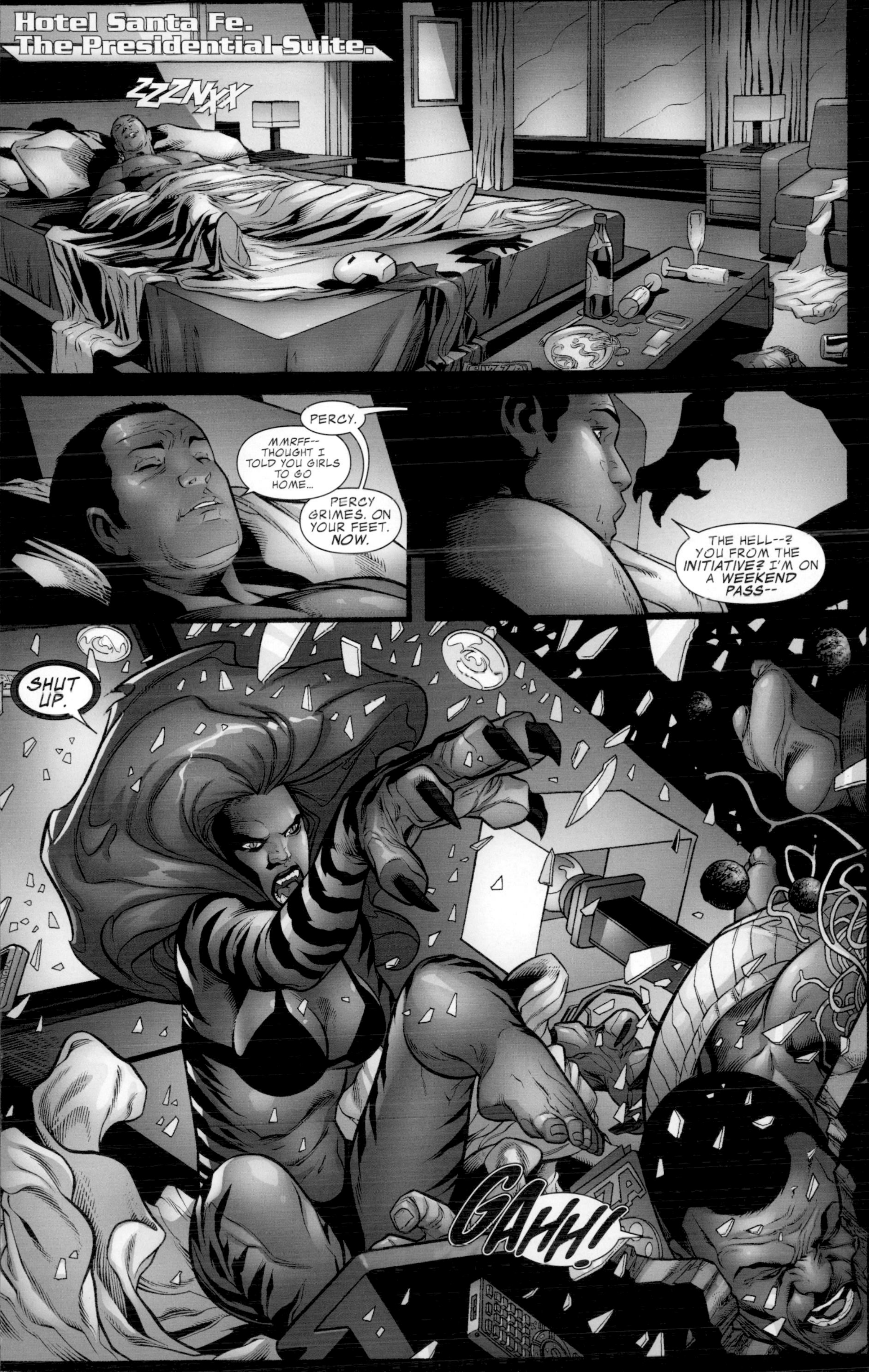
Hotel Santa Fe.
The Presidential Suite.
ZZZNXX
PERCY.
MMRFF-- THOUGHT I TOLD YOU GIRLS TO GO HOME...
PERCY GRIMES. ON YOUR FEET. NOW.
THE HELL--? YOU FROM THE INITIATIVE? I'M ON A WEEKEND PASS--
SHUT UP.
GAHH!

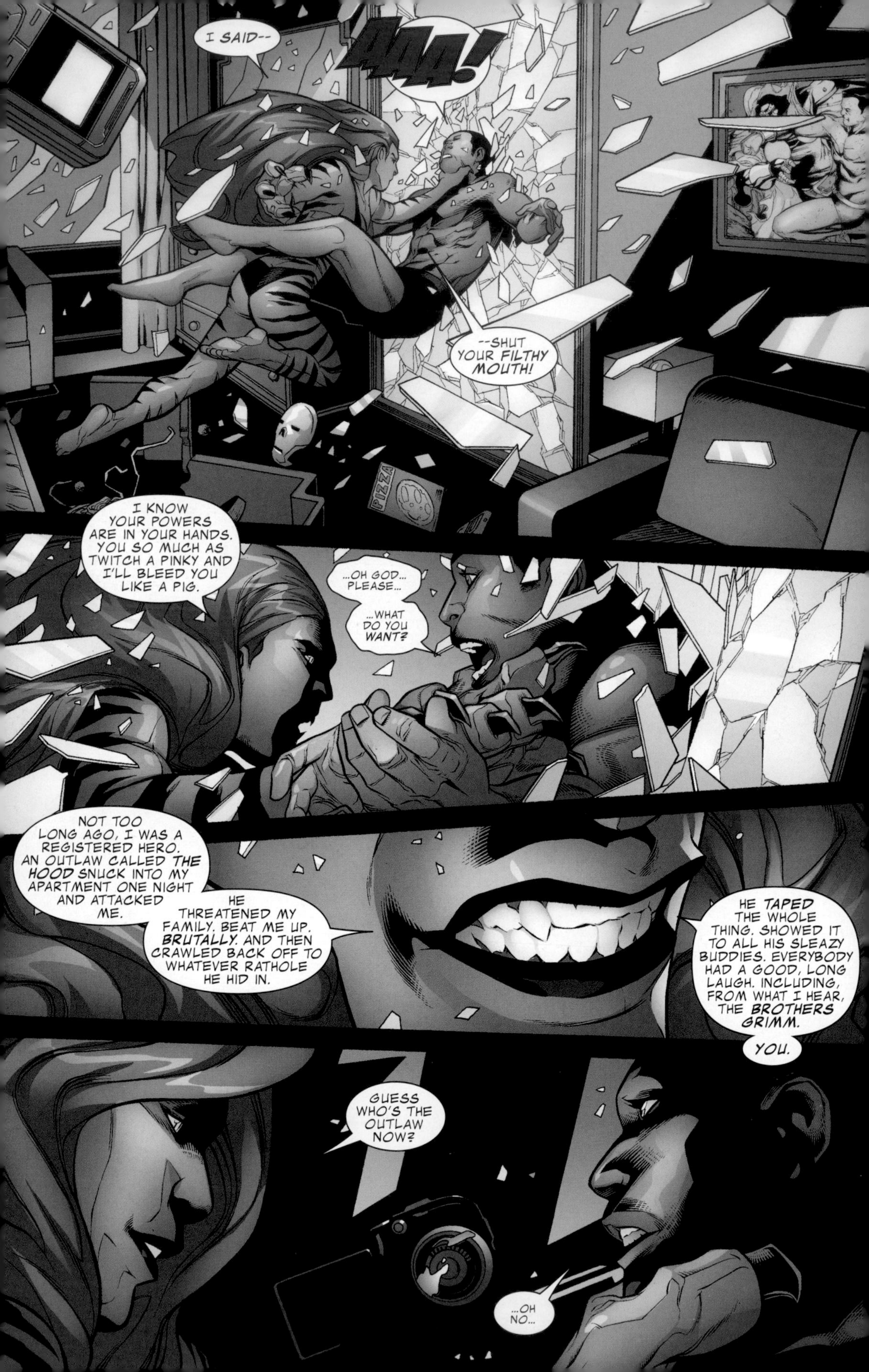
I SAID--
AAA!
--SHUT YOUR FILTHY MOUTH!
PIZZA
I KNOW YOUR POWERS ARE IN YOUR HANDS. YOU SO MUCH AS TWITCH A PINKY AND I'LL BLEED YOU LIKE A PIG.
...OH GOD... PLEASE...
...WHAT DO YOU WANT?
NOT TOO LONG AGO, I WAS A REGISTERED HERO. AN OUTLAW CALLED THE HOOD SNUCK INTO MY APARTMENT ONE NIGHT AND ATTACKED ME.
HE THREATENED MY FAMILY. BEAT ME UP. BRUTALLY. AND THEN CRAWLED BACK OFF TO WHATEVER RATHOLE HE HID IN.
HE TAPED THE WHOLE THING. SHOWED IT TO ALL HIS SLEAZY BUDDIES. EVERYBODY HAD A GOOD, LONG LAUGH. INCLUDING, FROM WHAT I HEAR, THE BROTHERS GRIMM.
YOU.
GUESS WHO'S THE OUTLAW NOW?
...OH NO...

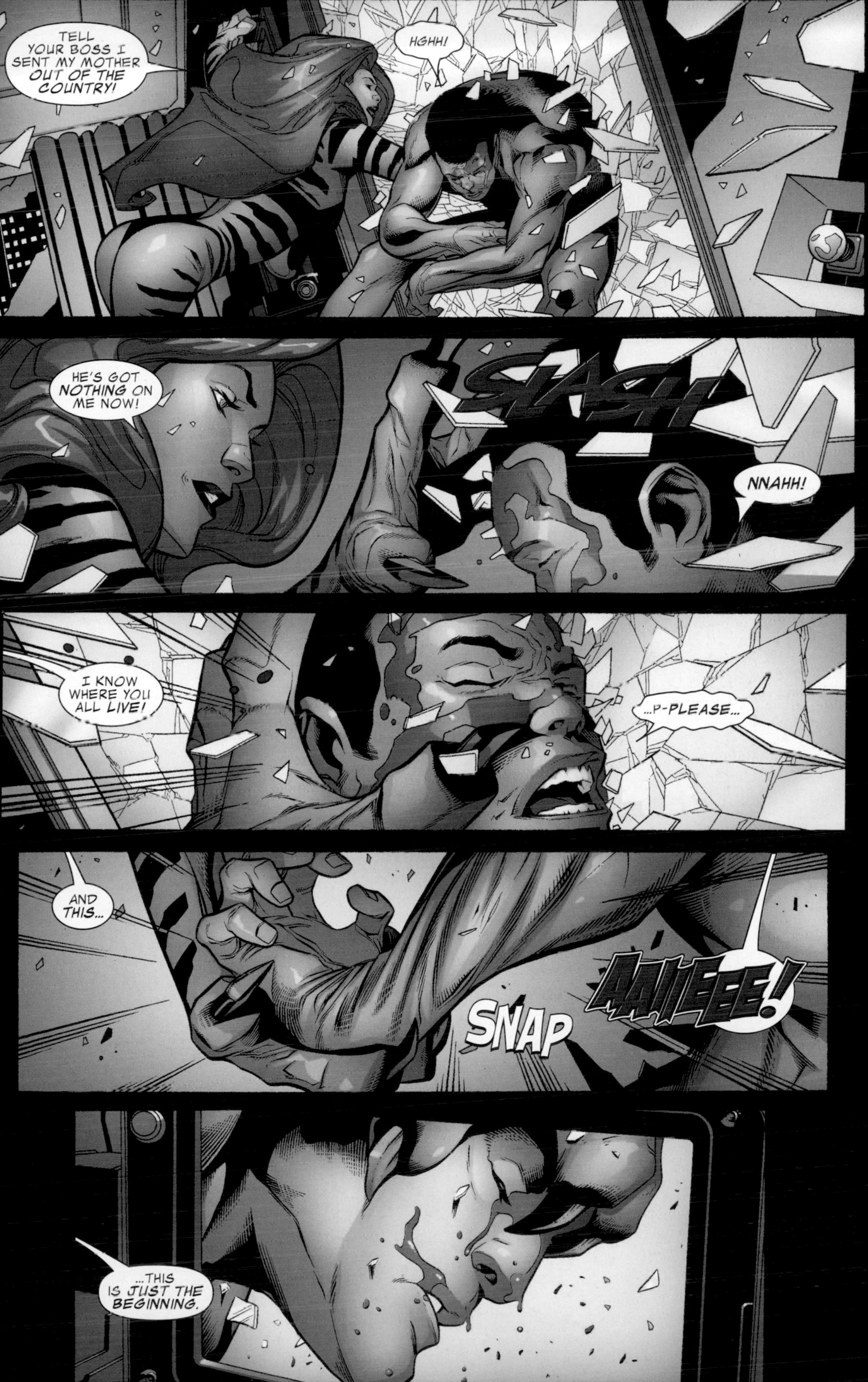
TELL YOUR BOSS I SENT MY MOTHER OUT OF THE COUNTRY!
HGHH!
HE'S GOT NOTHING ON ME NOW!
SLASH
NNAHH!
I KNOW WHERE YOU ALL LIVE!
...P-PLEASE...
AND THIS...
AAIIEEE!
SNAP
...THIS IS JUST THE BEGINNING.

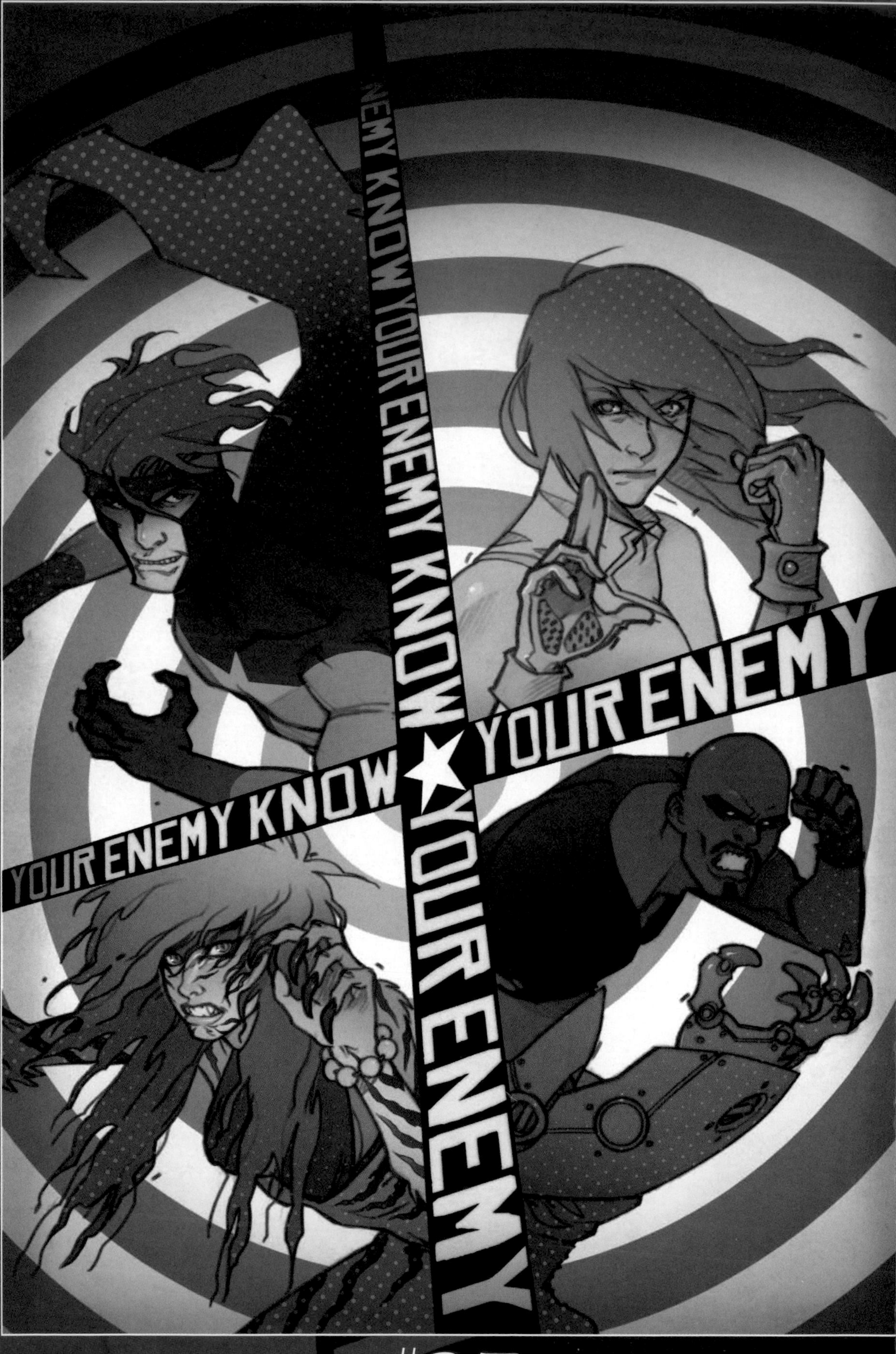
NEMY KNOW YOUR ENEMY KNOW
YOUR ENEMY
YOUR ENEMY KNOW
YOUR ENEMY

#27

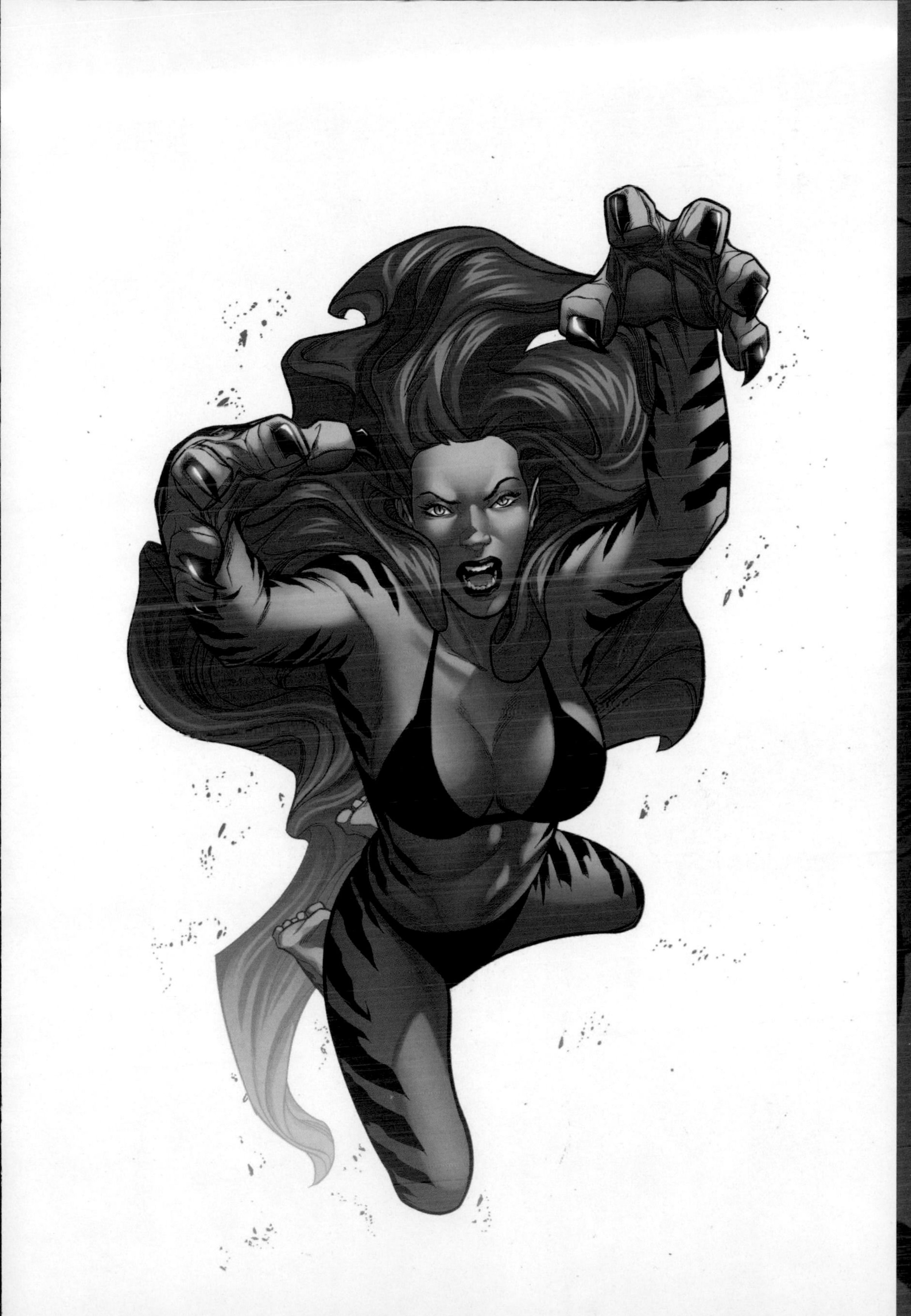

#27 70TH ANNIVERSARY FRAME VARIANT
BY RAFA SANDOVAL

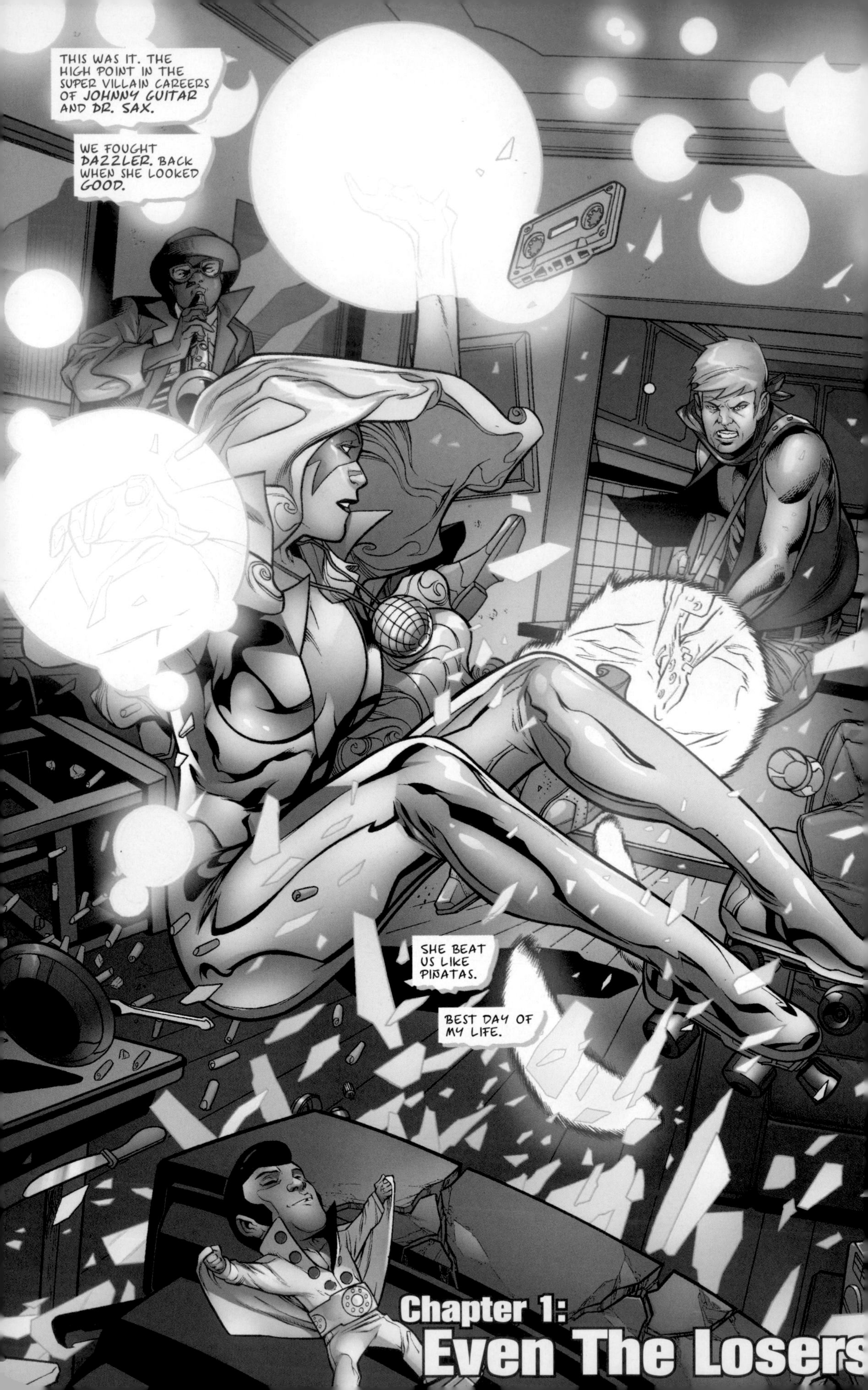
THIS WAS IT. THE HIGH POINT IN THE SUPER VILLAIN CAREERS OF JOHNNY GUITAR AND DR. SAX.
WE FOUGHT DAZZLER. BACK WHEN SHE LOOKED GOOD.
SHE BEAT US LIKE PIÑATAS.
BEST DAY OF MY LIFE.
Chapter 1:
Even The Losers

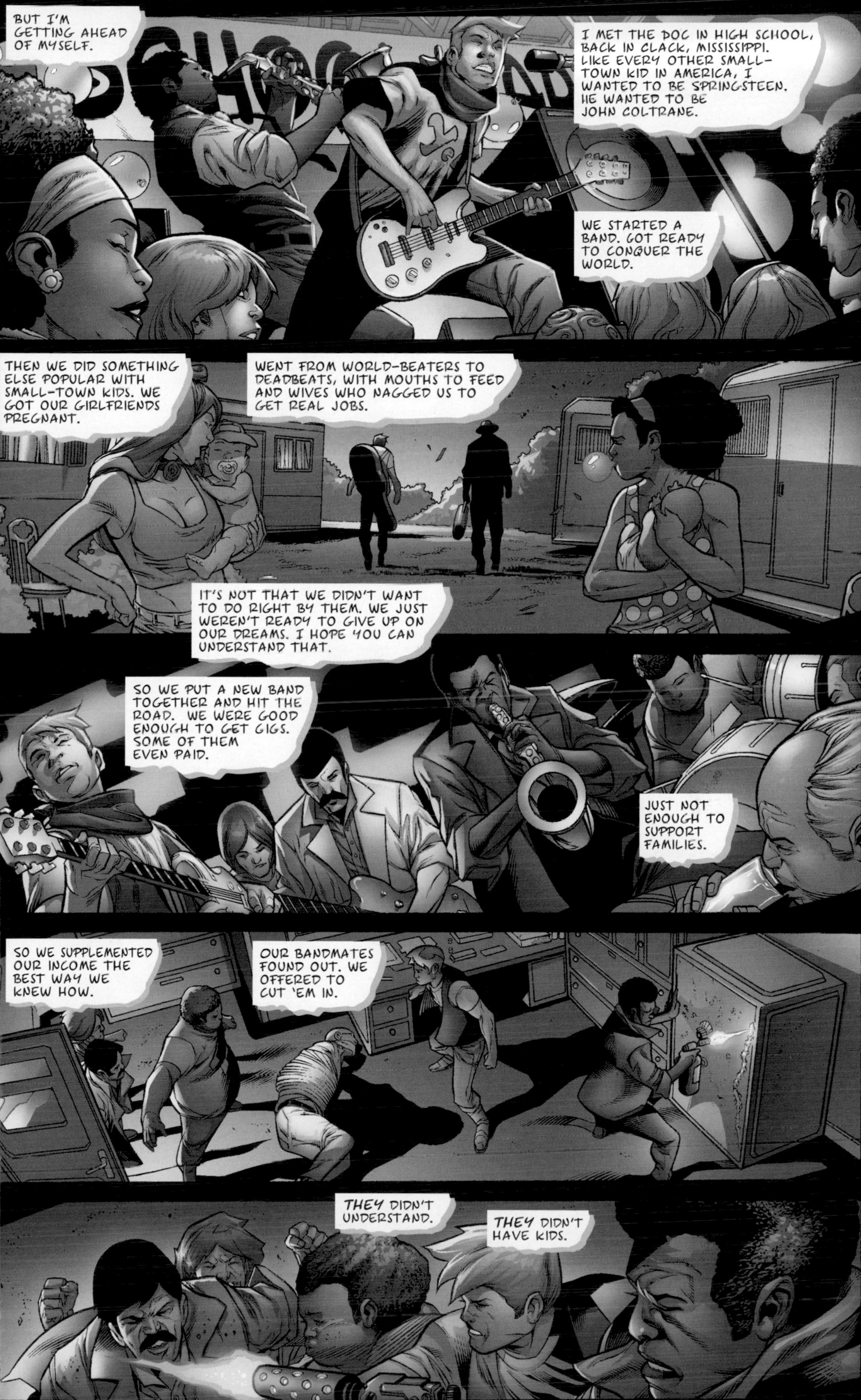

BUT I'M GETTING AHEAD OF MYSELF.
I MET THE DOC IN HIGH SCHOOL, BACK IN CLACK, MISSISSIPPI. LIKE EVERY OTHER SMALL-TOWN KID IN AMERICA, I WANTED TO BE SPRINGSTEEN. HE WANTED TO BE JOHN COLTRANE.
WE STARTED A BAND. GOT READY TO CONQUER THE WORLD.
THEN WE DID SOMETHING ELSE POPULAR WITH SMALL-TOWN KIDS. WE GOT OUR GIRLFRIENDS PREGNANT.
WENT FROM WORLD-BEATERS TO DEADBEATS, WITH MOUTHS TO FEED AND WIVES WHO NAGGED US TO GET REAL JOBS.
IT'S NOT THAT WE DIDN'T WANT TO DO RIGHT BY THEM. WE JUST WEREN'T READY TO GIVE UP ON OUR DREAMS. I HOPE YOU CAN UNDERSTAND THAT.
SO WE PUT A NEW BAND TOGETHER AND HIT THE ROAD. WE WERE GOOD ENOUGH TO GET GIGS. SOME OF THEM EVEN PAID.
JUST NOT ENOUGH TO SUPPORT FAMILIES.
SO WE SUPPLEMENTED OUR INCOME THE BEST WAY WE KNEW HOW.
OUR BANDMATES FOUND OUT. WE OFFERED TO CUT 'EM IN.
THEY DIDN'T UNDERSTAND.
THEY DIDN'T HAVE KIDS.

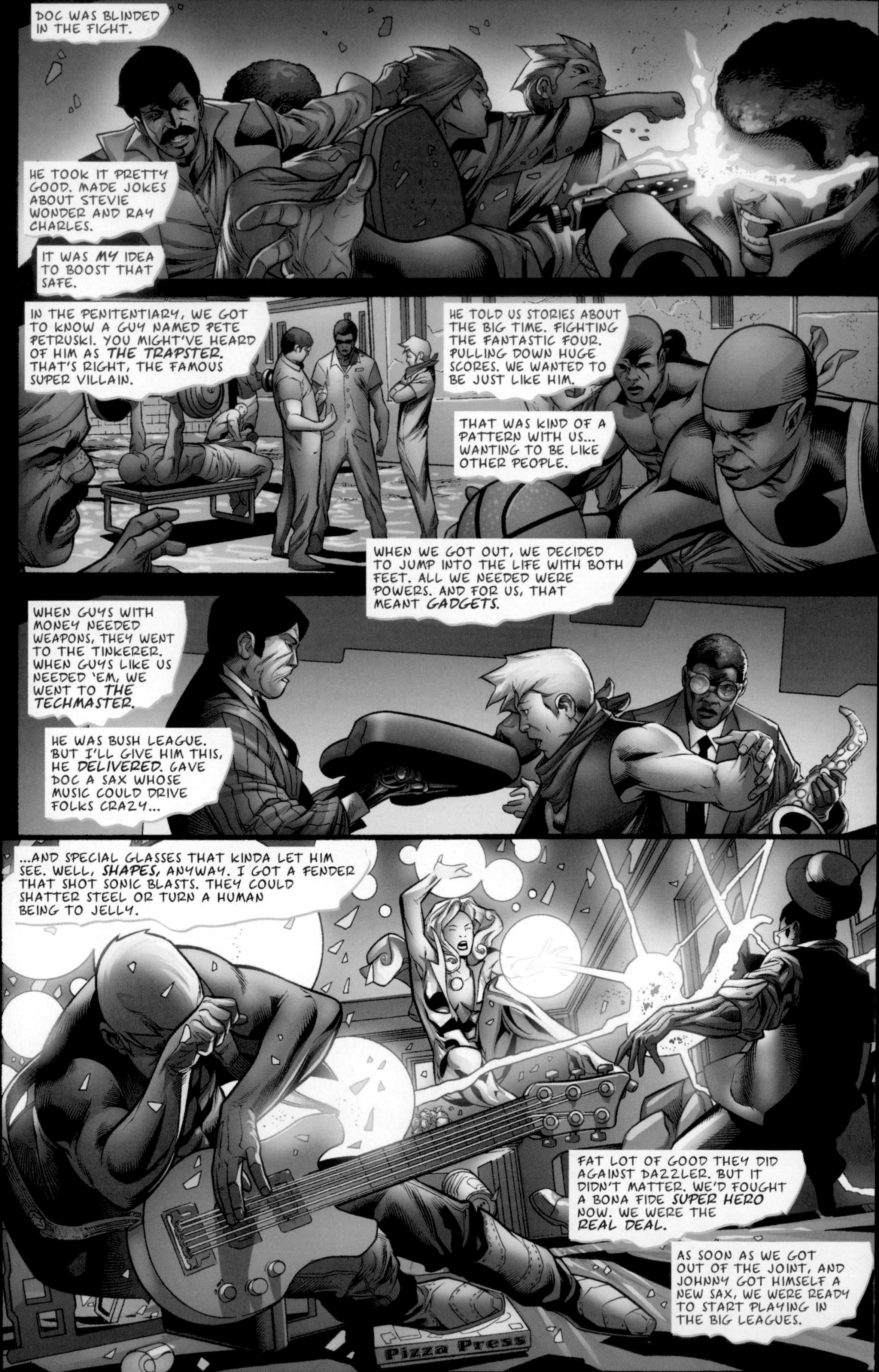
DOC WAS BLINDED IN THE FIGHT.
HE TOOK IT PRETTY GOOD. MADE JOKES ABOUT STEVIE WONDER AND RAY CHARLES.
IT WAS MY IDEA TO BOOST THAT SAFE.
IN THE PENITENTIARY, WE GOT TO KNOW A GUY NAMED PETE PETRUSKI. YOU MIGHT'VE HEARD OF HIM AS THE TRAPSTER. THAT'S RIGHT, THE FAMOUS SUPER VILLAIN.
HE TOLD US STORIES ABOUT THE BIG TIME. FIGHTING THE FANTASTIC FOUR. PULLING DOWN HUGE SCORES. WE WANTED TO BE JUST LIKE HIM.
THAT WAS KIND OF A PATTERN WITH US... WANTING TO BE LIKE OTHER PEOPLE.
WHEN WE GOT OUT, WE DECIDED TO JUMP INTO THE LIFE WITH BOTH FEET. ALL WE NEEDED WERE POWERS. AND FOR US, THAT MEANT GADGETS.
WHEN GUYS WITH MONEY NEEDED WEAPONS, THEY WENT TO THE TINKERER. WHEN GUYS LIKE US NEEDED 'EM, WE WENT TO THE TECHMASTER.
HE WAS BUSH LEAGUE. BUT I'LL GIVE HIM THIS, HE DELIVERED. GAVE DOC A SAX WHOSE MUSIC COULD DRIVE FOLKS CRAZY...
...AND SPECIAL GLASSES THAT KINDA LET HIM SEE. WELL, SHAPES, ANYWAY. I GOT A FENDER THAT SHOT SONIC BLASTS. THEY COULD SHATTER STEEL OR TURN A HUMAN BEING TO JELLY.
FAT LOT OF GOOD THEY DID AGAINST DAZZLER. BUT IT DIDN'T MATTER. WE'D FOUGHT A BONA FIDE SUPER HERO NOW. WE WERE THE REAL DEAL.
AS SOON AS WE GOT OUT OF THE JOINT, AND JOHNNY GOT HIMSELF A NEW SAX, WE WERE READY TO START PLAYING IN THE BIG LEAGUES.
Pizza Press

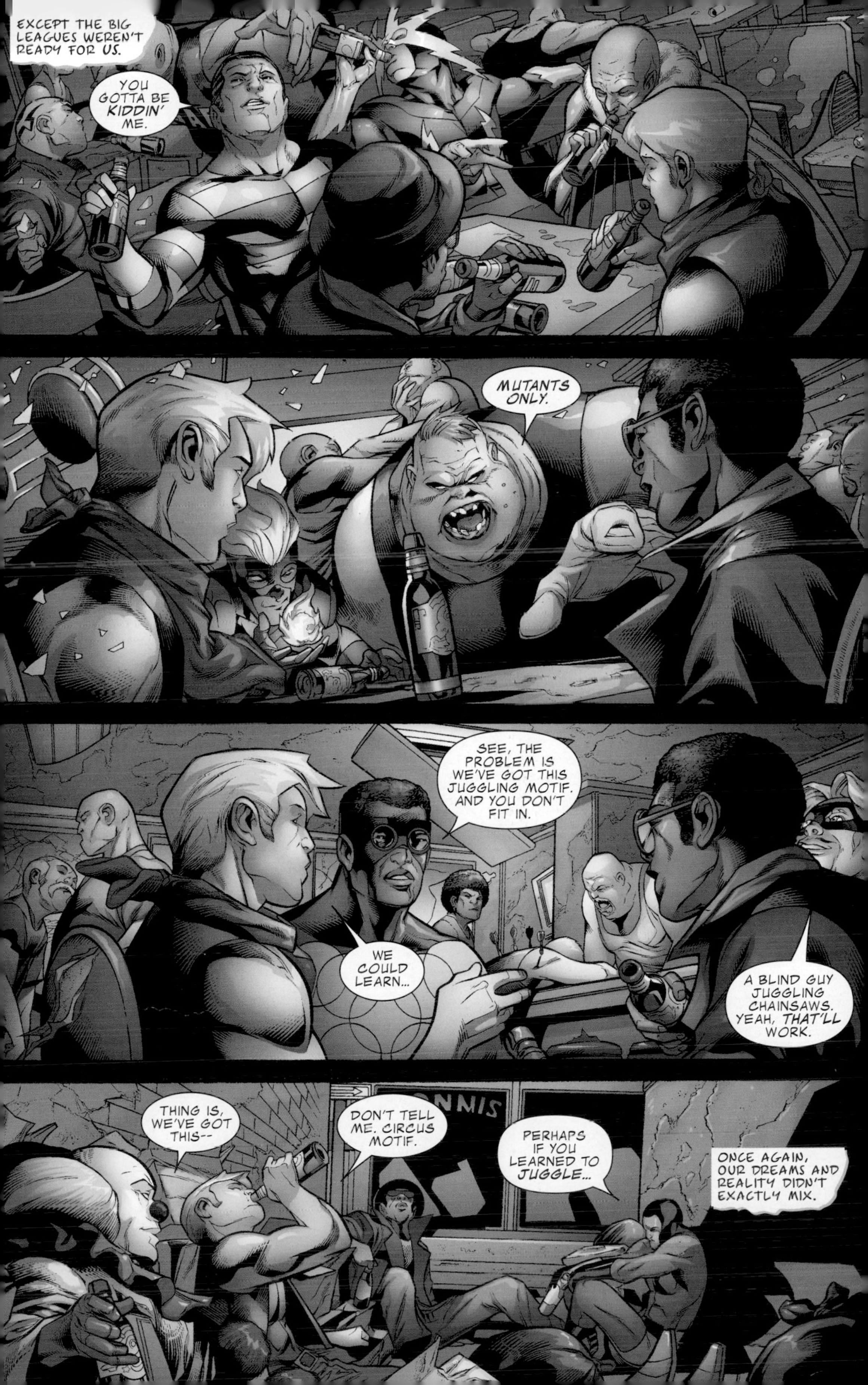
EXCEPT THE BIG LEAGUES WEREN'T READY FOR US.
YOU GOTTA BE KIDDIN' ME.
MUTANTS ONLY.
SEE, THE PROBLEM IS WE'VE GOT THIS JUGGLING MOTIF. AND YOU DON'T FIT IN.
WE COULD LEARN...
A BLIND GUY JUGGLING CHAINSAWS. YEAH, THAT'LL WORK.
THING IS, WE'VE GOT THIS--
DON'T TELL ME. CIRCUS MOTIF.
PERHAPS IF YOU LEARNED TO JUGGLE...
ONCE AGAIN, OUR DREAMS AND REALITY DIDN'T EXACTLY MIX.

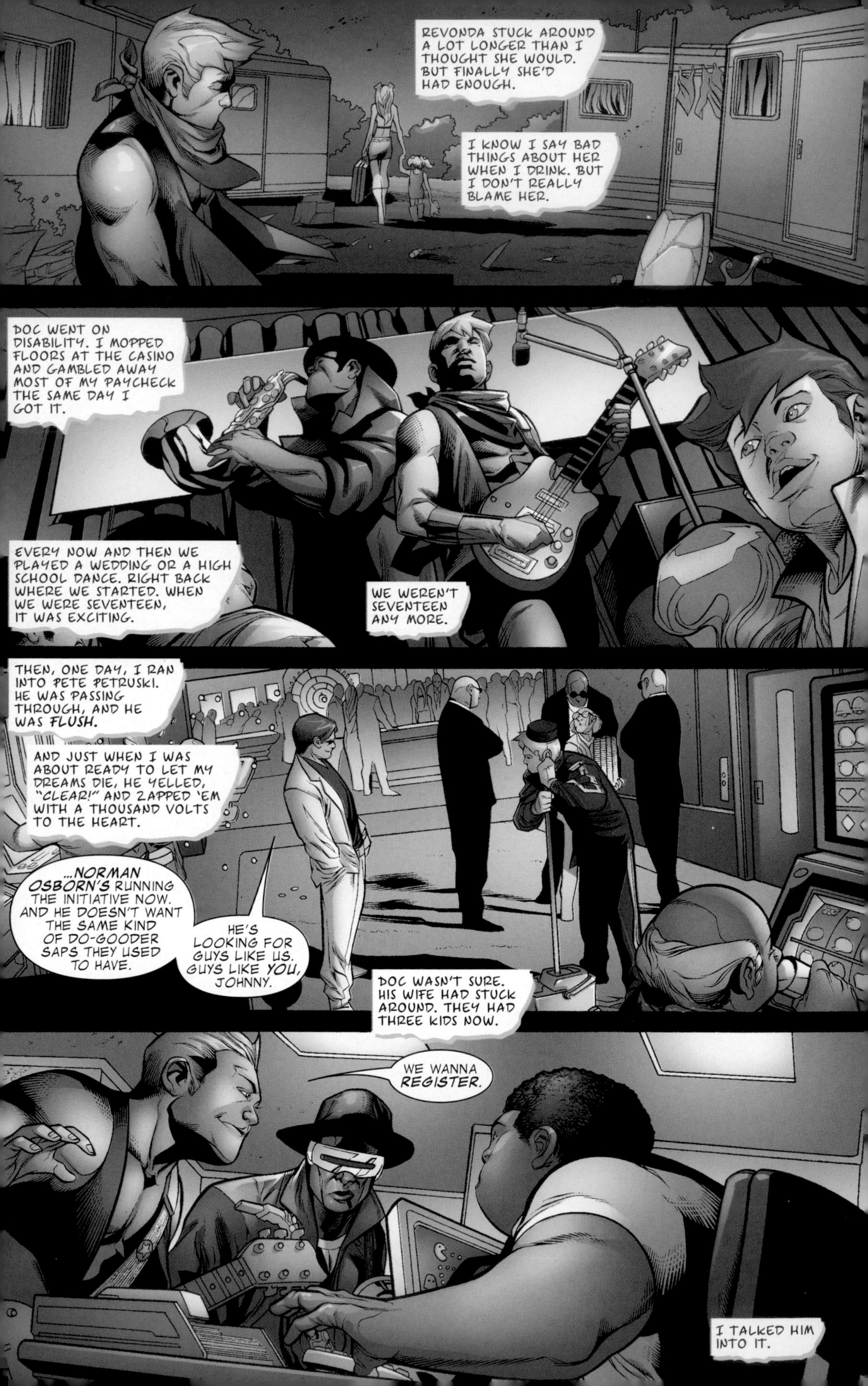
REVONDA STUCK AROUND A LOT LONGER THAN I THOUGHT SHE WOULD. BUT FINALLY SHE'D HAD ENOUGH.
I KNOW I SAY BAD THINGS ABOUT HER WHEN I DRINK. BUT I DON'T REALLY BLAME HER.
DOC WENT ON DISABILITY. I MOPPED FLOORS AT THE CASINO AND GAMBLED AWAY MOST OF MY PAYCHECK THE SAME DAY I GOT IT.
EVERY NOW AND THEN WE PLAYED A WEDDING OR A HIGH SCHOOL DANCE. RIGHT BACK WHERE WE STARTED. WHEN WE WERE SEVENTEEN, IT WAS EXCITING.
WE WEREN'T SEVENTEEN ANY MORE.
THEN, ONE DAY, I RAN INTO PETE PETRUSKI. HE WAS PASSING THROUGH, AND HE WAS FLUSH.
AND JUST WHEN I WAS ABOUT READY TO LET MY DREAMS DIE, HE YELLED, "CLEAR!" AND ZAPPED 'EM WITH A THOUSAND VOLTS TO THE HEART.
...NORMAN OSBORN'S RUNNING THE INITIATIVE NOW. AND HE DOESN'T WANT THE SAME KIND OF DO-GOODER SAPS THEY USED TO HAVE.
HE'S LOOKING FOR GUYS LIKE US. GUYS LIKE YOU, JOHNNY.
DOC WASN'T SURE. HIS WIFE HAD STUCK AROUND. THEY HAD THREE KIDS NOW.
WE WANNA REGISTER.
I TALKED HIM INTO IT.

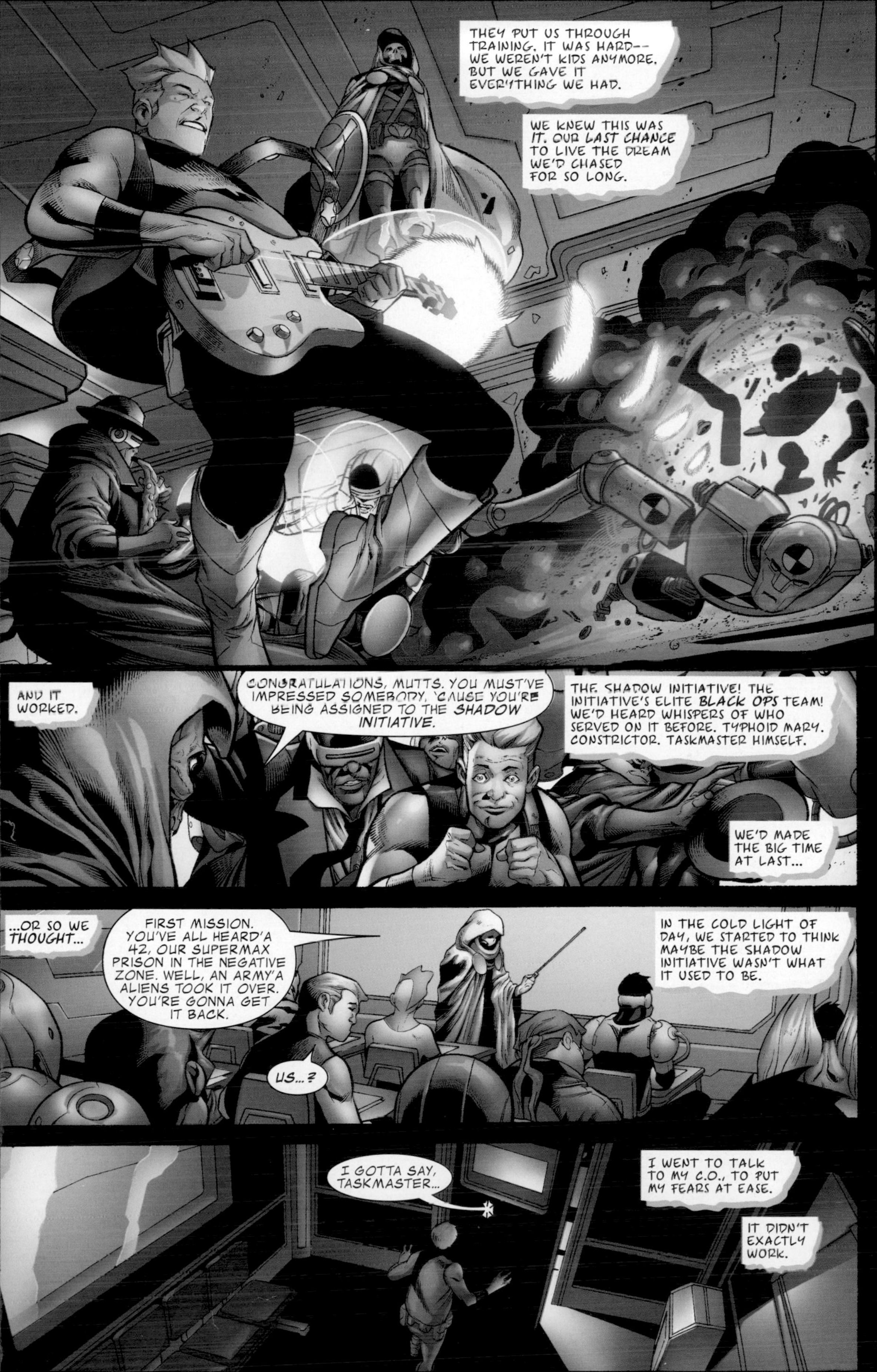
THEY PUT US THROUGH TRAINING. IT WAS HARD-- WE WEREN'T KIDS ANYMORE. BUT WE GAVE IT EVERYTHING WE HAD.
WE KNEW THIS WAS IT. OUR LAST CHANCE TO LIVE THE DREAM WE'D CHASED FOR SO LONG.
AND IT WORKED.
CONGRATULATIONS, MUTTS. YOU MUST'VE IMPRESSED SOMEBODY, 'CAUSE YOU'RE BEING ASSIGNED TO THE SHADOW INITIATIVE.
THE SHADOW INITIATIVE! THE INITIATIVE'S ELITE BLACK OPS TEAM! WE'D HEARD WHISPERS OF WHO SERVED ON IT BEFORE. TYPHOID MARY. CONSTRICTOR. TASKMASTER HIMSELF.
WE'D MADE THE BIG TIME AT LAST...
...OR SO WE THOUGHT...
FIRST MISSION. YOU'VE ALL HEARD'A 42, OUR SUPERMAX PRISON IN THE NEGATIVE ZONE. WELL, AN ARMY'A ALIENS TOOK IT OVER. YOU'RE GONNA GET IT BACK.
US...?
IN THE COLD LIGHT OF DAY, WE STARTED TO THINK MAYBE THE SHADOW INITIATIVE WASN'T WHAT IT USED TO BE.
I GOTTA SAY, TASKMASTER...
I WENT TO TALK TO MY C.O., TO PUT MY FEARS AT EASE.
IT DIDN'T EXACTLY WORK.

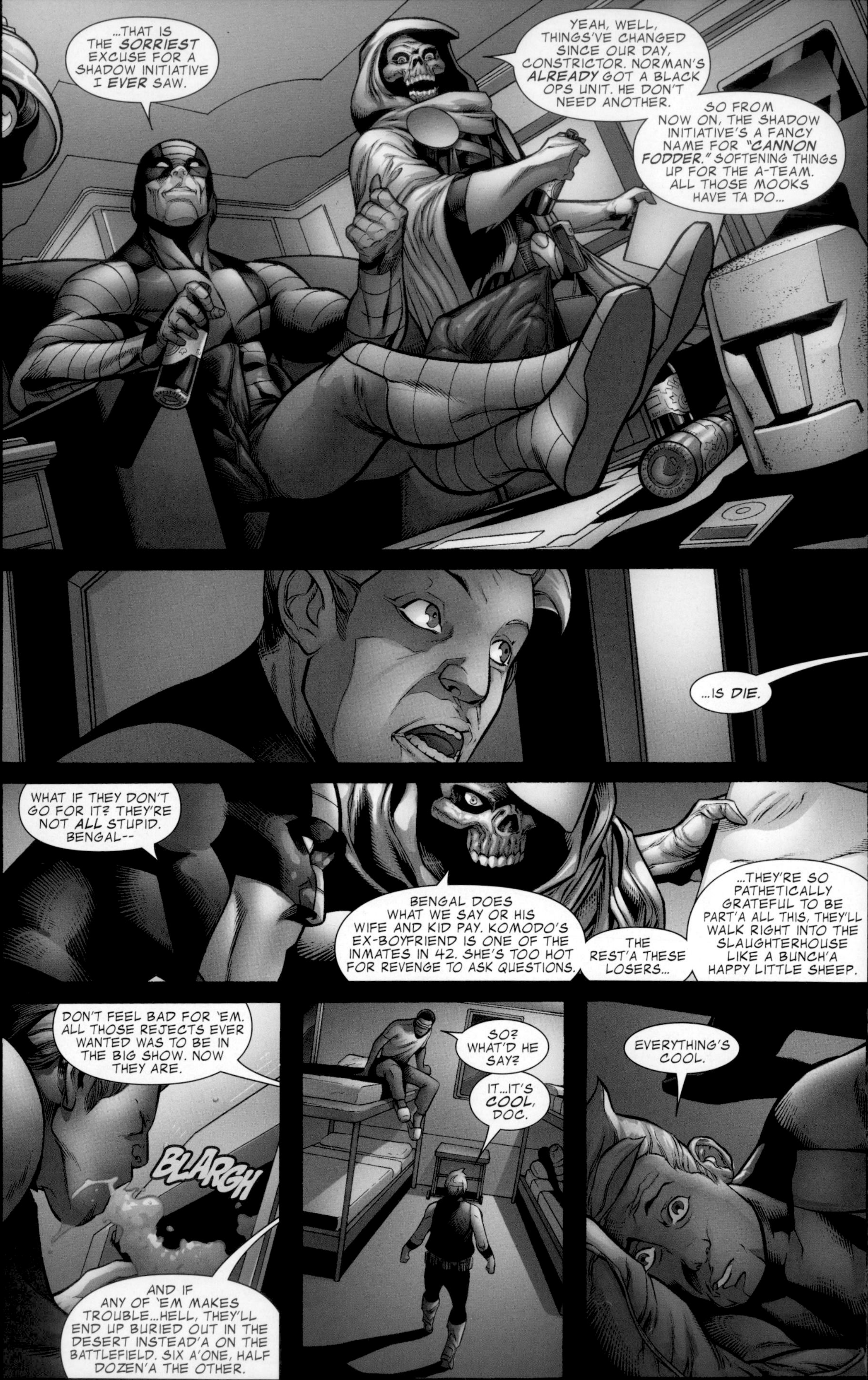
...THAT IS THE SORRIEST EXCUSE FOR A SHADOW INITIATIVE I EVER SAW.
YEAH, WELL, THINGS'VE CHANGED SINCE OUR DAY, CONSTRICTOR. NORMAN'S ALREADY GOT A BLACK OPS UNIT. HE DON'T NEED ANOTHER.
SO FROM NOW ON, THE SHADOW INITIATIVE'S A FANCY NAME FOR "CANNON FODDER." SOFTENING THINGS UP FOR THE A-TEAM. ALL THOSE MOOKS HAVE TA DO...
...IS DIE.
WHAT IF THEY DON'T GO FOR IT? THEY'RE NOT ALL STUPID. BENGAL--
BENGAL DOES WHAT WE SAY OR HIS WIFE AND KID PAY. KOMODO'S EX-BOYFRIEND IS ONE OF THE INMATES IN 42. SHE'S TOO HOT FOR REVENGE TO ASK QUESTIONS.
THE REST'A THESE LOSERS...
...THEY'RE SO PATHETICALLY GRATEFUL TO BE PART'A ALL THIS, THEY'LL WALK RIGHT INTO THE SLAUGHTERHOUSE LIKE A BUNCH'A HAPPY LITTLE SHEEP.
DON'T FEEL BAD FOR 'EM. ALL THOSE REJECTS EVER WANTED WAS TO BE IN THE BIG SHOW. NOW THEY ARE.
BLARGH
AND IF ANY OF 'EM MAKES TROUBLE...HELL, THEY'LL END UP BURIED OUT IN THE DESERT INSTEAD'A ON THE BATTLEFIELD. SIX A'ONE, HALF DOZEN'A THE OTHER.
SO? WHAT'D HE SAY?
IT...IT'S COOL, DOC.
EVERYTHING'S COOL.

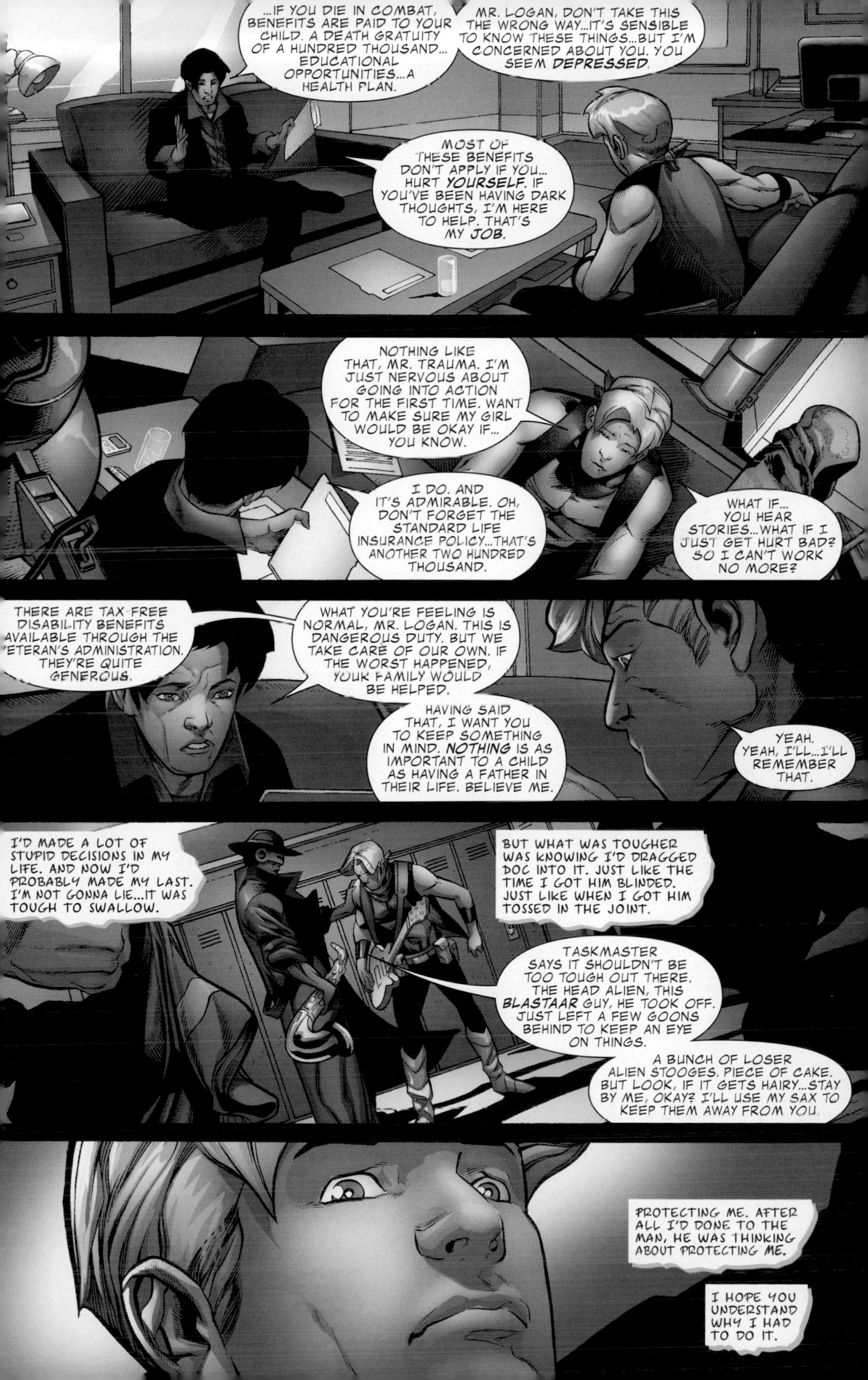
...IF YOU DIE IN COMBAT, BENEFITS ARE PAID TO YOUR CHILD. A DEATH GRATUITY OF A HUNDRED THOUSAND... EDUCATIONAL OPPORTUNITIES...A HEALTH PLAN.
MR. LOGAN, DON'T TAKE THIS THE WRONG WAY...IT'S SENSIBLE TO KNOW THESE THINGS...BUT I'M CONCERNED ABOUT YOU. YOU SEEM DEPRESSED.
MOST OF THESE BENEFITS DON'T APPLY IF YOU... HURT YOURSELF. IF YOU'VE BEEN HAVING DARK THOUGHTS, I'M HERE TO HELP. THAT'S MY JOB.
NOTHING LIKE THAT, MR. TRAUMA. I'M JUST NERVOUS ABOUT GOING INTO ACTION FOR THE FIRST TIME. WANT TO MAKE SURE MY GIRL WOULD BE OKAY IF... YOU KNOW.
I DO. AND IT'S ADMIRABLE. OH, DON'T FORGET THE STANDARD LIFE INSURANCE POLICY...THAT'S ANOTHER TWO HUNDRED THOUSAND.
WHAT IF... YOU HEAR STORIES...WHAT IF I JUST GET HURT BAD? SO I CAN'T WORK NO MORE?
THERE ARE TAX FREE DISABILITY BENEFITS AVAILABLE THROUGH THE VETERAN'S ADMINISTRATION. THEY'RE QUITE GENEROUS.
WHAT YOU'RE FEELING IS NORMAL, MR. LOGAN. THIS IS DANGEROUS DUTY. BUT WE TAKE CARE OF OUR OWN. IF THE WORST HAPPENED, YOUR FAMILY WOULD BE HELPED.
HAVING SAID THAT, I WANT YOU TO KEEP SOMETHING IN MIND. NOTHING IS AS IMPORTANT TO A CHILD AS HAVING A FATHER IN THEIR LIFE. BELIEVE ME.
YEAH. YEAH, I'LL...I'LL REMEMBER THAT.
I'D MADE A LOT OF STUPID DECISIONS IN MY LIFE. AND NOW I'D PROBABLY MADE MY LAST. I'M NOT GONNA LIE...IT WAS TOUGH TO SWALLOW.
BUT WHAT WAS TOUGHER WAS KNOWING I'D DRAGGED DOC INTO IT. JUST LIKE THE TIME I GOT HIM BLINDED. JUST LIKE WHEN I GOT HIM TOSSED IN THE JOINT.
TASKMASTER SAYS IT SHOULDN'T BE TOO TOUGH OUT THERE. THE HEAD ALIEN, THIS BLASTAAR GUY, HE TOOK OFF. JUST LEFT A FEW GOONS BEHIND TO KEEP AN EYE ON THINGS.
A BUNCH OF LOSER ALIEN STOOGES. PIECE OF CAKE. BUT LOOK, IF IT GETS HAIRY...STAY BY ME, OKAY? I'LL USE MY SAX TO KEEP THEM AWAY FROM YOU.
PROTECTING ME. AFTER ALL I'D DONE TO THE MAN, HE WAS THINKING ABOUT PROTECTING ME.
I HOPE YOU UNDERSTAND WHY I HAD TO DO IT.

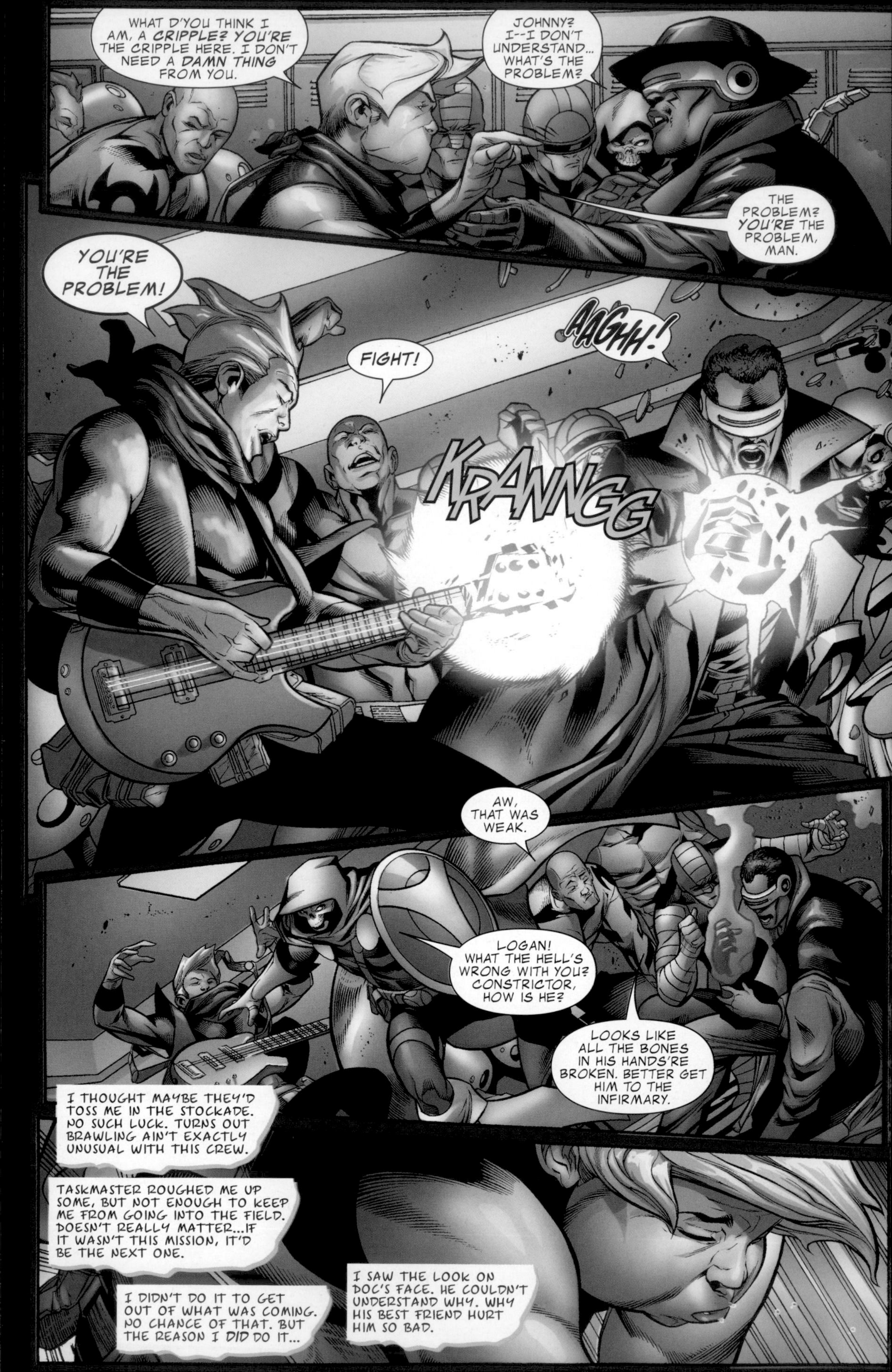
WHAT D'YOU THINK I AM, A CRIPPLE? YOU'RE THE CRIPPLE HERE. I DON'T NEED A DAMN THING FROM YOU.
JOHNNY? I--I DON'T UNDERSTAND... WHAT'S THE PROBLEM?
THE PROBLEM? YOU'RE THE PROBLEM, MAN.
YOU'RE THE PROBLEM!
FIGHT!
AAGHH!
KRANNGG
AW, THAT WAS WEAK.
LOGAN! WHAT THE HELL'S WRONG WITH YOU? CONSTRICTOR, HOW IS HE?
LOOKS LIKE ALL THE BONES IN HIS HANDS'RE BROKEN. BETTER GET HIM TO THE INFIRMARY.
I THOUGHT MAYBE THEY'D TOSS ME IN THE STOCKADE. NO SUCH LUCK. TURNS OUT BRAWLING AIN'T EXACTLY UNUSUAL WITH THIS CREW.
TASKMASTER ROUGHED ME UP SOME, BUT NOT ENOUGH TO KEEP ME FROM GOING INTO THE FIELD. DOESN'T REALLY MATTER...IF IT WASN'T THIS MISSION, IT'D BE THE NEXT ONE.
I DIDN'T DO IT TO GET OUT OF WHAT WAS COMING. NO CHANCE OF THAT. BUT THE REASON I DID DO IT...
I SAW THE LOOK ON DOC'S FACE. HE COULDN'T UNDERSTAND WHY. WHY HIS BEST FRIEND HURT HIM SO BAD.

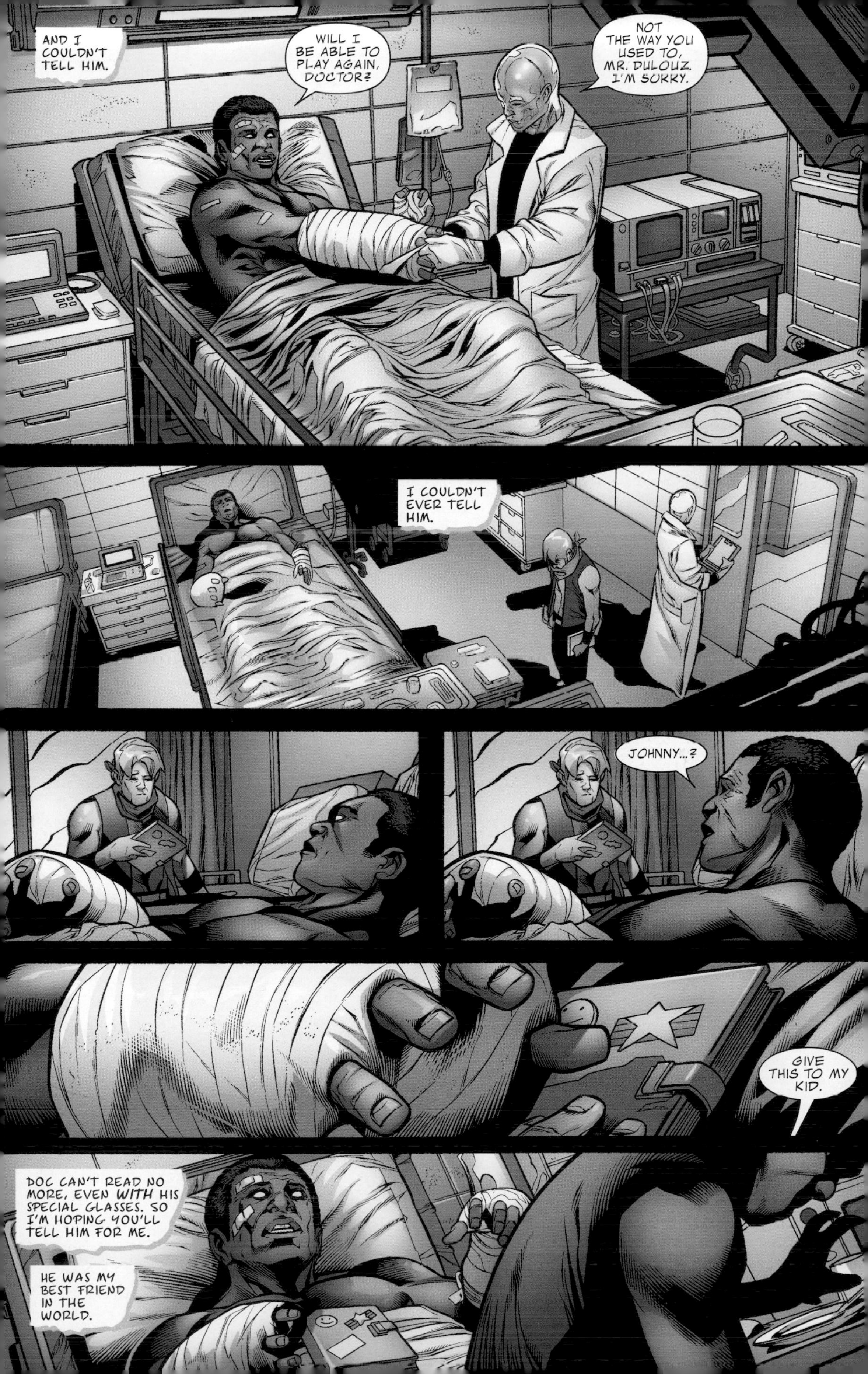
AND I COULDN'T TELL HIM.
WILL I BE ABLE TO PLAY AGAIN, DOCTOR?
NOT THE WAY YOU USED TO, MR. DULOUZ. I'M SORRY.
I COULDN'T EVER TELL HIM.
JOHNNY...?
GIVE THIS TO MY KID.
DOC CAN'T READ NO MORE, EVEN WITH HIS SPECIAL GLASSES. SO I'M HOPING YOU'LL TELL HIM FOR ME.
HE WAS MY BEST FRIEND IN THE WORLD.

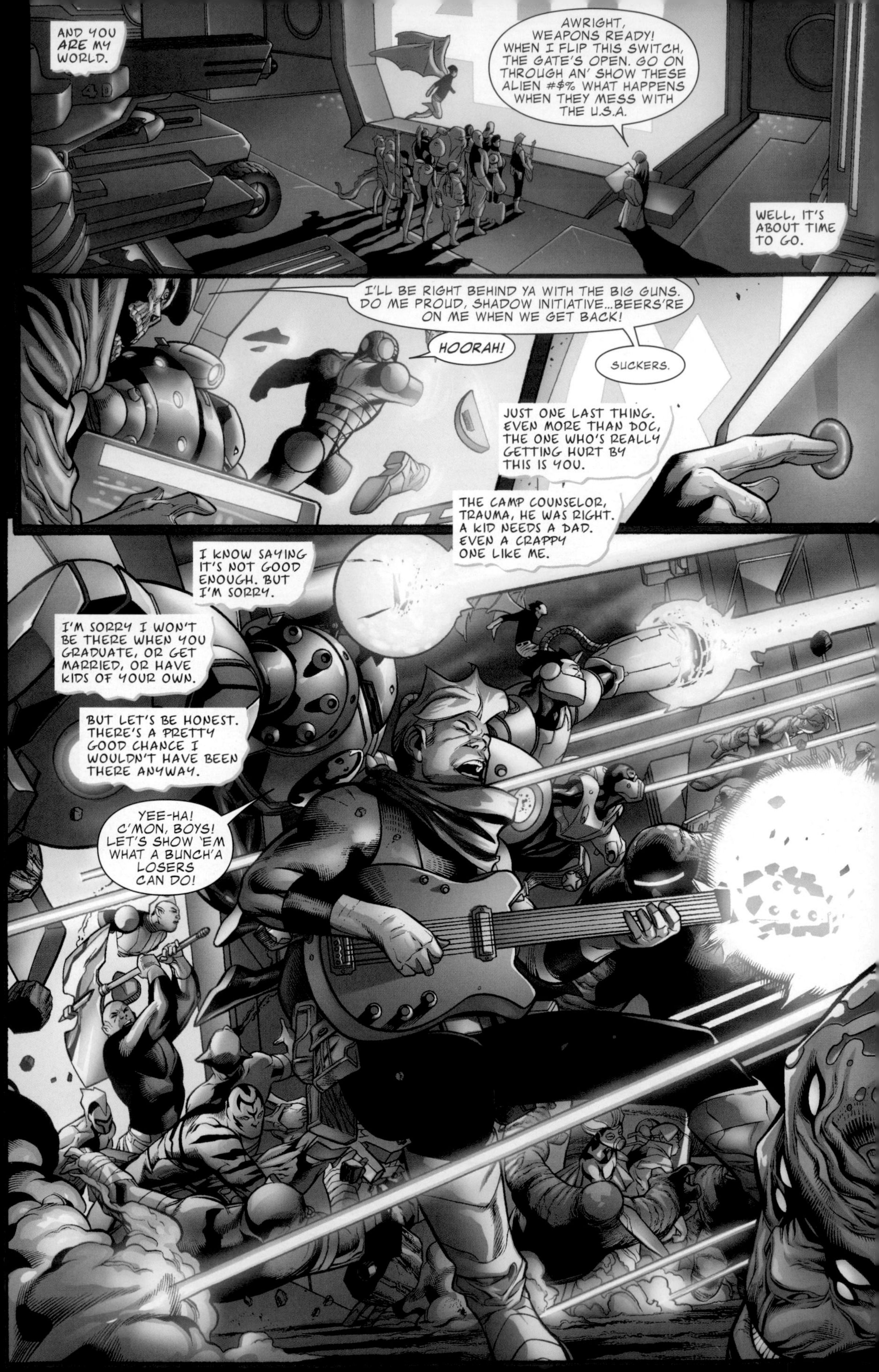
AND YOU ARE MY WORLD.
AWRIGHT, WEAPONS READY! WHEN I FLIP THIS SWITCH, THE GATE'S OPEN. GO ON THROUGH AN' SHOW THESE ALIEN #$% WHAT HAPPENS WHEN THEY MESS WITH THE U.S.A.
WELL, IT'S ABOUT TIME TO GO.
I'LL BE RIGHT BEHIND YA WITH THE BIG GUNS. DO ME PROUD, SHADOW INITIATIVE...BEERS'RE ON ME WHEN WE GET BACK!
HOORAH!
SUCKERS.
JUST ONE LAST THING. EVEN MORE THAN DOC, THE ONE WHO'S REALLY GETTING HURT BY THIS IS YOU.
THE CAMP COUNSELOR, TRAUMA, HE WAS RIGHT. A KID NEEDS A DAD. EVEN A CRAPPY ONE LIKE ME.
I KNOW SAYING IT'S NOT GOOD ENOUGH. BUT I'M SORRY.
I'M SORRY I WON'T BE THERE WHEN YOU GRADUATE, OR GET MARRIED, OR HAVE KIDS OF YOUR OWN.
BUT LET'S BE HONEST. THERE'S A PRETTY GOOD CHANCE I WOULDN'T HAVE BEEN THERE ANYWAY.
YEE-HA! C'MON, BOYS! LET'S SHOW 'EM WHAT A BUNCH'A LOSERS CAN DO!

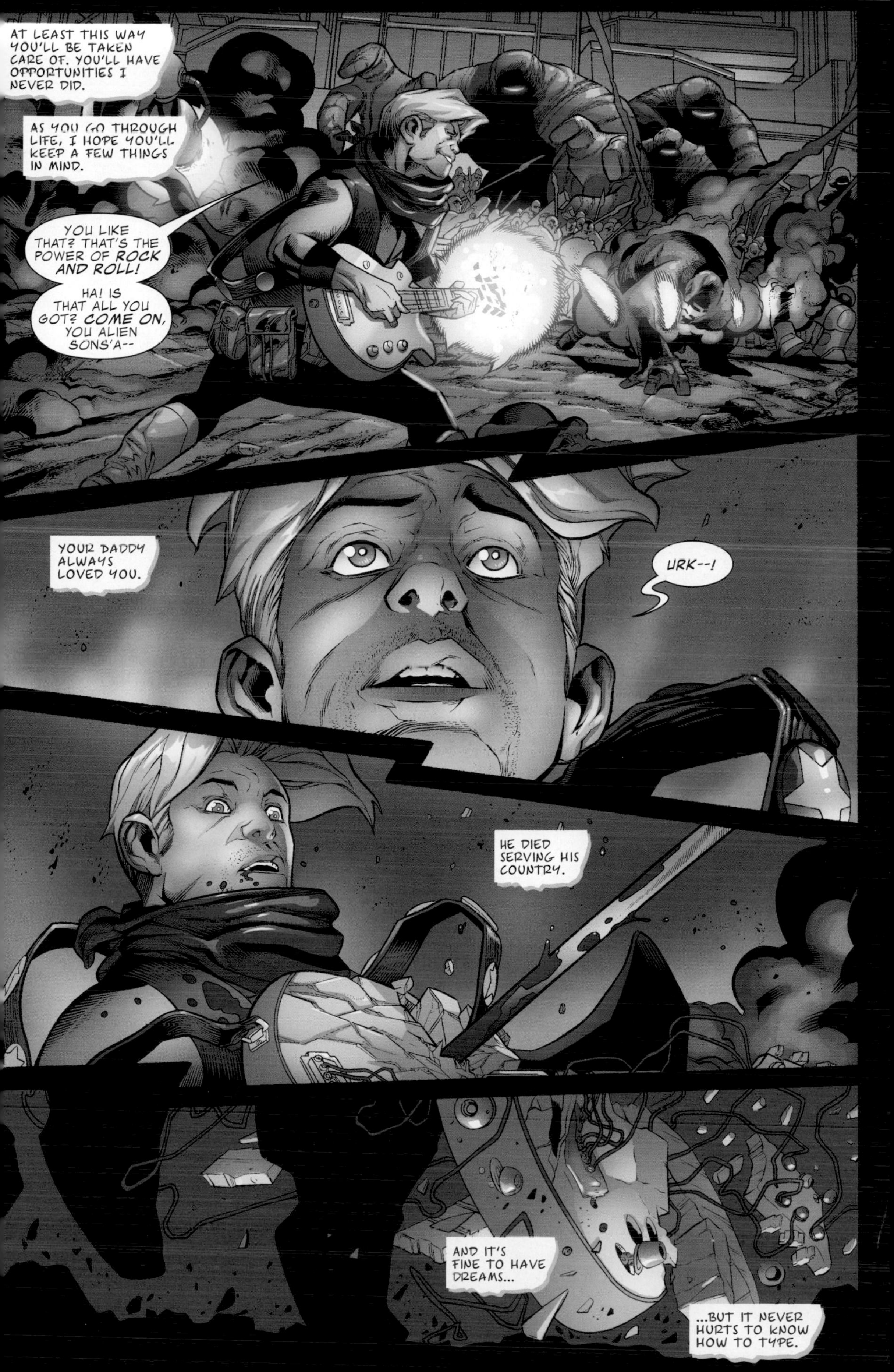
AT LEAST THIS WAY YOU'LL BE TAKEN CARE OF. YOU'LL HAVE OPPORTUNITIES I NEVER DID.
AS YOU GO THROUGH LIFE, I HOPE YOU'LL KEEP A FEW THINGS IN MIND.
YOU LIKE THAT? THAT'S THE POWER OF ROCK AND ROLL!
HA! IS THAT ALL YOU GOT? COME ON, YOU ALIEN SONS'A--
YOUR DADDY ALWAYS LOVED YOU.
URK--!
HE DIED SERVING HIS COUNTRY.
AND IT'S FINE TO HAVE DREAMS...
...BUT IT NEVER HURTS TO KNOW HOW TO TYPE.

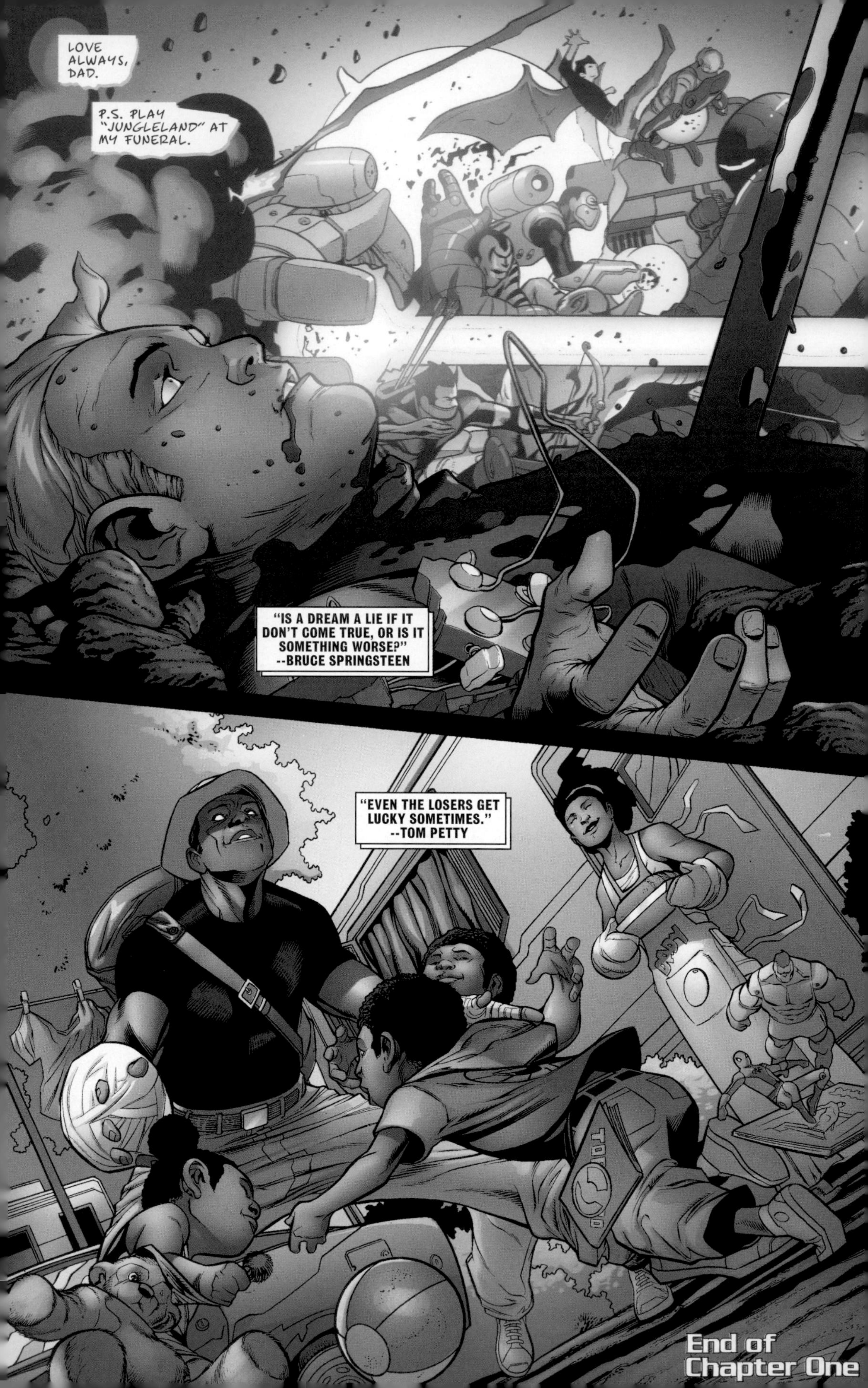
LOVE ALWAYS, DAD.
P.S. PLAY "JUNGLELAND" AT MY FUNERAL.
"IS A DREAM A LIE IF IT DON'T COME TRUE, OR IS IT SOMETHING WORSE?" --BRUCE SPRINGSTEEN
"EVEN THE LOSERS GET LUCKY SOMETIMES." --TOM PETTY
End of Chapter One

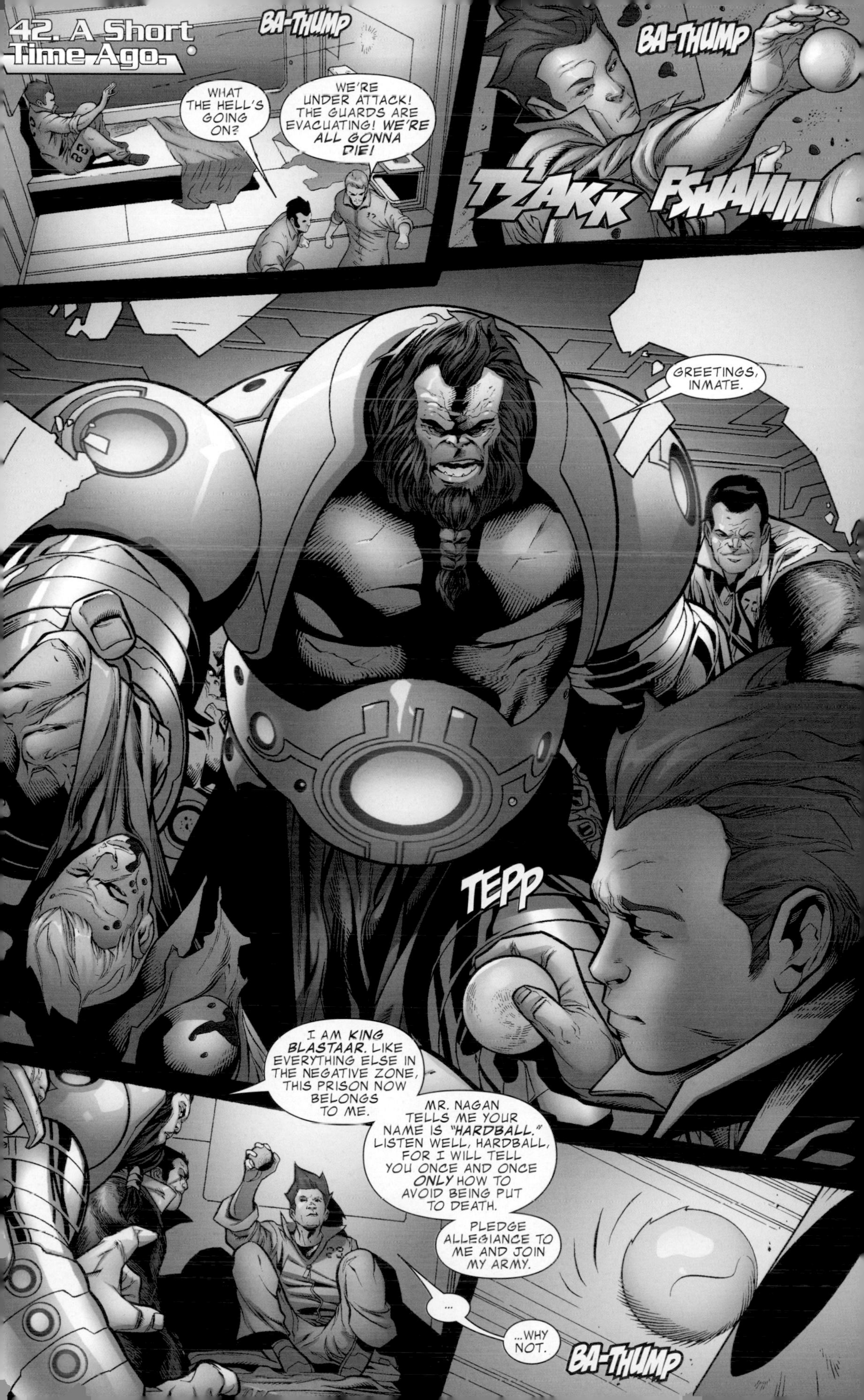
42. A Short Time Ago.
BA-THUMP
WHAT THE HELL'S GOING ON?
WE'RE UNDER ATTACK! THE GUARDS ARE EVACUATING! WE'RE ALL GONNA DIE!
BA-THUMP
TZAKK
FSHAMM
GREETINGS, INMATE.
TEPP
I AM KING BLASTAAR. LIKE EVERYTHING ELSE IN THE NEGATIVE ZONE, THIS PRISON NOW BELONGS TO ME.
MR. NAGAN TELLS ME YOUR NAME IS "HARDBALL." LISTEN WELL, HARDBALL, FOR I WILL TELL YOU ONCE AND ONCE ONLY HOW TO AVOID BEING PUT TO DEATH.
PLEDGE ALLEGIANCE TO ME AND JOIN MY ARMY.
...
...WHY NOT.
BA-THUMP

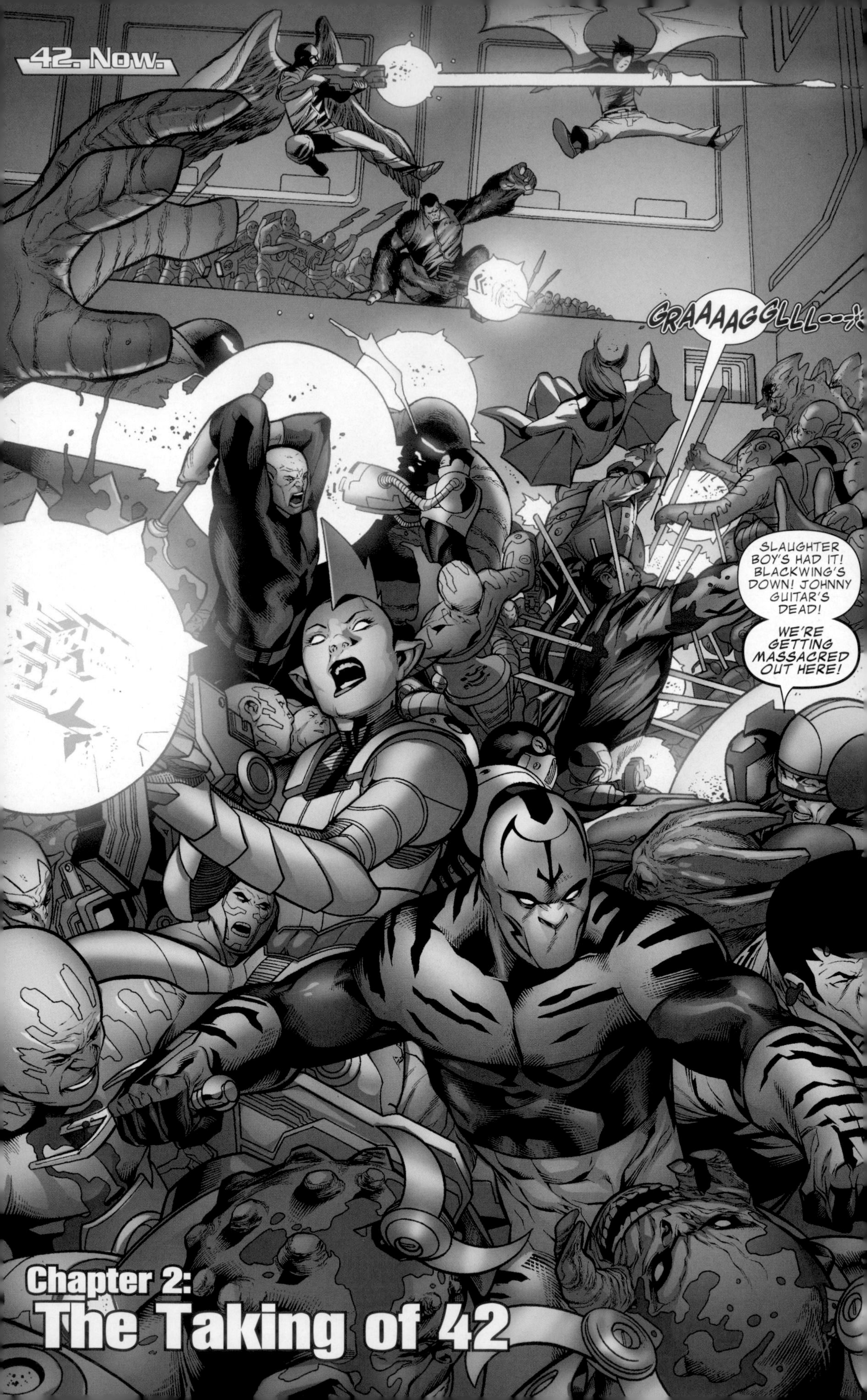
42. Now.
GRAAAAGGLLL--!
SLAUGHTER BOY'S HAD IT! BLACKWING'S DOWN! JOHNNY GUITAR'S DEAD!
WE'RE GETTING MASSACRED OUT HERE!

Chapter 2: The Taking of 42

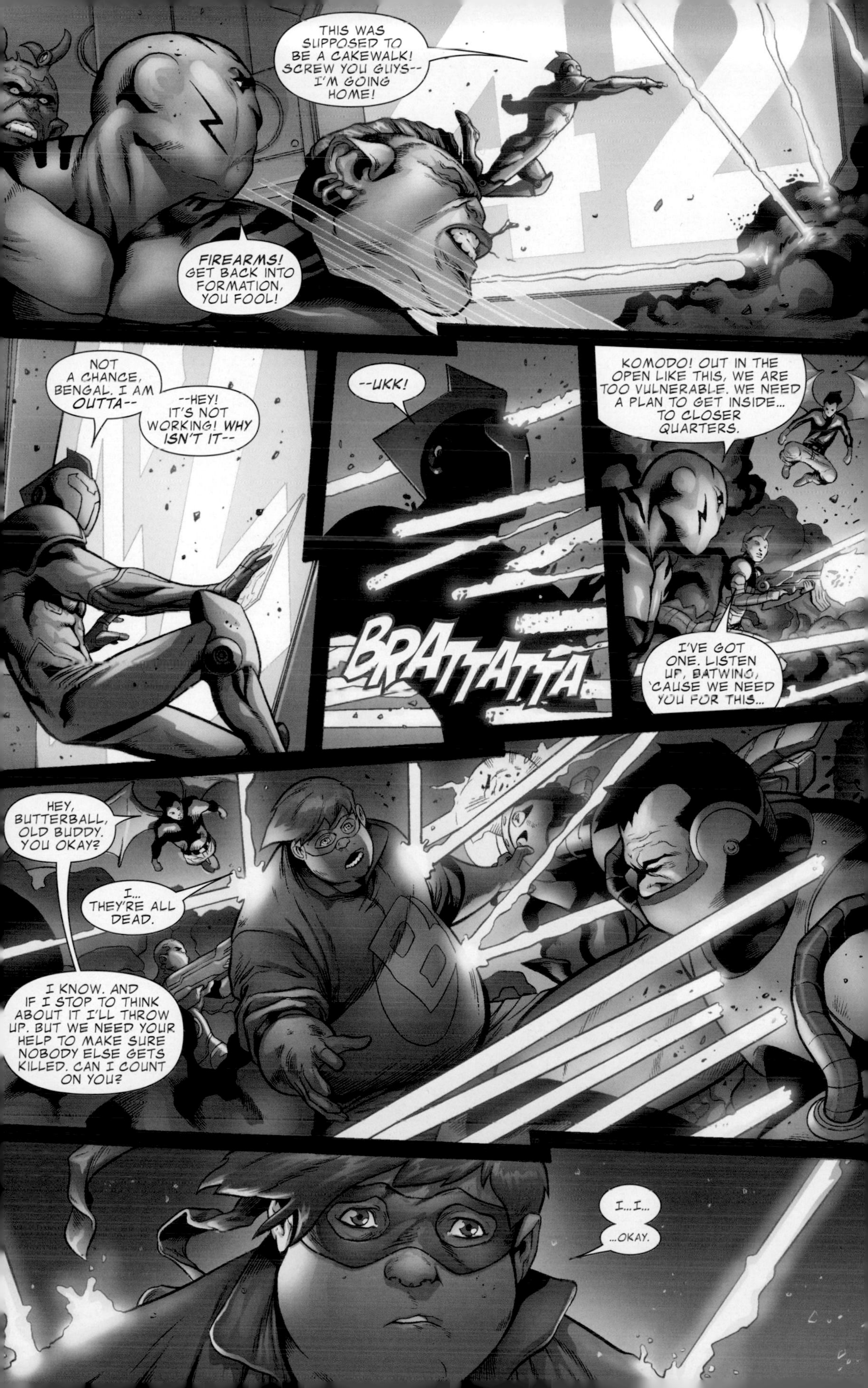

THIS WAS SUPPOSED TO BE A CAKEWALK! SCREW YOU GUYS-- I'M GOING HOME!
FIREARMS! GET BACK INTO FORMATION, YOU FOOL!
NOT A CHANCE, BENGAL. I AM OUTTA--
--HEY! IT'S NOT WORKING! WHY ISN'T IT--
--UKK!
BRATTATTA
KOMODO! OUT IN THE OPEN LIKE THIS, WE ARE TOO VULNERABLE. WE NEED A PLAN TO GET INSIDE... TO CLOSER QUARTERS.
I'VE GOT ONE. LISTEN UP, BATWING, 'CAUSE WE NEED YOU FOR THIS...
HEY, BUTTERBALL, OLD BUDDY. YOU OKAY?
I... THEY'RE ALL DEAD.
I KNOW. AND IF I STOP TO THINK ABOUT IT I'LL THROW UP. BUT WE NEED YOUR HELP TO MAKE SURE NOBODY ELSE GETS KILLED. CAN I COUNT ON YOU?
I...I...
...OKAY.

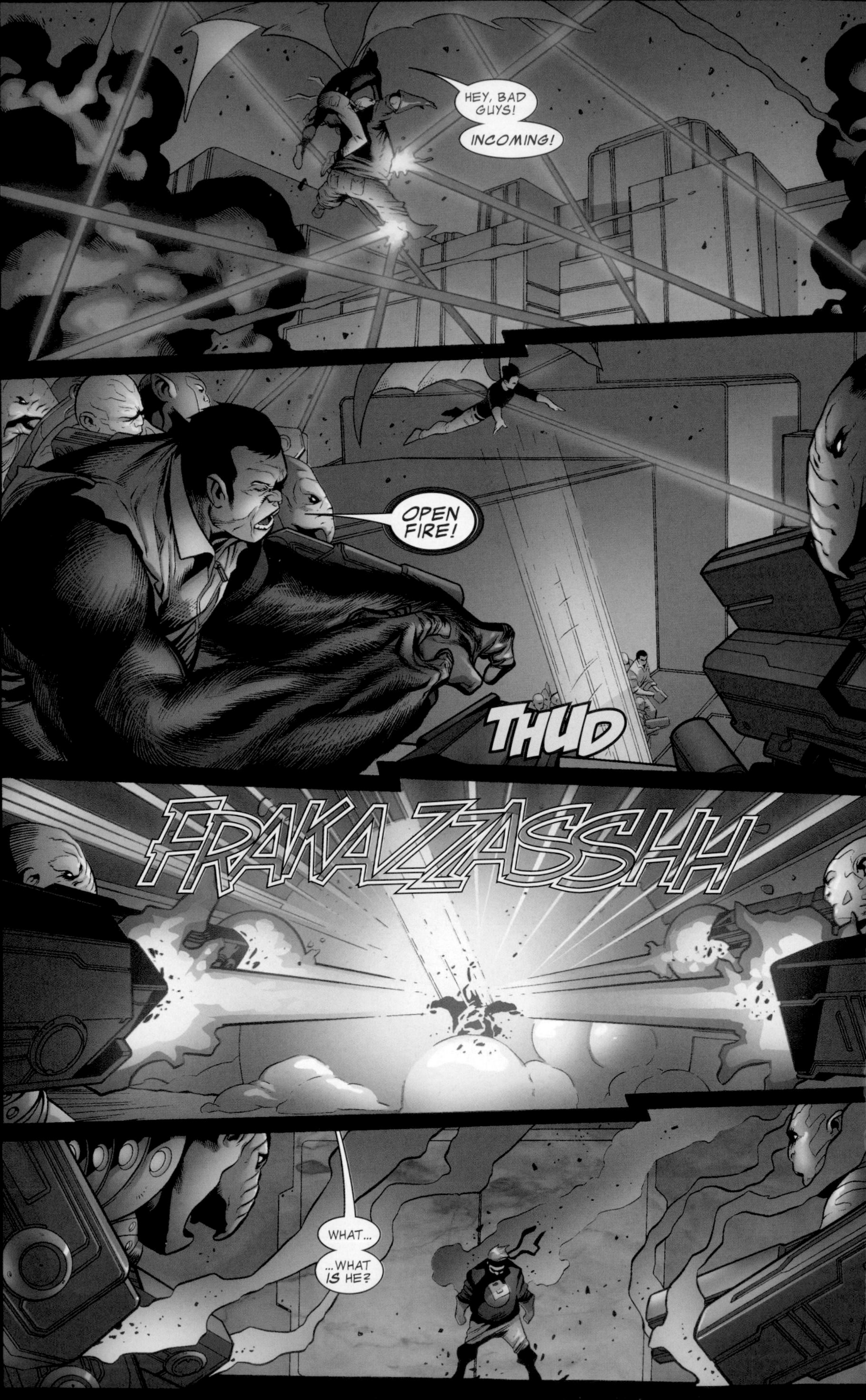
HEY, BAD GUYS!
INCOMING!
OPEN FIRE!
THUD
FRAKAZZASSHH
WHAT...
...WHAT IS HE?

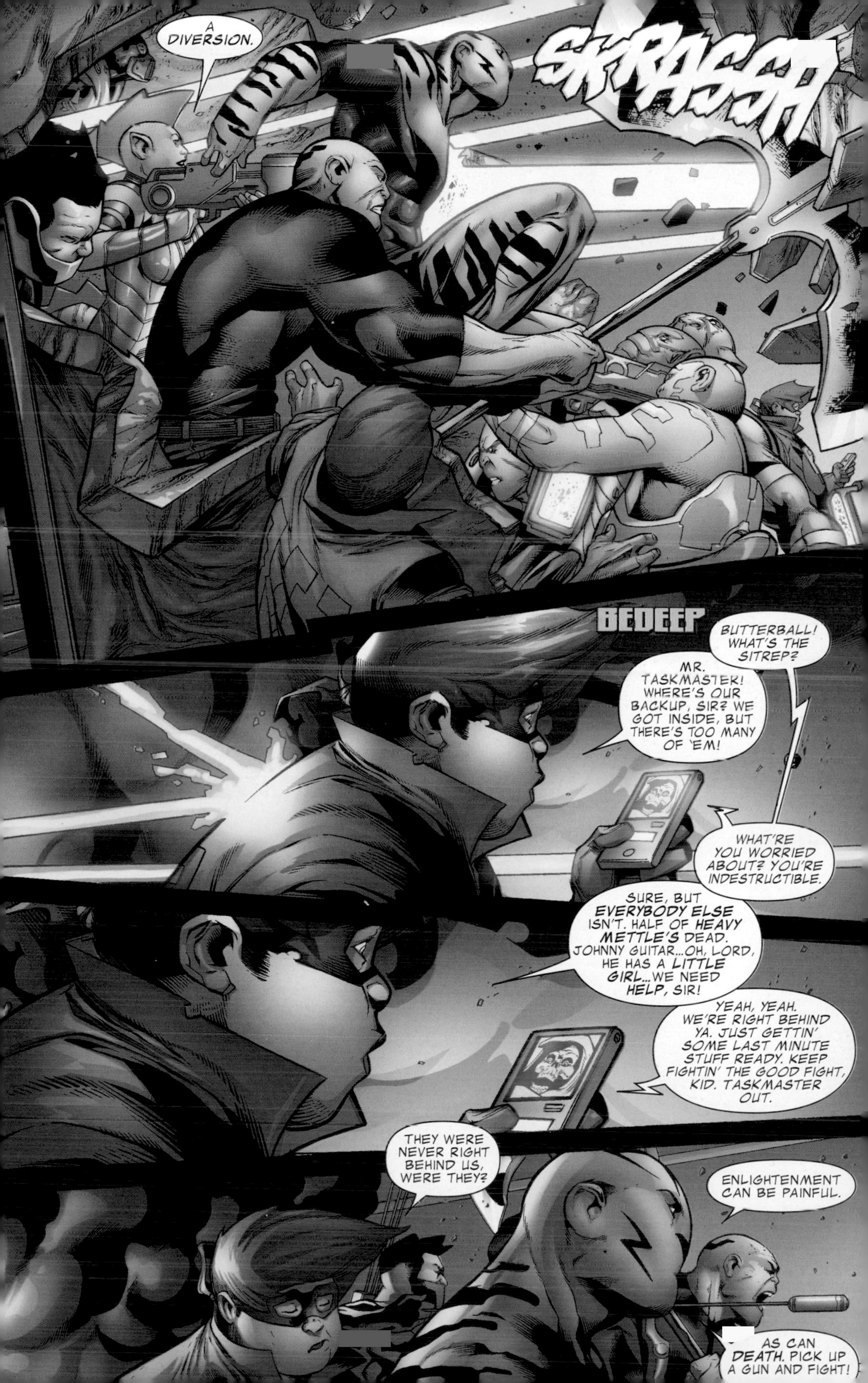
A DIVERSION.
SKRASSA
BEDEEP
BUTTERBALL! WHAT'S THE SITREP?
MR. TASKMASTER! WHERE'S OUR BACKUP, SIR? WE GOT INSIDE, BUT THERE'S TOO MANY OF 'EM!
WHAT'RE YOU WORRIED ABOUT? YOU'RE INDESTRUCTIBLE.
SURE, BUT EVERYBODY ELSE ISN'T. HALF OF HEAVY METTLE'S DEAD. JOHNNY GUITAR...OH, LORD, HE HAS A LITTLE GIRL...WE NEED HELP, SIR!
YEAH, YEAH. WE'RE RIGHT BEHIND YA. JUST GETTIN' SOME LAST MINUTE STUFF READY. KEEP FIGHTIN' THE GOOD FIGHT, KID. TASKMASTER OUT.
THEY WERE NEVER RIGHT BEHIND US, WERE THEY?
ENLIGHTENMENT CAN BE PAINFUL.
AS CAN DEATH. PICK UP A GUN AND FIGHT!

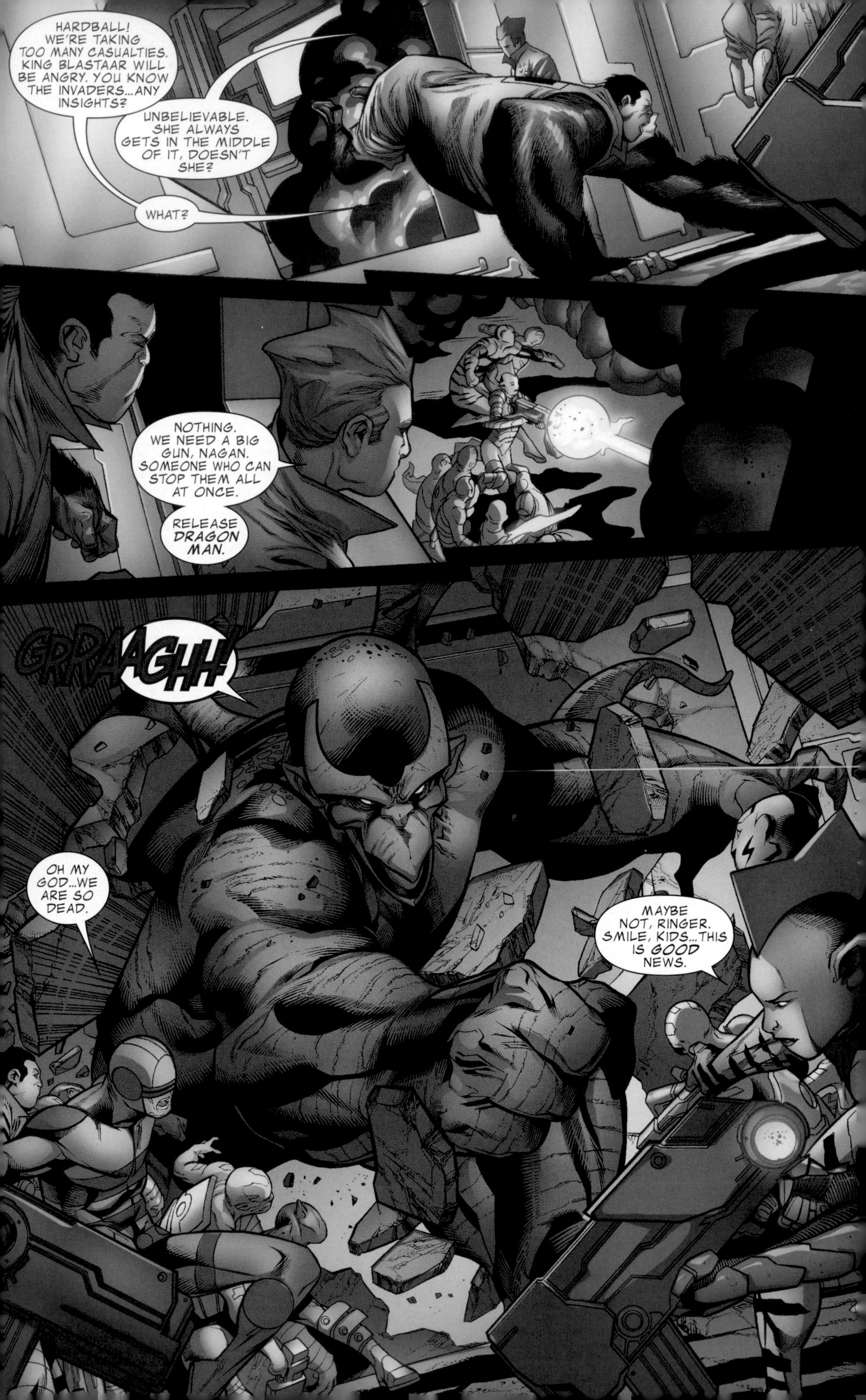
HARDBALL! WE'RE TAKING TOO MANY CASUALTIES. KING BLASTAAR WILL BE ANGRY. YOU KNOW THE INVADERS...ANY INSIGHTS?
UNBELIEVABLE. SHE ALWAYS GETS IN THE MIDDLE OF IT, DOESN'T SHE?
WHAT?
NOTHING. WE NEED A BIG GUN, NAGAN. SOMEONE WHO CAN STOP THEM ALL AT ONCE.
RELEASE *DRAGON MAN.*
GRRAAGHH!
OH MY GOD...WE ARE SO DEAD.
MAYBE NOT, RINGER. SMILE, KIDS...THIS IS *GOOD* NEWS.

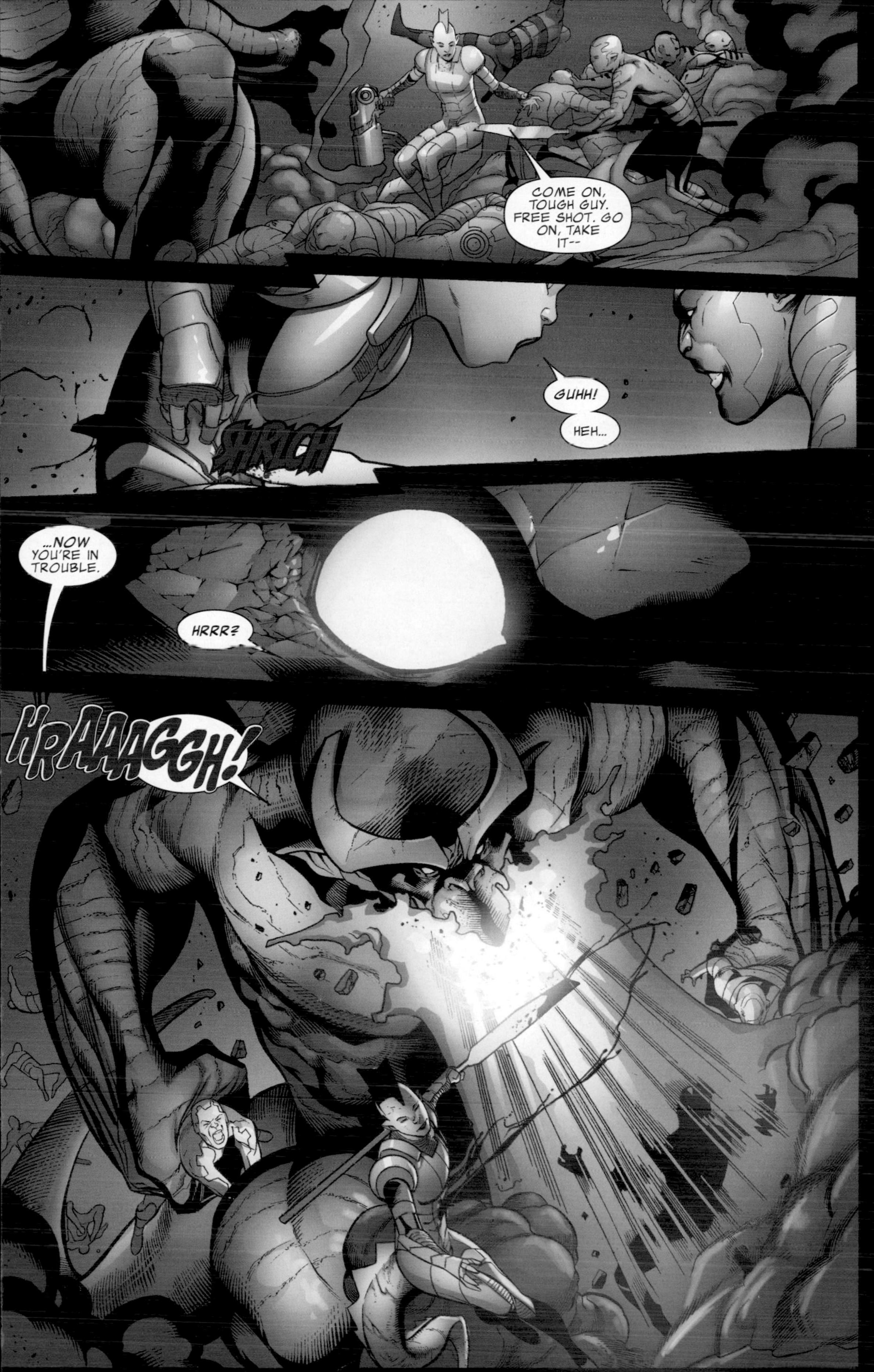

COME ON, TOUGH GUY. FREE SHOT. GO ON, TAKE IT--
SHRICH
GUHH!
HEH...
...NOW YOU'RE IN TROUBLE.
HRRR?
HRAAAAGGH!

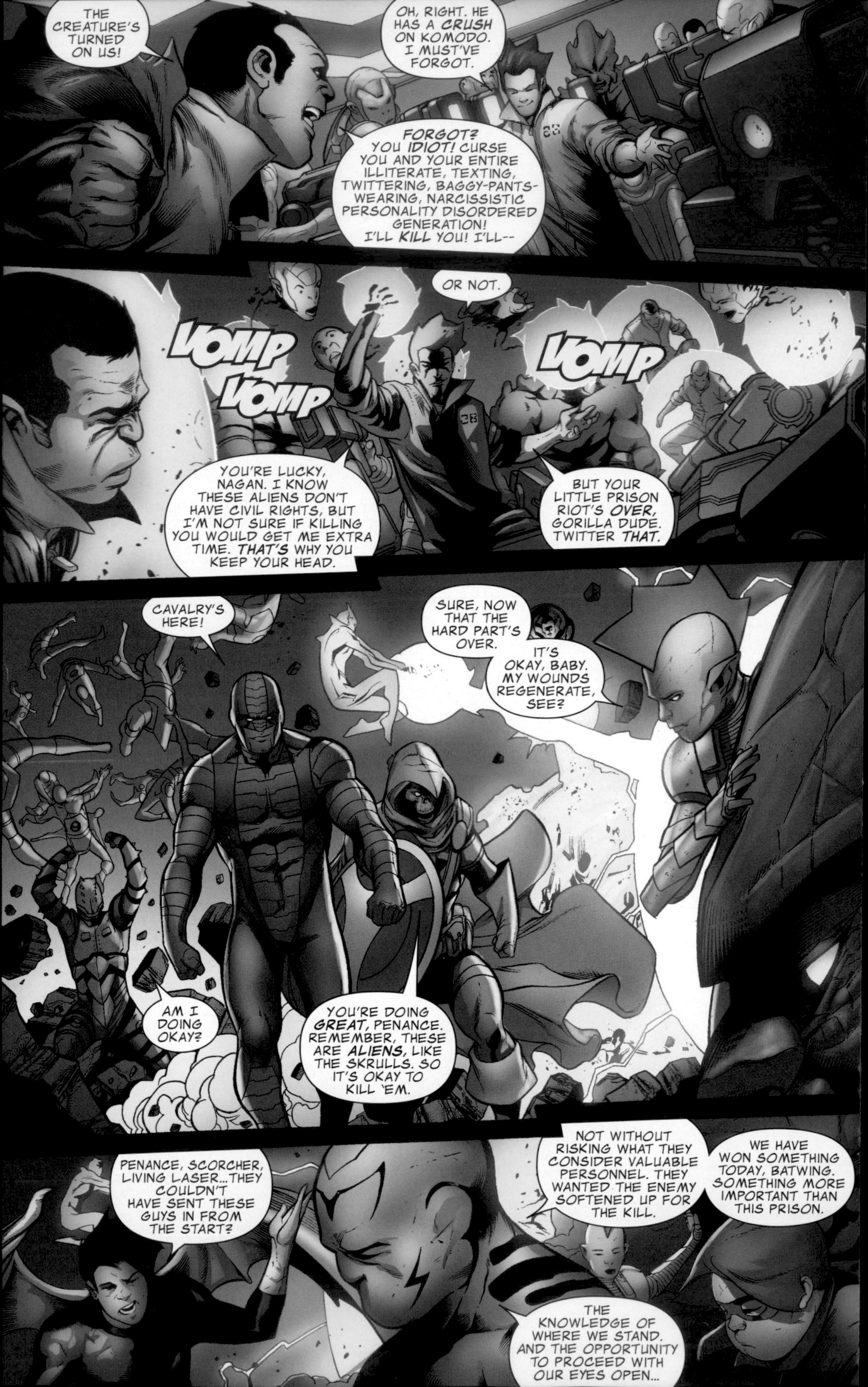
THE CREATURE'S TURNED ON US!
OH, RIGHT. HE HAS A CRUSH ON KOMODO. I MUST'VE FORGOT.
FORGOT? YOU IDIOT! CURSE YOU AND YOUR ENTIRE ILLITERATE, TEXTING, TWITTERING, BAGGY-PANTS-WEARING, NARCISSISTIC PERSONALITY DISORDERED GENERATION! I'LL KILL YOU! I'LL--
OR NOT.
VOMP
VOMP
VOMP
YOU'RE LUCKY, NAGAN. I KNOW THESE ALIENS DON'T HAVE CIVIL RIGHTS, BUT I'M NOT SURE IF KILLING YOU WOULD GET ME EXTRA TIME. THAT'S WHY YOU KEEP YOUR HEAD.
BUT YOUR LITTLE PRISON RIOT'S OVER, GORILLA DUDE. TWITTER THAT.
CAVALRY'S HERE!
SURE, NOW THAT THE HARD PART'S OVER.
IT'S OKAY, BABY. MY WOUNDS REGENERATE, SEE?
AM I DOING OKAY?
YOU'RE DOING GREAT, PENANCE. REMEMBER, THESE ARE ALIENS, LIKE THE SKRULLS. SO IT'S OKAY TO KILL 'EM.
PENANCE, SCORCHER, LIVING LASER...THEY COULDN'T HAVE SENT THESE GUYS IN FROM THE START?
NOT WITHOUT RISKING WHAT THEY CONSIDER VALUABLE PERSONNEL. THEY WANTED THE ENEMY SOFTENED UP FOR THE KILL.
WE HAVE WON SOMETHING TODAY, BATWING. SOMETHING MORE IMPORTANT THAN THIS PRISON.
THE KNOWLEDGE OF WHERE WE STAND. AND THE OPPORTUNITY TO PROCEED WITH OUR EYES OPEN...

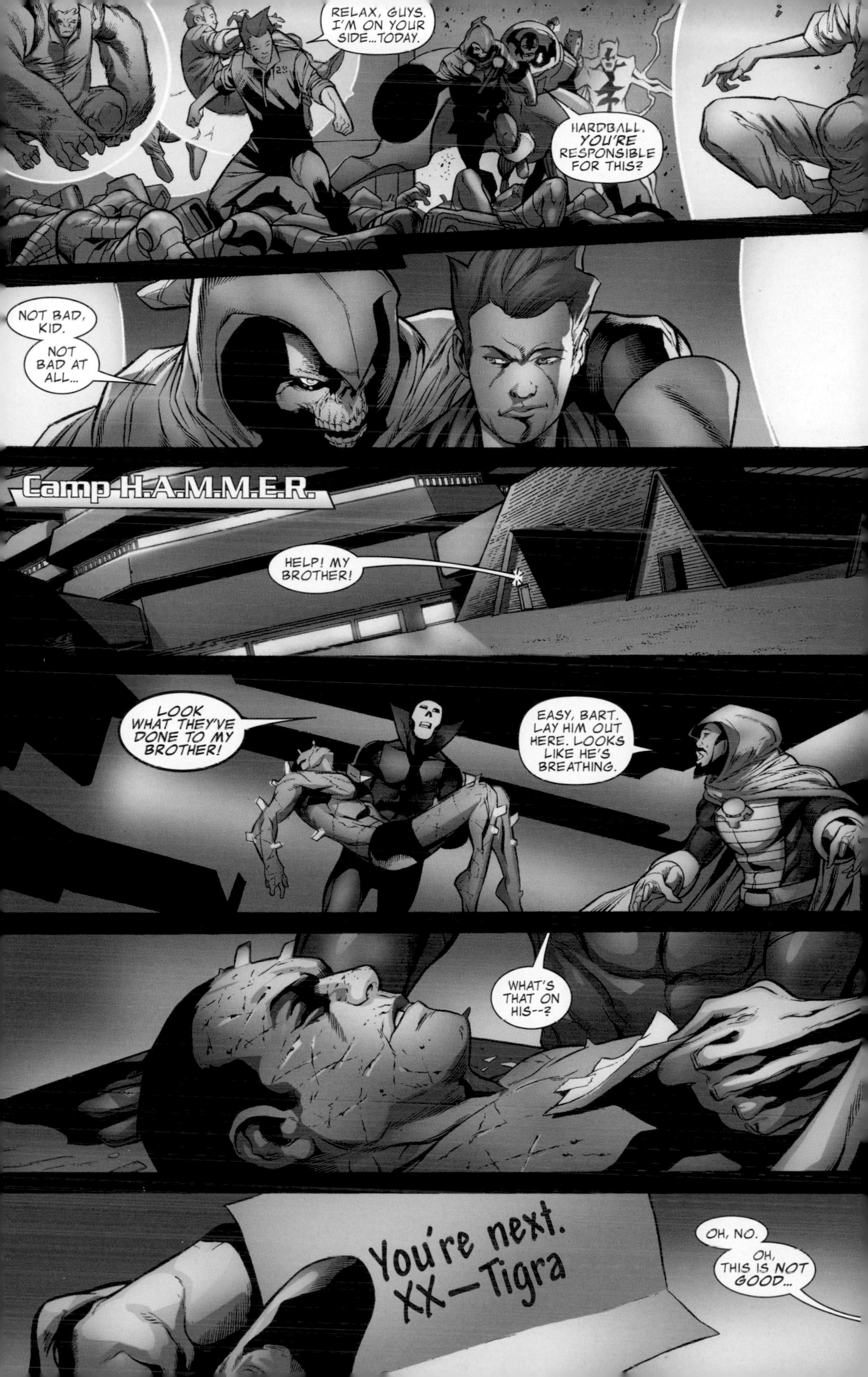
RELAX, GUYS. I'M ON YOUR SIDE...TODAY.
HARDBALL. YOU'RE RESPONSIBLE FOR THIS?
NOT BAD, KID.
NOT BAD AT ALL...
Camp H.A.M.M.E.R.
HELP! MY BROTHER!
LOOK WHAT THEY'VE DONE TO MY BROTHER!
EASY, BART. LAY HIM OUT HERE. LOOKS LIKE HE'S BREATHING.
WHAT'S THAT ON HIS--?
You're next. XX—Tigra
OH, NO.
OH, THIS IS NOT GOOD...

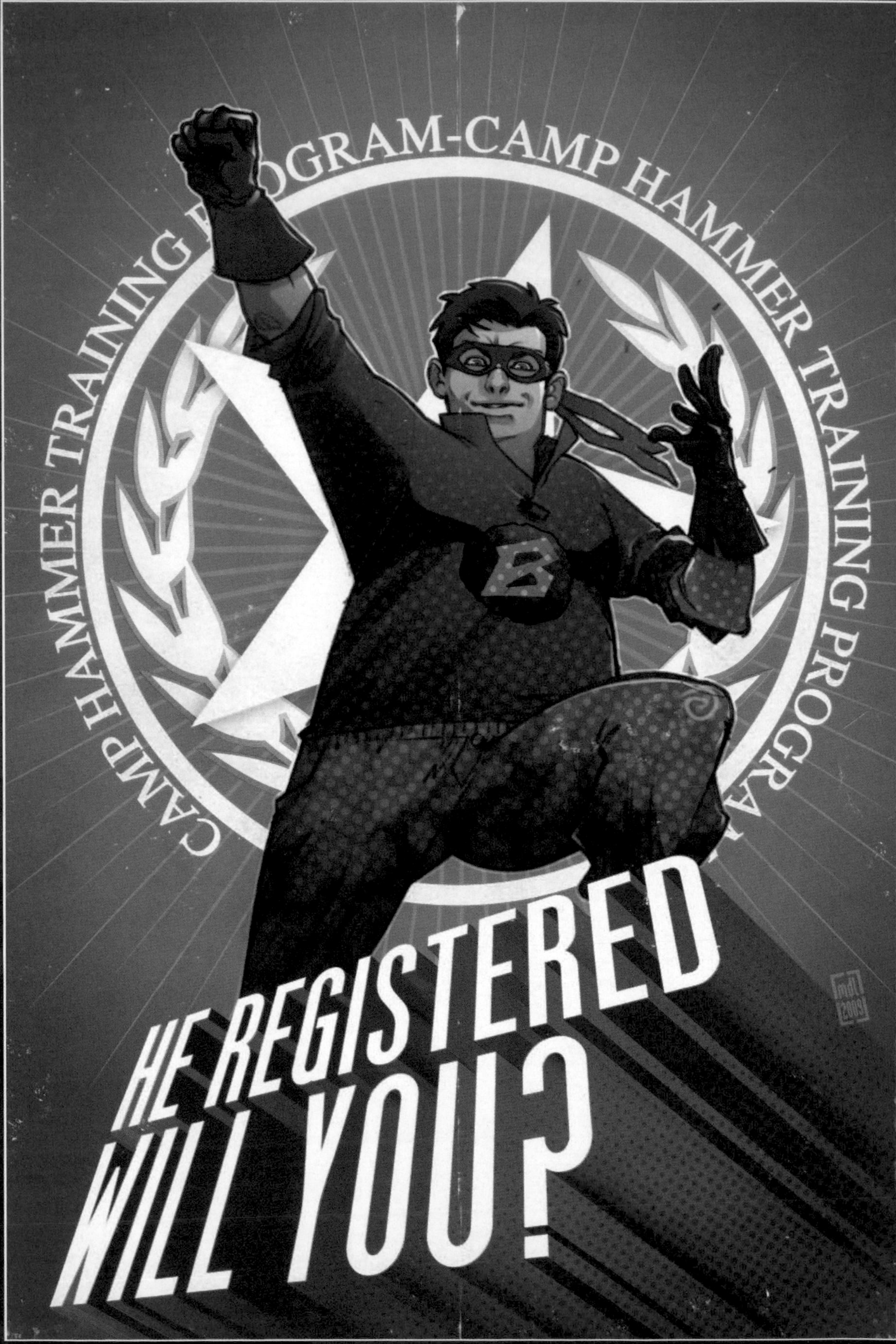
CAMP HAMMER TRAINING
OGRAM-CAMP HAMMER TRAINING PROGRA
HE REGISTERED
WILL YOU?

#28

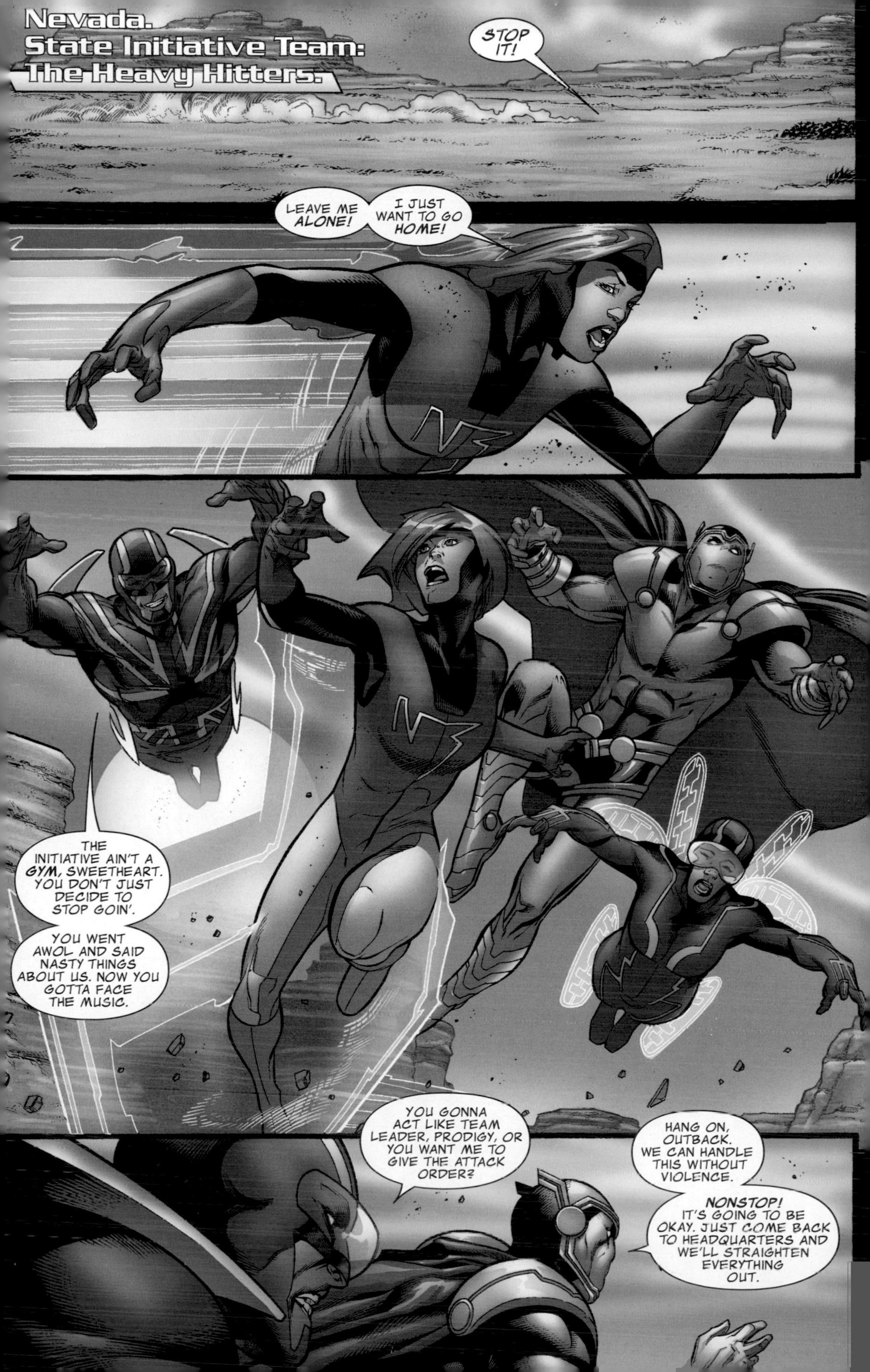

Nevada.
State Initiative Team:
The Heavy Hitters.
STOP IT!
LEAVE ME ALONE!
I JUST WANT TO GO HOME!
THE INITIATIVE AIN'T A GYM, SWEETHEART. YOU DON'T JUST DECIDE TO STOP GOIN'.
YOU WENT AWOL AND SAID NASTY THINGS ABOUT US. NOW YOU GOTTA FACE THE MUSIC.
YOU GONNA ACT LIKE TEAM LEADER, PRODIGY, OR YOU WANT ME TO GIVE THE ATTACK ORDER?
HANG ON, OUTBACK. WE CAN HANDLE THIS WITHOUT VIOLENCE.
NONSTOP! IT'S GOING TO BE OKAY. JUST COME BACK TO HEADQUARTERS AND WE'LL STRAIGHTEN EVERYTHING OUT.

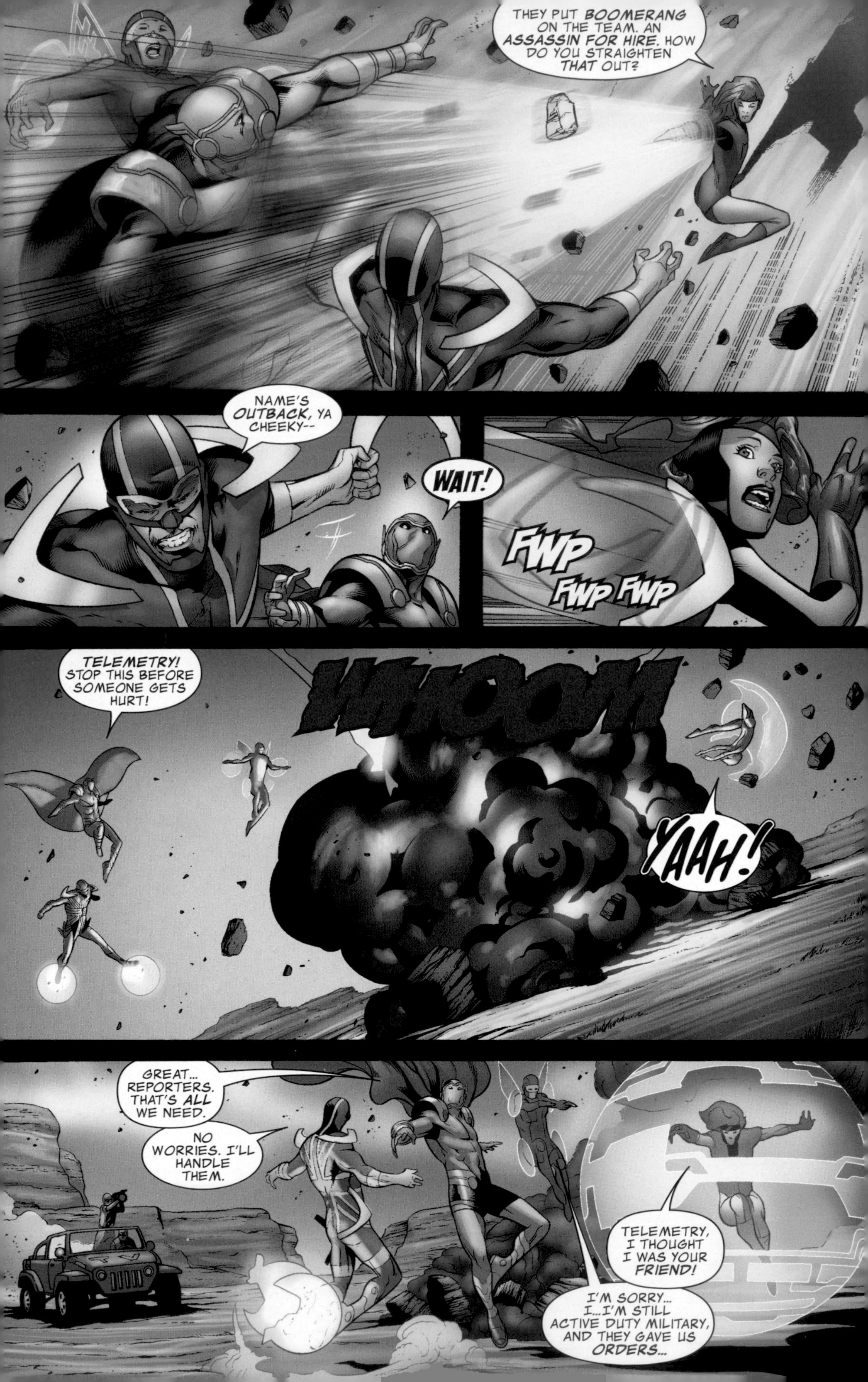
THEY PUT BOOMERANG ON THE TEAM. AN ASSASSIN FOR HIRE. HOW DO YOU STRAIGHTEN THAT OUT?
NAME'S OUTBACK, YA CHEEKY--
WAIT!
FWP FWP FWP
TELEMETRY! STOP THIS BEFORE SOMEONE GETS HURT!
WHOOM
YAAH!
GREAT... REPORTERS. THAT'S ALL WE NEED.
NO WORRIES. I'LL HANDLE THEM.
TELEMETRY, I THOUGHT I WAS YOUR FRIEND!
I'M SORRY... I...I'M STILL ACTIVE DUTY MILITARY, AND THEY GAVE US ORDERS...

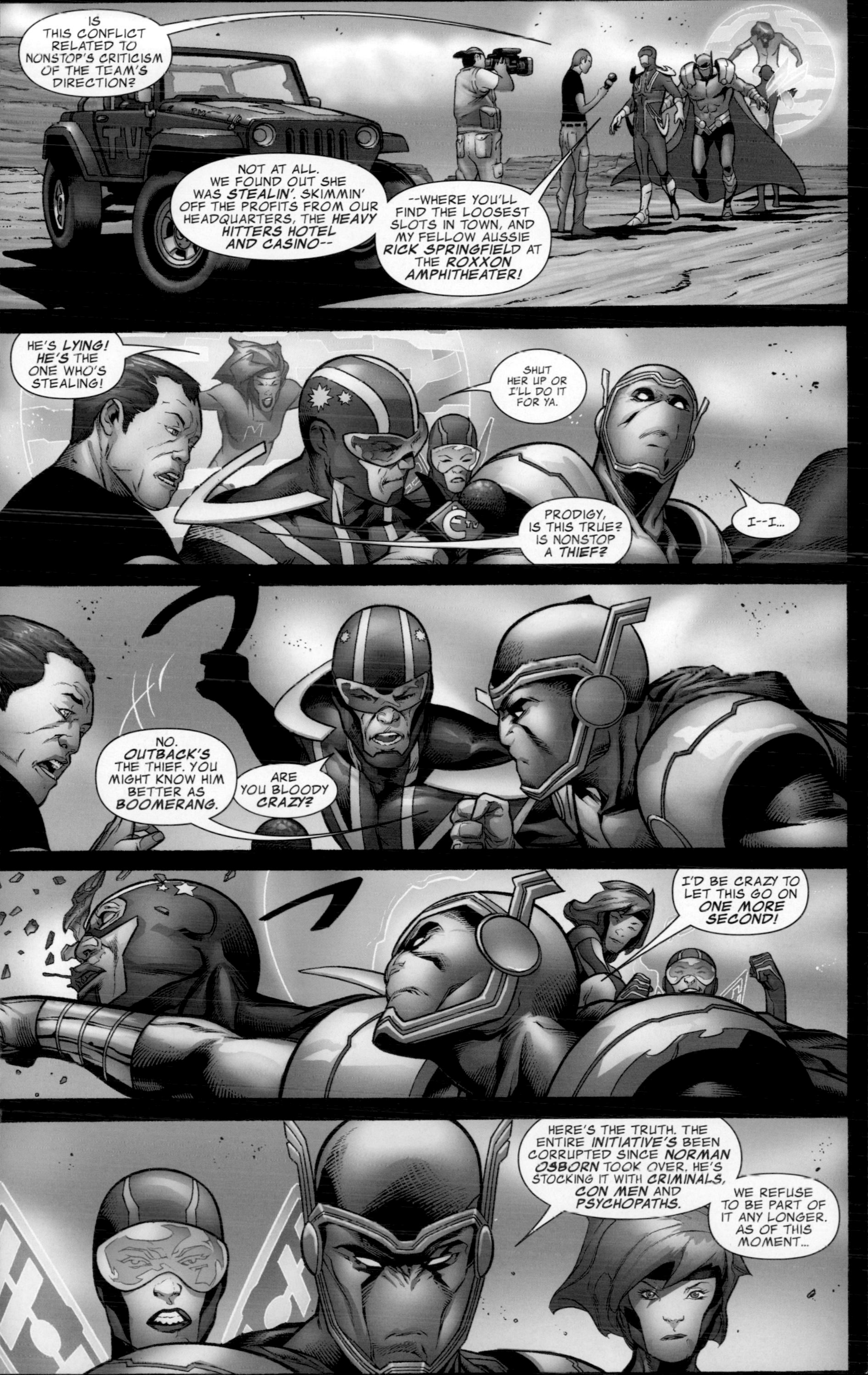

IS THIS CONFLICT RELATED TO NONSTOP'S CRITICISM OF THE TEAM'S DIRECTION?
NOT AT ALL. WE FOUND OUT SHE WAS STEALIN'. SKIMMIN' OFF THE PROFITS FROM OUR HEADQUARTERS, THE HEAVY HITTERS HOTEL AND CASINO--
--WHERE YOU'LL FIND THE LOOSEST SLOTS IN TOWN, AND MY FELLOW AUSSIE RICK SPRINGFIELD AT THE ROXXON AMPHITHEATER!
HE'S LYING! HE'S THE ONE WHO'S STEALING!
SHUT HER UP OR I'LL DO IT FOR YA.
PRODIGY, IS THIS TRUE? IS NONSTOP A THIEF?
I--I...
NO. OUTBACK'S THE THIEF. YOU MIGHT KNOW HIM BETTER AS BOOMERANG.
ARE YOU BLOODY CRAZY?
I'D BE CRAZY TO LET THIS GO ON ONE MORE SECOND!
HERE'S THE TRUTH. THE ENTIRE INITIATIVE'S BEEN CORRUPTED SINCE NORMAN OSBORN TOOK OVER. HE'S STOCKING IT WITH CRIMINALS, CON MEN AND PSYCHOPATHS.
WE REFUSE TO BE PART OF IT ANY LONGER. AS OF THIS MOMENT...

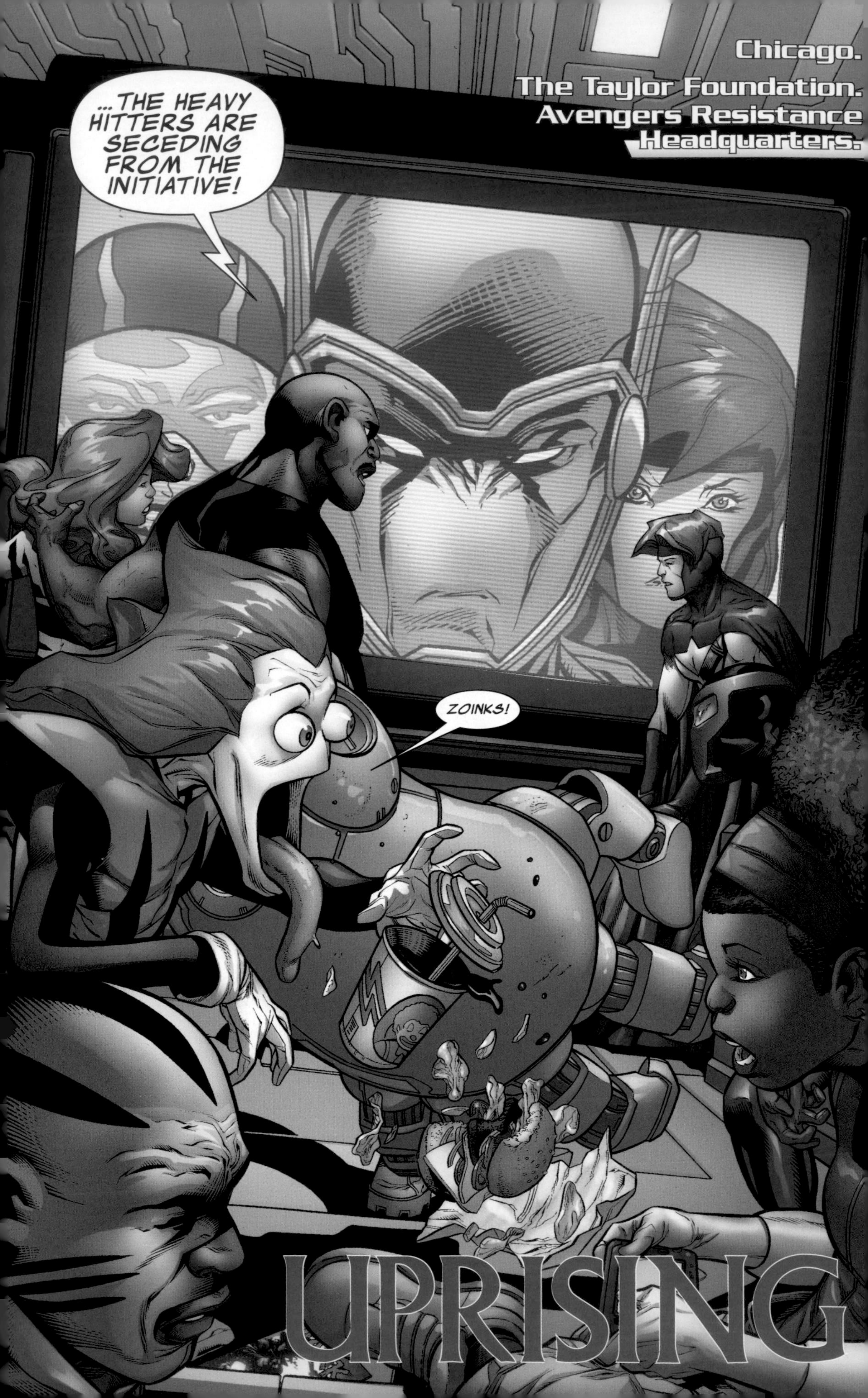
Chicago.
The Taylor Foundation.
Avengers Resistance
Headquarters.
...THE HEAVY HITTERS ARE SECEDING FROM THE INITIATIVE!
ZOINKS!
UPRISING

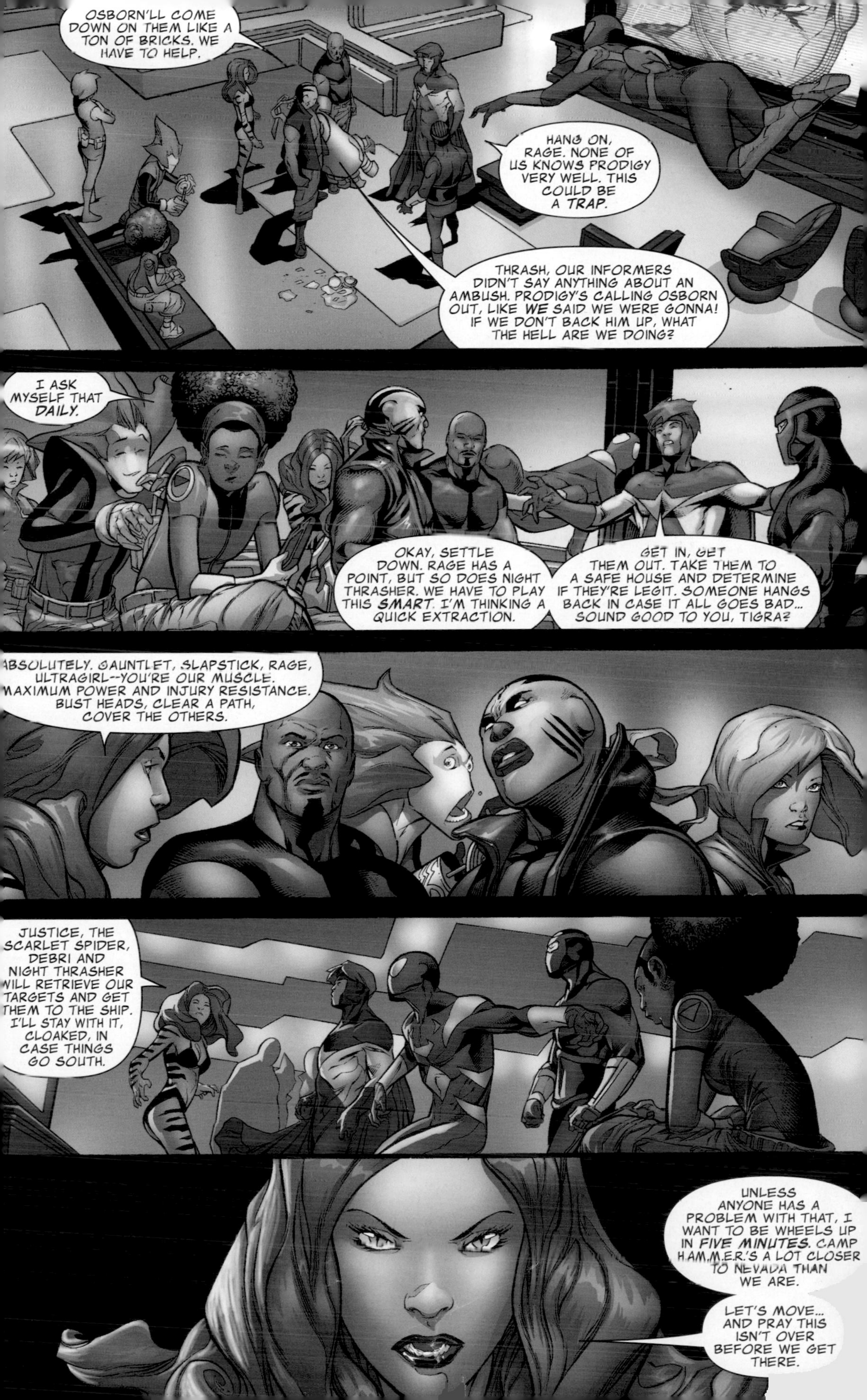

OSBORN'LL COME DOWN ON THEM LIKE A TON OF BRICKS. WE HAVE TO HELP.
HANG ON, RAGE. NONE OF US KNOWS PRODIGY VERY WELL. THIS COULD BE A TRAP.
THRASH, OUR INFORMERS DIDN'T SAY ANYTHING ABOUT AN AMBUSH. PRODIGY'S CALLING OSBORN OUT, LIKE WE SAID WE WERE GONNA! IF WE DON'T BACK HIM UP, WHAT THE HELL ARE WE DOING?
I ASK MYSELF THAT DAILY.
OKAY, SETTLE DOWN. RAGE HAS A POINT, BUT SO DOES NIGHT THRASHER. WE HAVE TO PLAY THIS SMART. I'M THINKING A QUICK EXTRACTION.
GET IN, GET THEM OUT. TAKE THEM TO A SAFE HOUSE AND DETERMINE IF THEY'RE LEGIT. SOMEONE HANGS BACK IN CASE IT ALL GOES BAD... SOUND GOOD TO YOU, TIGRA?
ABSOLUTELY. GAUNTLET, SLAPSTICK, RAGE, ULTRAGIRL--YOU'RE OUR MUSCLE. MAXIMUM POWER AND INJURY RESISTANCE. BUST HEADS, CLEAR A PATH, COVER THE OTHERS.
JUSTICE, THE SCARLET SPIDER, DEBRI AND NIGHT THRASHER WILL RETRIEVE OUR TARGETS AND GET THEM TO THE SHIP. I'LL STAY WITH IT, CLOAKED, IN CASE THINGS GO SOUTH.
UNLESS ANYONE HAS A PROBLEM WITH THAT, I WANT TO BE WHEELS UP IN FIVE MINUTES. CAMP H.A.M.M.E.R.'S A LOT CLOSER TO NEVADA THAN WE ARE.
LET'S MOVE... AND PRAY THIS ISN'T OVER BEFORE WE GET THERE.

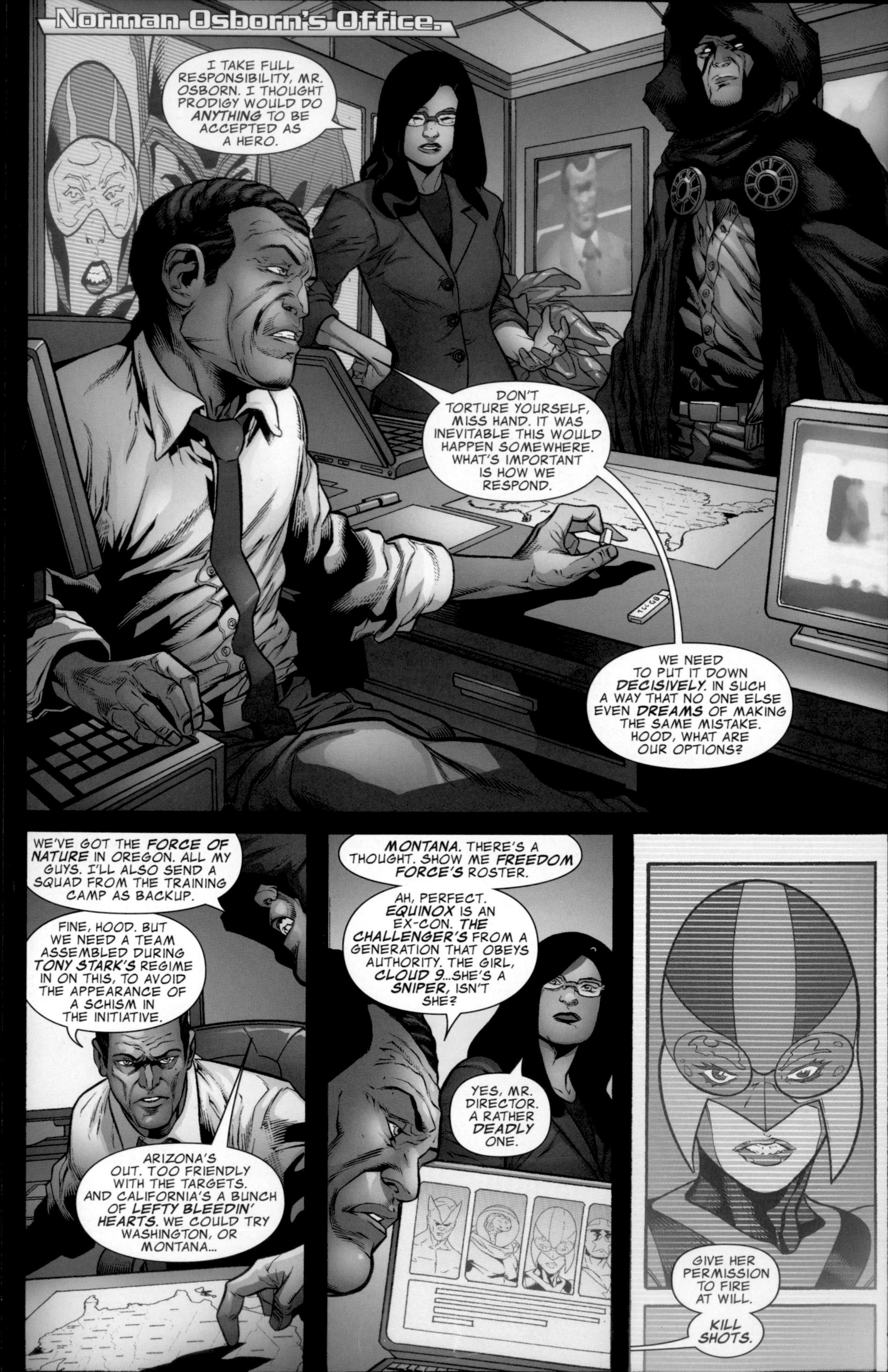
Norman Osborn's Office.
I TAKE FULL RESPONSIBILITY, MR. OSBORN. I THOUGHT PRODIGY WOULD DO ANYTHING TO BE ACCEPTED AS A HERO.
DON'T TORTURE YOURSELF, MISS HAND. IT WAS INEVITABLE THIS WOULD HAPPEN SOMEWHERE. WHAT'S IMPORTANT IS HOW WE RESPOND.
WE NEED TO PUT IT DOWN DECISIVELY. IN SUCH A WAY THAT NO ONE ELSE EVEN DREAMS OF MAKING THE SAME MISTAKE. HOOD, WHAT ARE OUR OPTIONS?
WE'VE GOT THE FORCE OF NATURE IN OREGON. ALL MY GUYS. I'LL ALSO SEND A SQUAD FROM THE TRAINING CAMP AS BACKUP.
FINE, HOOD. BUT WE NEED A TEAM ASSEMBLED DURING TONY STARK'S REGIME IN ON THIS, TO AVOID THE APPEARANCE OF A SCHISM IN THE INITIATIVE.
ARIZONA'S OUT. TOO FRIENDLY WITH THE TARGETS. AND CALIFORNIA'S A BUNCH OF LEFTY BLEEDIN' HEARTS. WE COULD TRY WASHINGTON, OR MONTANA...
MONTANA. THERE'S A THOUGHT. SHOW ME FREEDOM FORCE'S ROSTER.
AH, PERFECT. EQUINOX IS AN EX-CON. THE CHALLENGER'S FROM A GENERATION THAT OBEYS AUTHORITY. THE GIRL, CLOUD 9...SHE'S A SNIPER, ISN'T SHE?
YES, MR. DIRECTOR. A RATHER DEADLY ONE.
GIVE HER PERMISSION TO FIRE AT WILL.
KILL SHOTS.

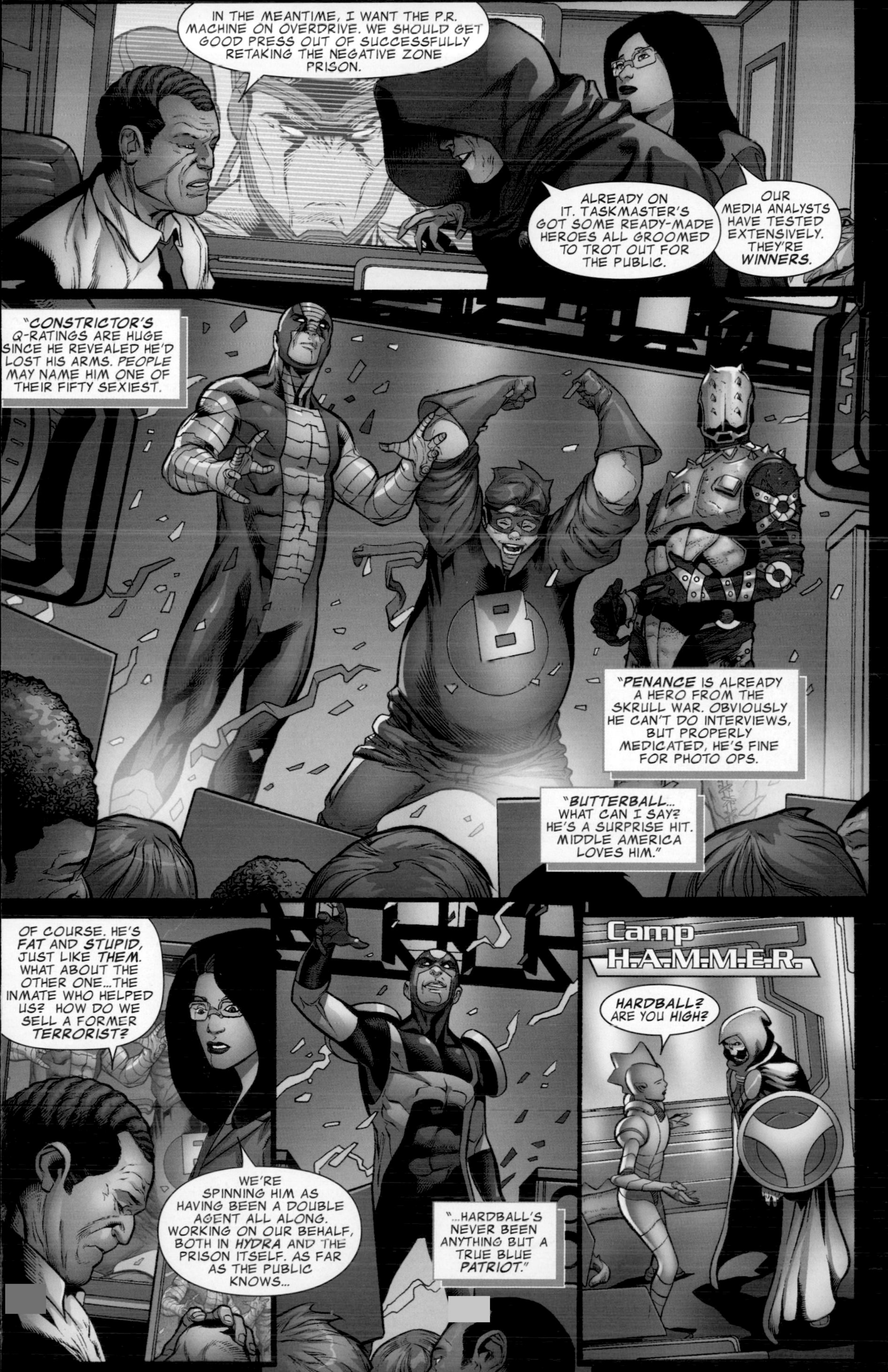
IN THE MEANTIME, I WANT THE P.R. MACHINE ON OVERDRIVE. WE SHOULD GET GOOD PRESS OUT OF SUCCESSFULLY RETAKING THE NEGATIVE ZONE PRISON.
ALREADY ON IT. TASKMASTER'S GOT SOME READY-MADE HEROES ALL GROOMED TO TROT OUT FOR THE PUBLIC.
OUR MEDIA ANALYSTS HAVE TESTED EXTENSIVELY. THEY'RE WINNERS.
"CONSTRICTOR'S Q-RATINGS ARE HUGE SINCE HE REVEALED HE'D LOST HIS ARMS. PEOPLE MAY NAME HIM ONE OF THEIR FIFTY SEXIEST.
"PENANCE IS ALREADY A HERO FROM THE SKRULL WAR. OBVIOUSLY HE CAN'T DO INTERVIEWS, BUT PROPERLY MEDICATED, HE'S FINE FOR PHOTO OPS.
"BUTTERBALL... WHAT CAN I SAY? HE'S A SURPRISE HIT. MIDDLE AMERICA LOVES HIM."
OF COURSE. HE'S FAT AND STUPID, JUST LIKE THEM. WHAT ABOUT THE OTHER ONE...THE INMATE WHO HELPED US? HOW DO WE SELL A FORMER TERRORIST?
WE'RE SPINNING HIM AS HAVING BEEN A DOUBLE AGENT ALL ALONG. WORKING ON OUR BEHALF, BOTH IN HYDRA AND THE PRISON ITSELF. AS FAR AS THE PUBLIC KNOWS...
"...HARDBALL'S NEVER BEEN ANYTHING BUT A TRUE BLUE PATRIOT."
Camp H.A.M.M.E.R.
HARDBALL? ARE YOU HIGH?

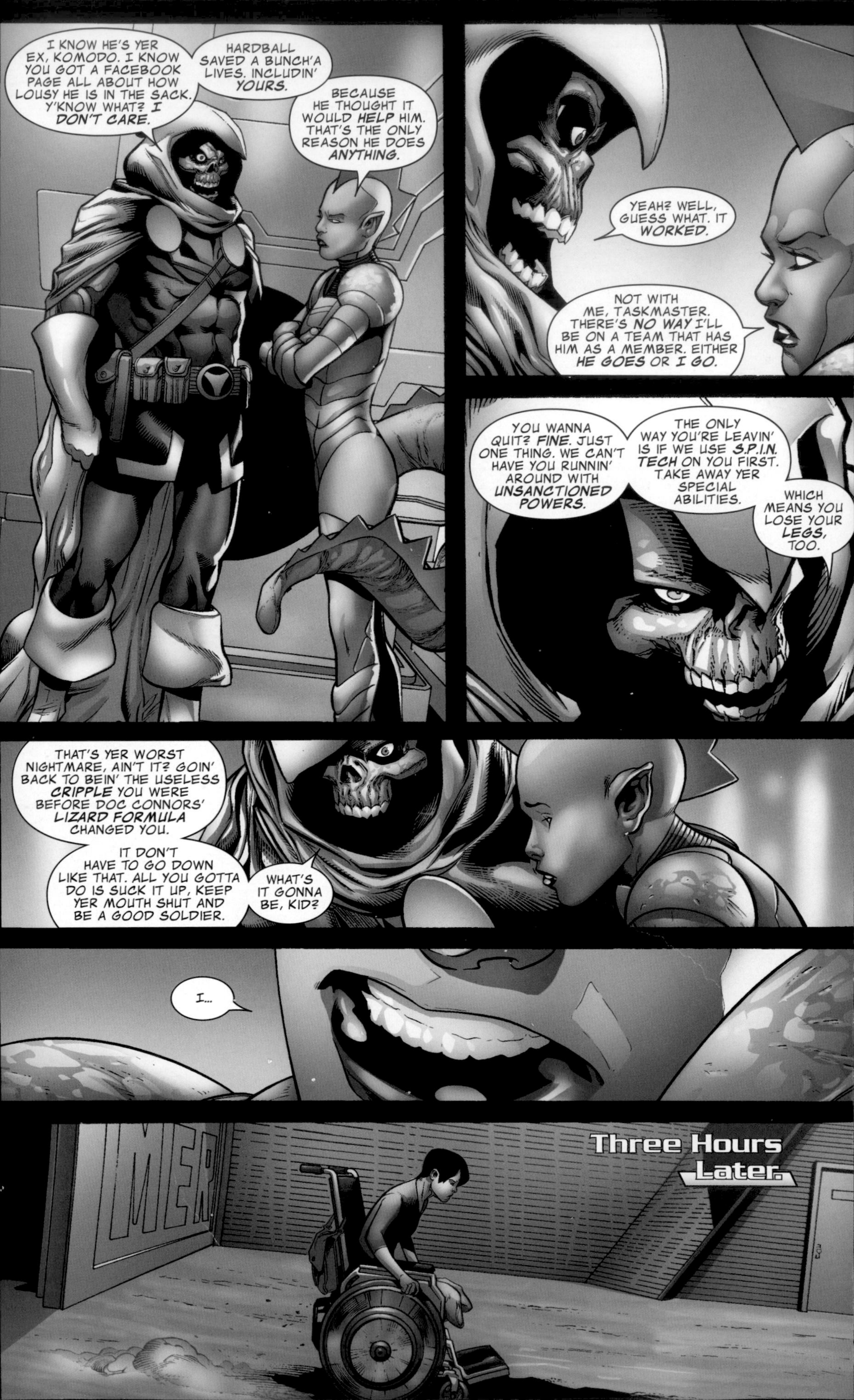
I KNOW HE'S YER EX, KOMODO. I KNOW YOU GOT A FACEBOOK PAGE ALL ABOUT HOW LOUSY HE IS IN THE SACK. Y'KNOW WHAT? I DON'T CARE.
HARDBALL SAVED A BUNCH'A LIVES. INCLUDIN' YOURS.
BECAUSE HE THOUGHT IT WOULD HELP HIM. THAT'S THE ONLY REASON HE DOES ANYTHING.
YEAH? WELL, GUESS WHAT. IT WORKED.
NOT WITH ME, TASKMASTER. THERE'S NO WAY I'LL BE ON A TEAM THAT HAS HIM AS A MEMBER. EITHER HE GOES OR I GO.
YOU WANNA QUIT? FINE. JUST ONE THING. WE CAN'T HAVE YOU RUNNIN' AROUND WITH UNSANCTIONED POWERS.
THE ONLY WAY YOU'RE LEAVIN' IS IF WE USE S.P.I.N. TECH ON YOU FIRST. TAKE AWAY YER SPECIAL ABILITIES.
WHICH MEANS YOU LOSE YOUR LEGS, TOO.
THAT'S YER WORST NIGHTMARE, AIN'T IT? GOIN' BACK TO BEIN' THE USELESS CRIPPLE YOU WERE BEFORE DOC CONNORS' LIZARD FORMULA CHANGED YOU.
IT DON'T HAVE TO GO DOWN LIKE THAT. ALL YOU GOTTA DO IS SUCK IT UP, KEEP YER MOUTH SHUT AND BE A GOOD SOLDIER.
WHAT'S IT GONNA BE, KID?
I...
Three Hours Later.

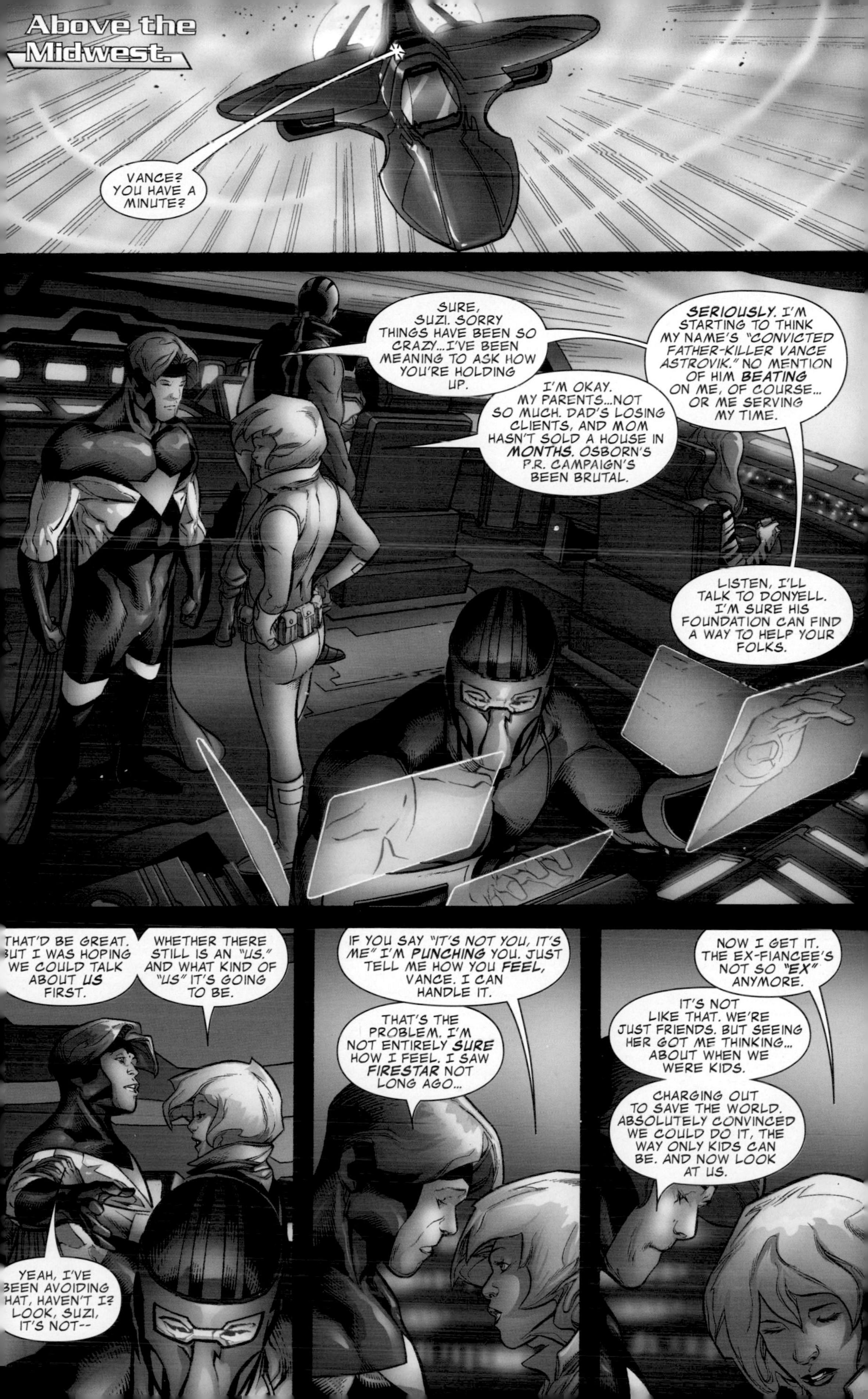
Above the Midwest.
VANCE? YOU HAVE A MINUTE?
SURE, SUZI. SORRY THINGS HAVE BEEN SO CRAZY...I'VE BEEN MEANING TO ASK HOW YOU'RE HOLDING UP.
I'M OKAY. MY PARENTS...NOT SO MUCH. DAD'S LOSING CLIENTS, AND MOM HASN'T SOLD A HOUSE IN MONTHS. OSBORN'S P.R. CAMPAIGN'S BEEN BRUTAL.
SERIOUSLY. I'M STARTING TO THINK MY NAME'S "CONVICTED FATHER-KILLER VANCE ASTROVIK." NO MENTION OF HIM BEATING ON ME, OF COURSE... OR ME SERVING MY TIME.
LISTEN, I'LL TALK TO DONYELL. I'M SURE HIS FOUNDATION CAN FIND A WAY TO HELP YOUR FOLKS.
THAT'D BE GREAT. BUT I WAS HOPING WE COULD TALK ABOUT US FIRST.
WHETHER THERE STILL IS AN "US." AND WHAT KIND OF "US" IT'S GOING TO BE.
YEAH, I'VE BEEN AVOIDING THAT, HAVEN'T I? LOOK, SUZI, IT'S NOT--
IF YOU SAY "IT'S NOT YOU, IT'S ME" I'M PUNCHING YOU. JUST TELL ME HOW YOU FEEL, VANCE. I CAN HANDLE IT.
THAT'S THE PROBLEM. I'M NOT ENTIRELY SURE HOW I FEEL. I SAW FIRESTAR NOT LONG AGO...
NOW I GET IT. THE EX-FIANCEE'S NOT SO "EX" ANYMORE.
IT'S NOT LIKE THAT. WE'RE JUST FRIENDS. BUT SEEING HER GOT ME THINKING... ABOUT WHEN WE WERE KIDS.
CHARGING OUT TO SAVE THE WORLD. ABSOLUTELY CONVINCED WE COULD DO IT, THE WAY ONLY KIDS CAN BE. AND NOW LOOK AT US.

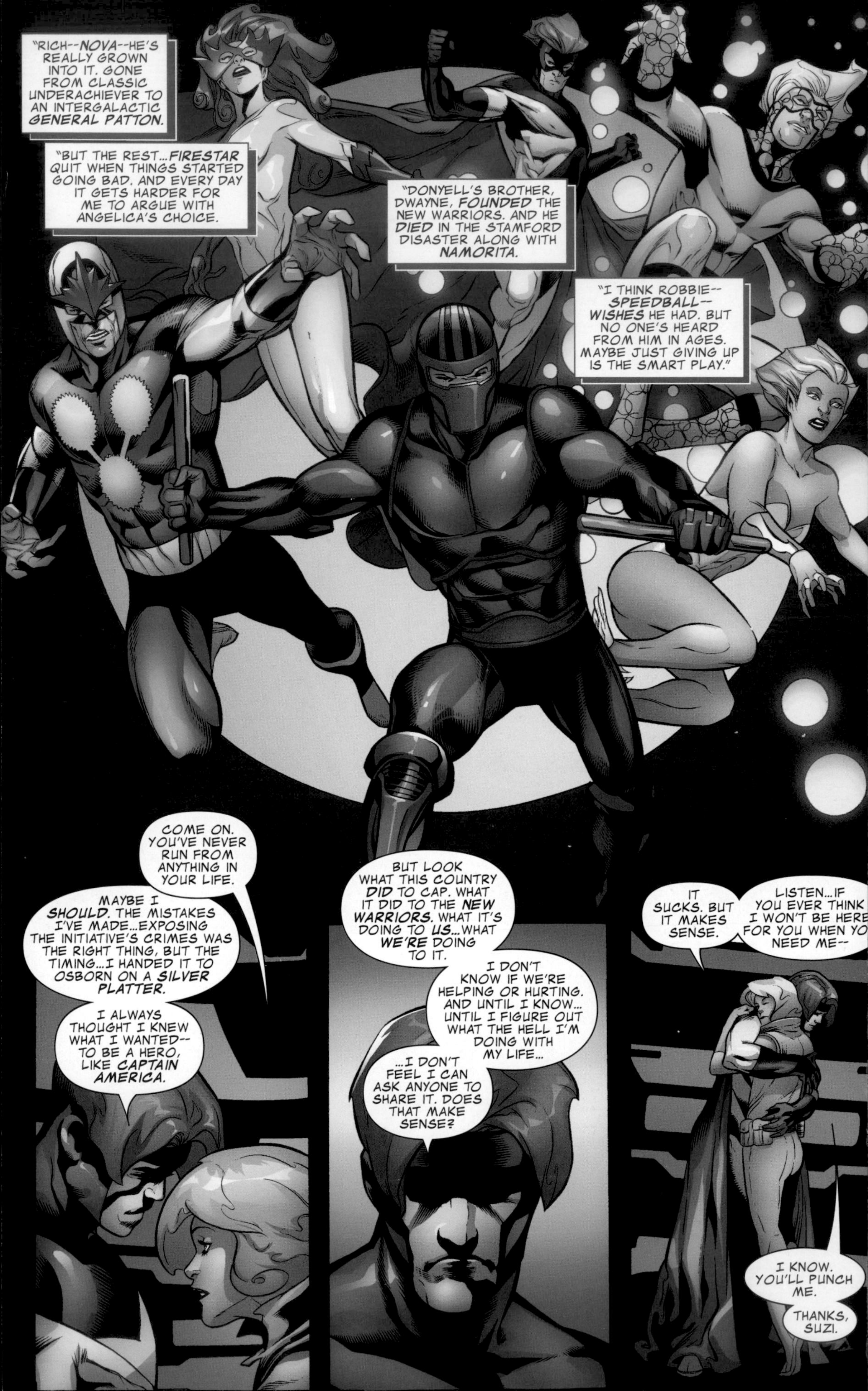
"RICH--NOVA--HE'S REALLY GROWN INTO IT. GONE FROM CLASSIC UNDERACHIEVER TO AN INTERGALACTIC GENERAL PATTON.
"BUT THE REST...FIRESTAR QUIT WHEN THINGS STARTED GOING BAD. AND EVERY DAY IT GETS HARDER FOR ME TO ARGUE WITH ANGELICA'S CHOICE.
"DONYELL'S BROTHER, DWAYNE, FOUNDED THE NEW WARRIORS. AND HE DIED IN THE STAMFORD DISASTER ALONG WITH NAMORITA.
"I THINK ROBBIE--SPEEDBALL--WISHES HE HAD. BUT NO ONE'S HEARD FROM HIM IN AGES. MAYBE JUST GIVING UP IS THE SMART PLAY."
COME ON. YOU'VE NEVER RUN FROM ANYTHING IN YOUR LIFE.
MAYBE I SHOULD. THE MISTAKES I'VE MADE...EXPOSING THE INITIATIVE'S CRIMES WAS THE RIGHT THING, BUT THE TIMING...I HANDED IT TO OSBORN ON A SILVER PLATTER.
I ALWAYS THOUGHT I KNEW WHAT I WANTED--TO BE A HERO, LIKE CAPTAIN AMERICA.
BUT LOOK WHAT THIS COUNTRY DID TO CAP. WHAT IT DID TO THE NEW WARRIORS. WHAT IT'S DOING TO US...WHAT WE'RE DOING TO IT.
I DON'T KNOW IF WE'RE HELPING OR HURTING. AND UNTIL I KNOW... UNTIL I FIGURE OUT WHAT THE HELL I'M DOING WITH MY LIFE...
...I DON'T FEEL I CAN ASK ANYONE TO SHARE IT. DOES THAT MAKE SENSE?
IT SUCKS. BUT IT MAKES SENSE.
LISTEN...IF YOU EVER THINK I WON'T BE HERE FOR YOU WHEN YO NEED ME--
I KNOW. YOU'LL PUNCH ME.
THANKS, SUZI.

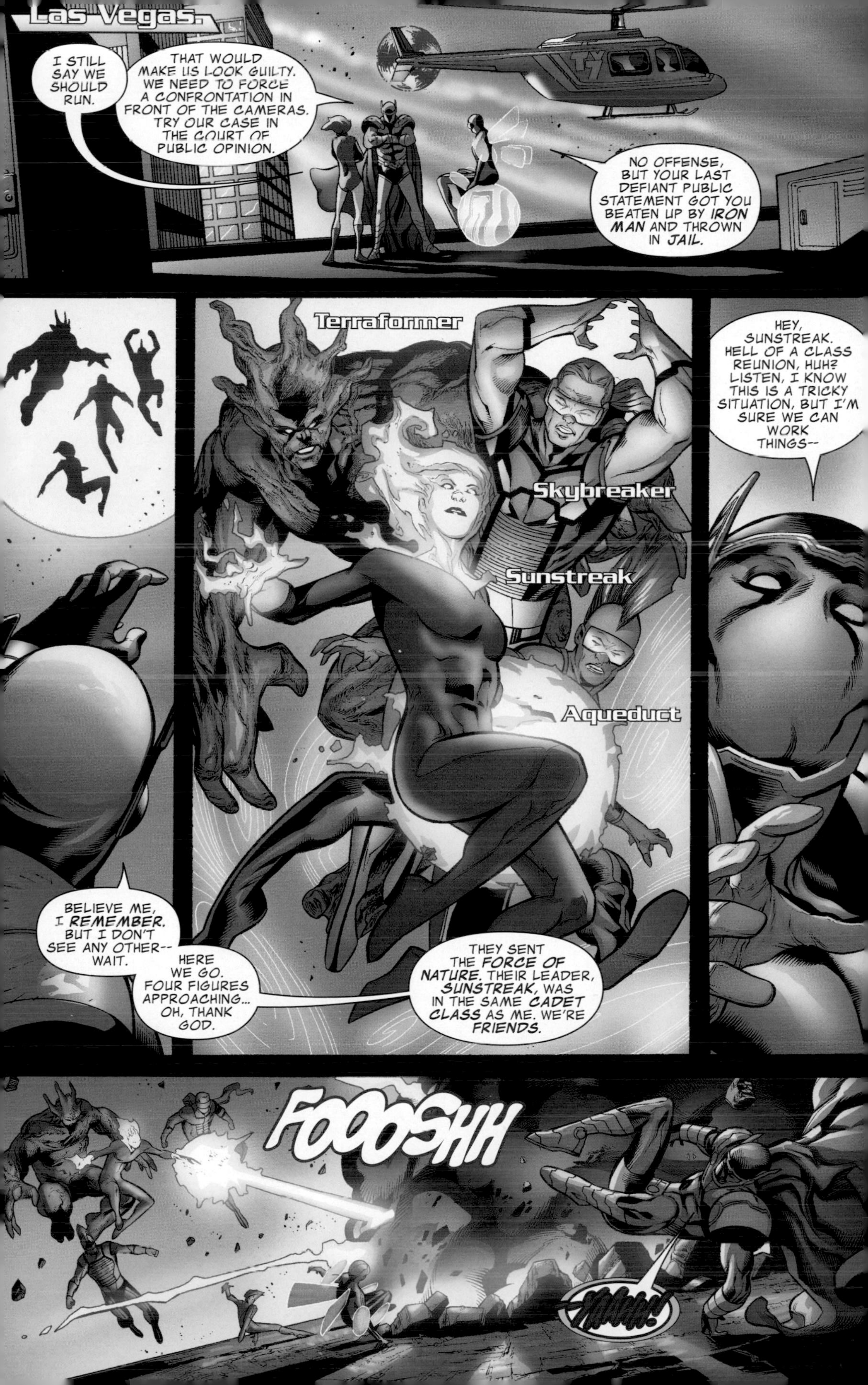

Las Vegas.
I STILL SAY WE SHOULD RUN.
THAT WOULD MAKE US LOOK GUILTY. WE NEED TO FORCE A CONFRONTATION IN FRONT OF THE CAMERAS. TRY OUR CASE IN THE COURT OF PUBLIC OPINION.
NO OFFENSE, BUT YOUR LAST DEFIANT PUBLIC STATEMENT GOT YOU BEATEN UP BY IRON MAN AND THROWN IN JAIL.
BELIEVE ME, I REMEMBER. BUT I DON'T SEE ANY OTHER-- WAIT.
HERE WE GO. FOUR FIGURES APPROACHING... OH, THANK GOD.
THEY SENT THE FORCE OF NATURE. THEIR LEADER, SUNSTREAK, WAS IN THE SAME CADET CLASS AS ME. WE'RE FRIENDS.
Terraformer
Skybreaker
Sunstreak
Aqueduct
HEY, SUNSTREAK. HELL OF A CLASS REUNION, HUH? LISTEN, I KNOW THIS IS A TRICKY SITUATION, BUT I'M SURE WE CAN WORK THINGS--
FOOOSHH

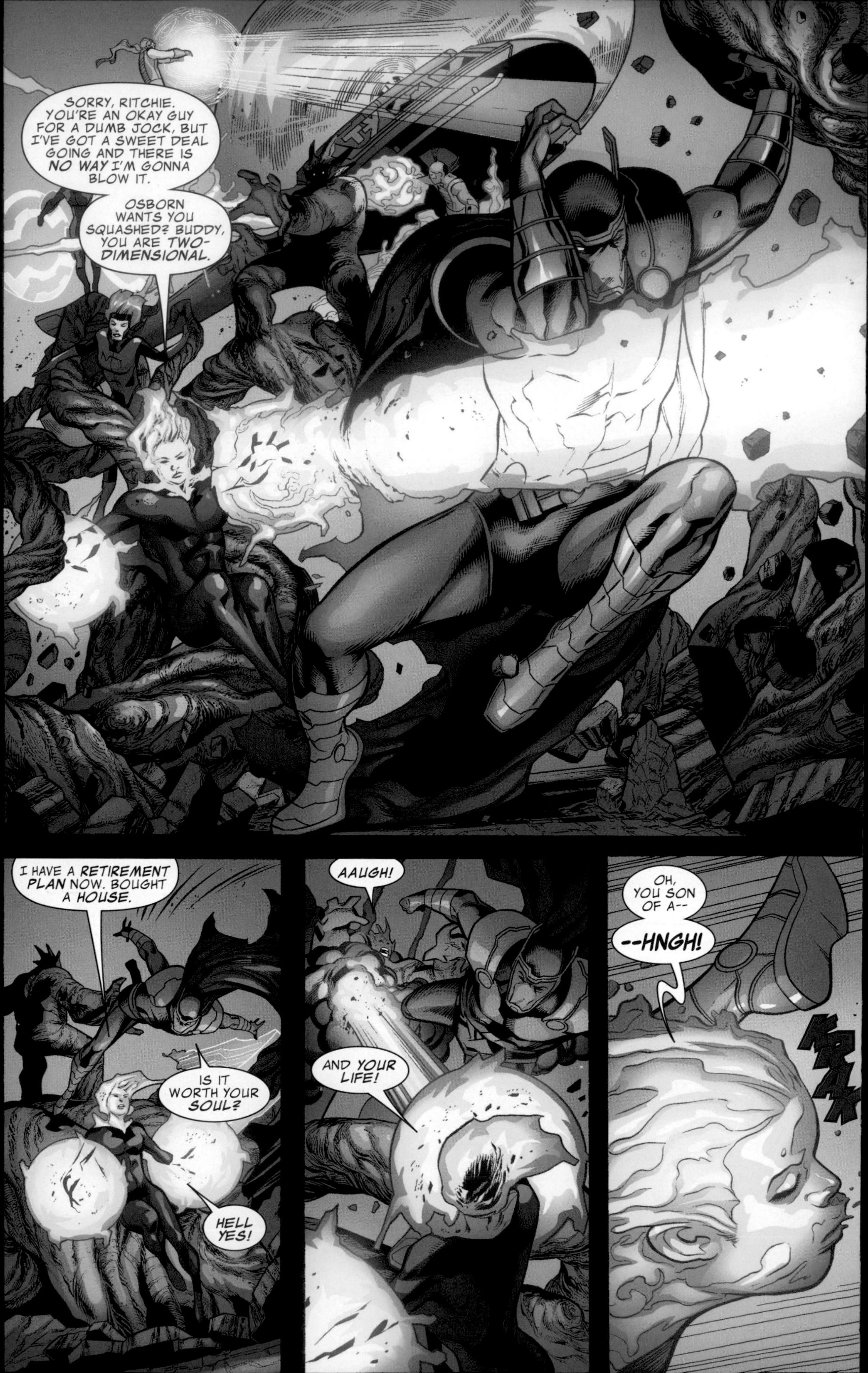
SORRY, RITCHIE. YOU'RE AN OKAY GUY FOR A DUMB JOCK, BUT I'VE GOT A SWEET DEAL GOING AND THERE IS NO WAY I'M GONNA BLOW IT.
OSBORN WANTS YOU SQUASHED? BUDDY, YOU ARE TWO-DIMENSIONAL.
I HAVE A RETIREMENT PLAN NOW. BOUGHT A HOUSE.
IS IT WORTH YOUR SOUL?
HELL YES!
AAUGH!
AND YOUR LIFE!
OH, YOU SON OF A--
--HNGH!
KRAK

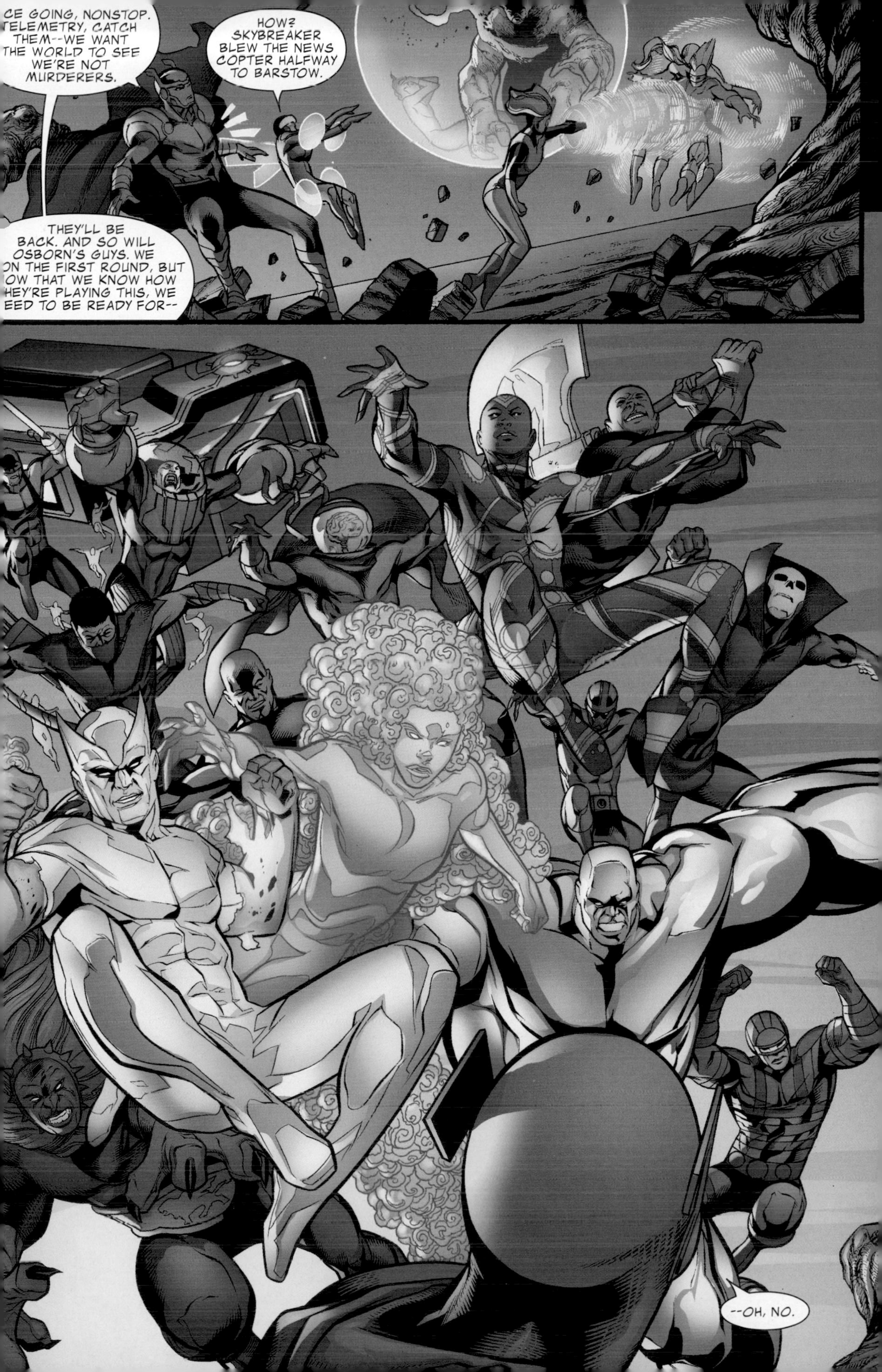
CE GOING, NONSTOP. TELEMETRY, CATCH THEM--WE WANT THE WORLD TO SEE WE'RE NOT MURDERERS.
HOW? SKYBREAKER BLEW THE NEWS COPTER HALFWAY TO BARSTOW.
THEY'LL BE BACK. AND SO WILL OSBORN'S GUYS. WE ON THE FIRST ROUND, BUT OW THAT WE KNOW HOW HEY'RE PLAYING THIS, WE EED TO BE READY FOR--
--OH, NO.

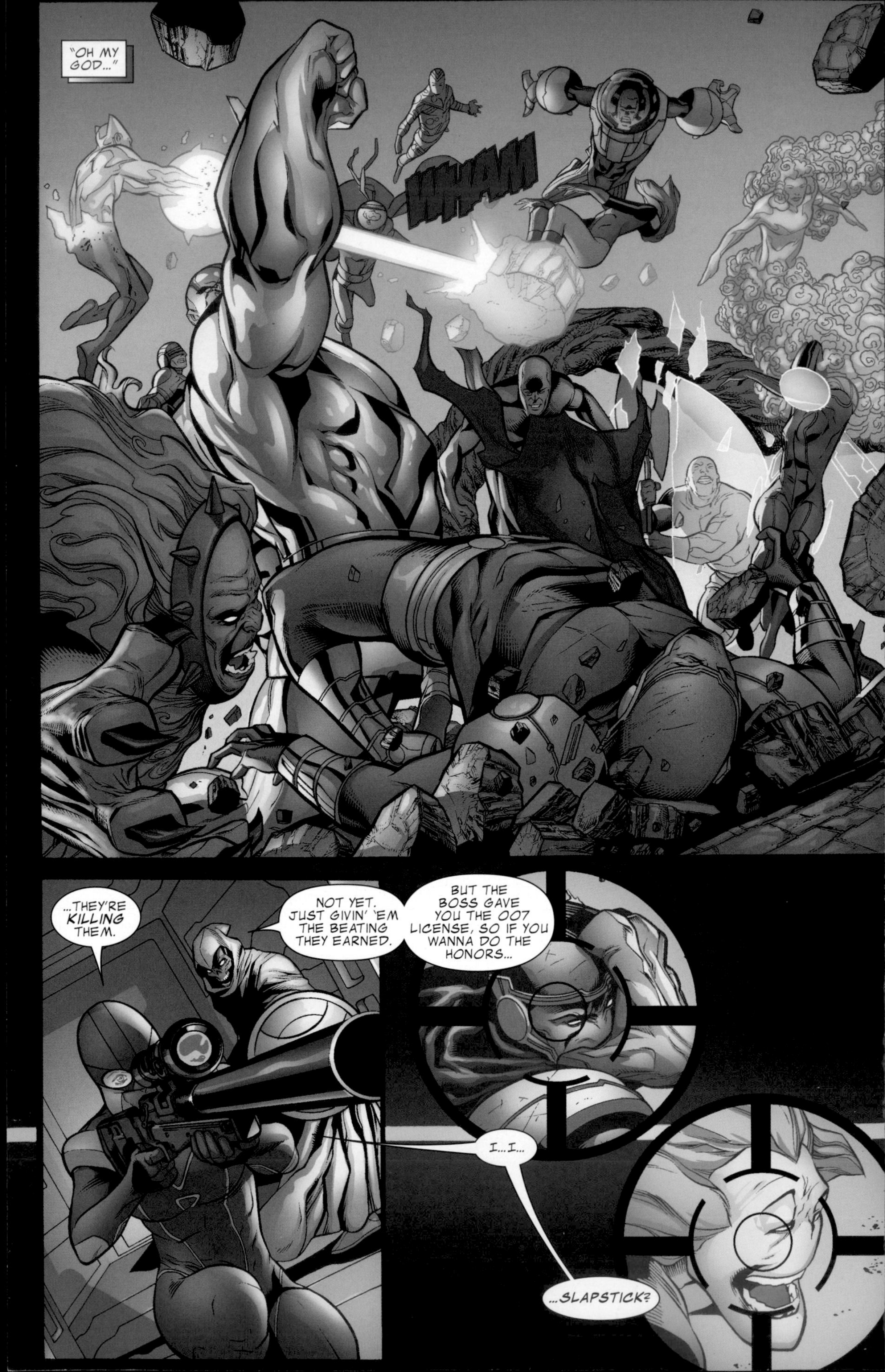
"OH MY GOD..."
WHAM
...THEY'RE KILLING THEM.
NOT YET. JUST GIVIN' 'EM THE BEATING THEY EARNED.
BUT THE BOSS GAVE YOU THE 007 LICENSE, SO IF YOU WANNA DO THE HONORS...
I...I...
...SLAPSTICK?

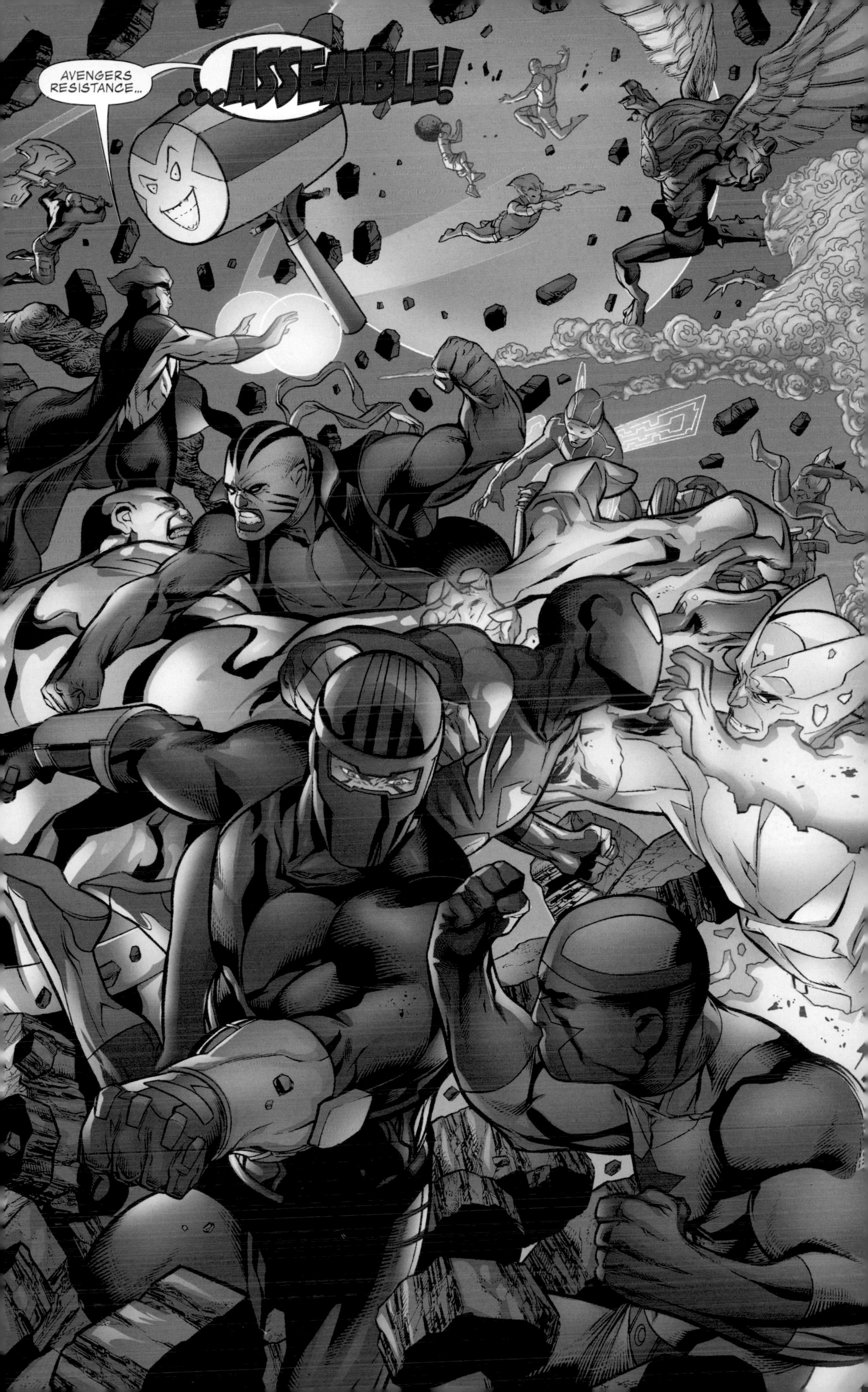
AVENGERS RESISTANCE...
...ASSEMBLE!

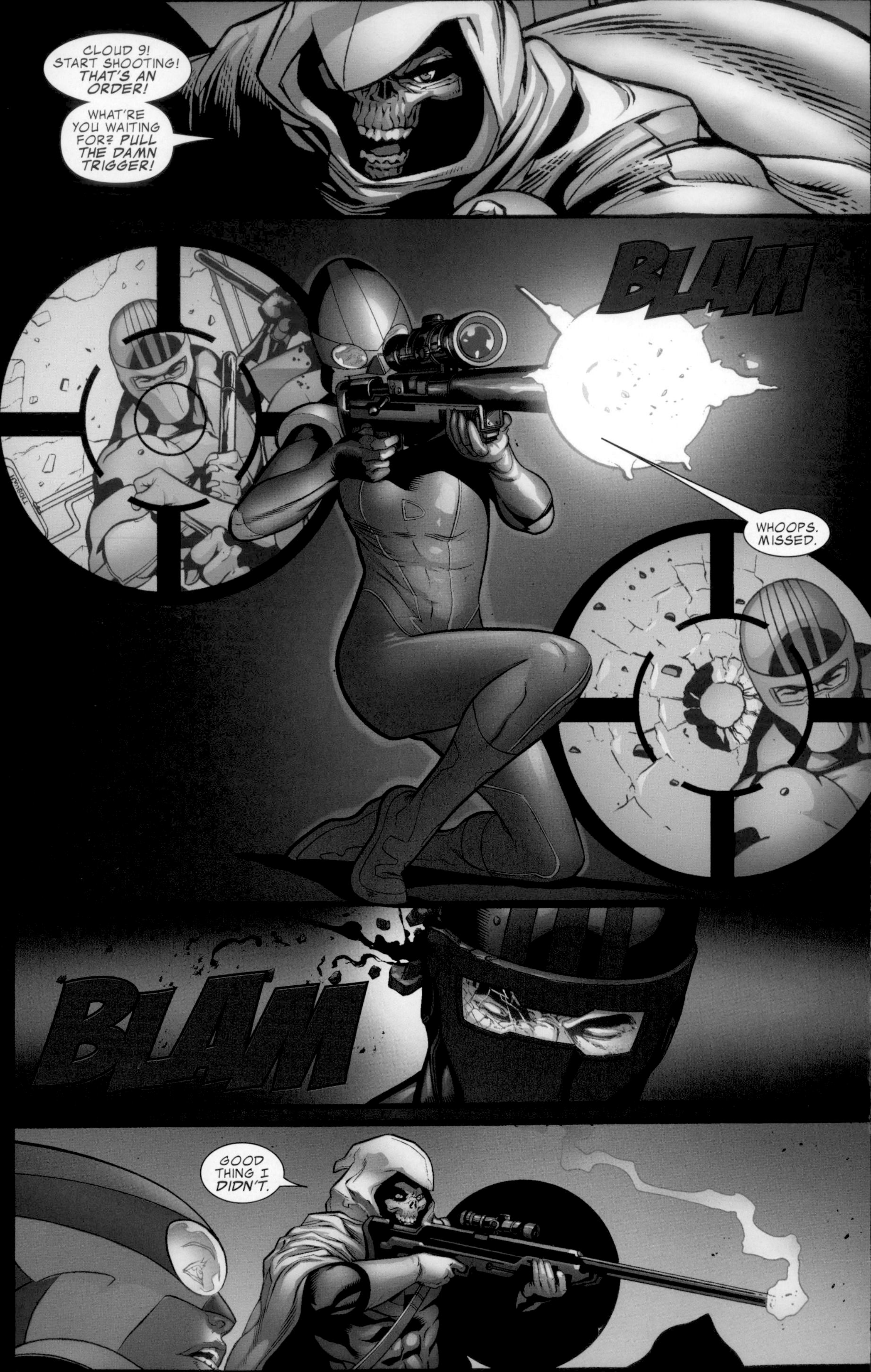
CLOUD 9! START SHOOTING! THAT'S AN ORDER!
WHAT'RE YOU WAITING FOR? PULL THE DAMN TRIGGER!
BLAM
WHOOPS. MISSED.
BLAM
GOOD THING I DIDN'T.

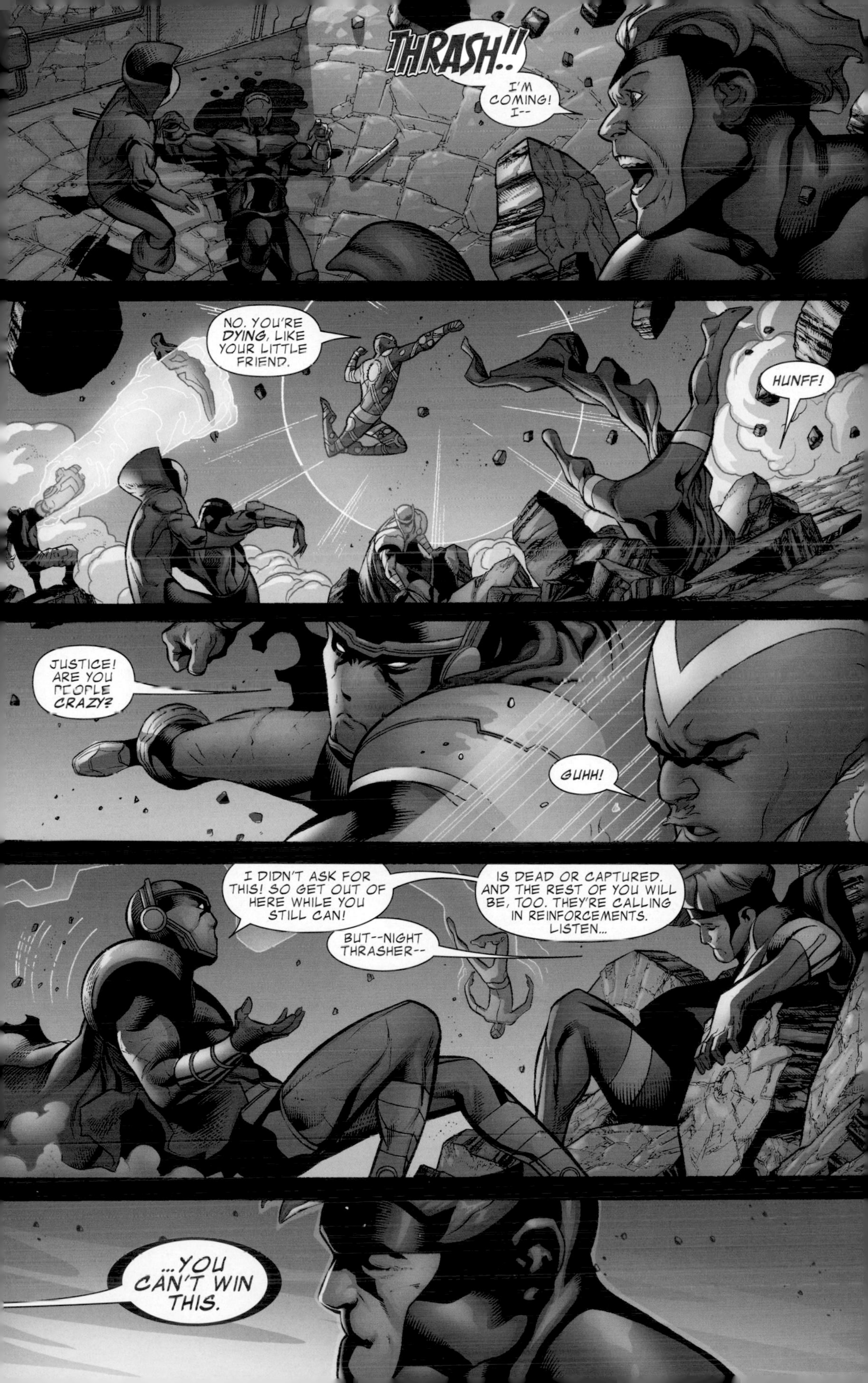
THRASH!!
I'M COMING! I--
NO. YOU'RE DYING, LIKE YOUR LITTLE FRIEND.
HUNFF!
JUSTICE! ARE YOU PEOPLE CRAZY?
GUHH!
I DIDN'T ASK FOR THIS! SO GET OUT OF HERE WHILE YOU STILL CAN!
BUT--NIGHT THRASHER--
IS DEAD OR CAPTURED. AND THE REST OF YOU WILL BE, TOO. THEY'RE CALLING IN REINFORCEMENTS. LISTEN...
...YOU CAN'T WIN THIS.

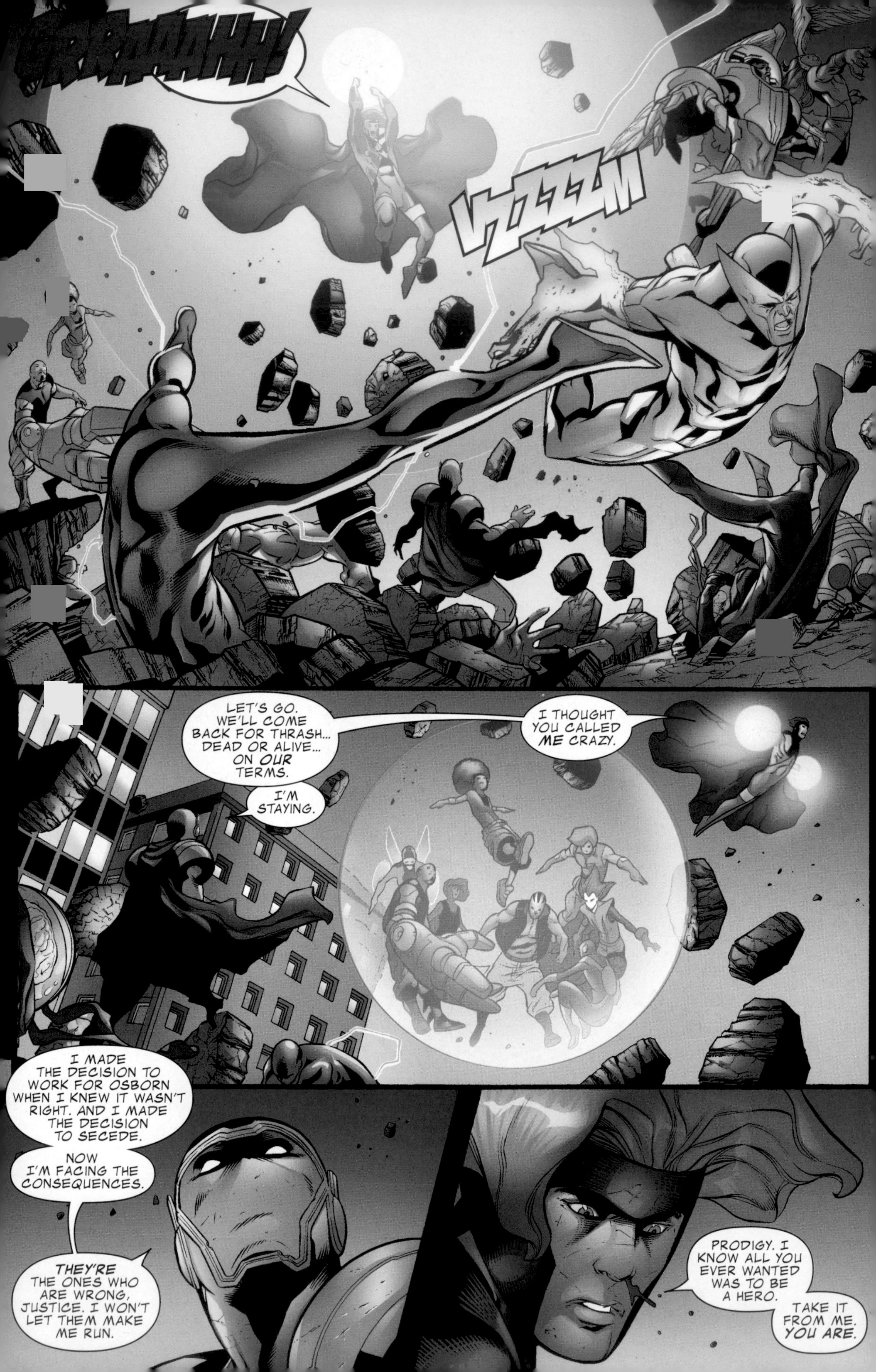
GRRAAAAHH!
VZZZZM
LET'S GO. WE'LL COME BACK FOR THRASH... DEAD OR ALIVE... ON OUR TERMS.
I THOUGHT YOU CALLED ME CRAZY.
I'M STAYING.
I MADE THE DECISION TO WORK FOR OSBORN WHEN I KNEW IT WASN'T RIGHT. AND I MADE THE DECISION TO SECEDE.
NOW I'M FACING THE CONSEQUENCES.
THEY'RE THE ONES WHO ARE WRONG, JUSTICE. I WON'T LET THEM MAKE ME RUN.
PRODIGY. I KNOW ALL YOU EVER WANTED WAS TO BE A HERO.
TAKE IT FROM ME. YOU ARE.

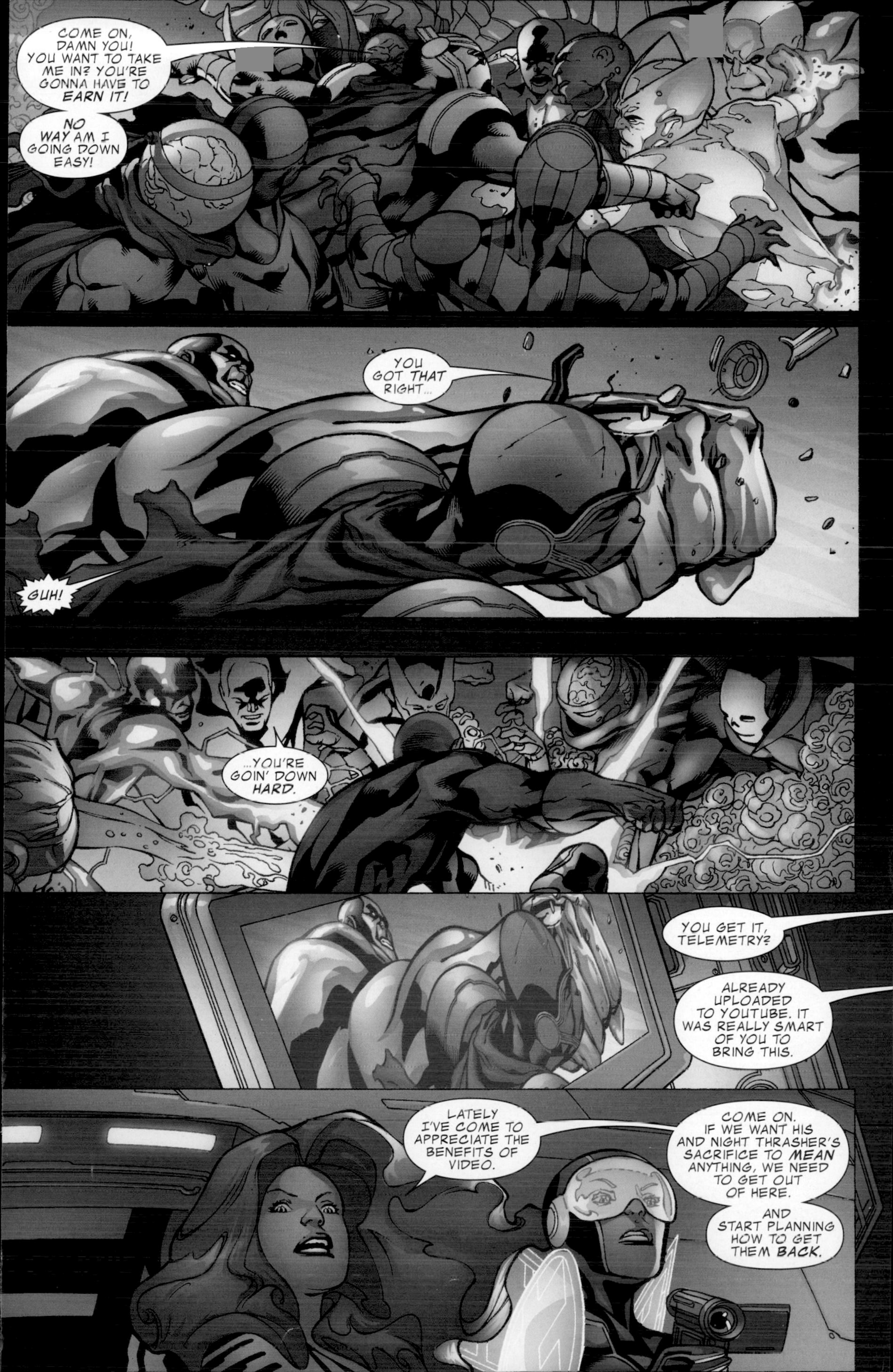
COME ON, DAMN YOU! YOU WANT TO TAKE ME IN? YOU'RE GONNA HAVE TO EARN IT!
NO WAY AM I GOING DOWN EASY!
YOU GOT THAT RIGHT...
GUH!
...YOU'RE GOIN' DOWN HARD.
YOU GET IT, TELEMETRY?
ALREADY UPLOADED TO YOUTUBE. IT WAS REALLY SMART OF YOU TO BRING THIS.
LATELY I'VE COME TO APPRECIATE THE BENEFITS OF VIDEO.
COME ON. IF WE WANT HIS AND NIGHT THRASHER'S SACRIFICE TO MEAN ANYTHING, WE NEED TO GET OUT OF HERE.
AND START PLANNING HOW TO GET THEM BACK.

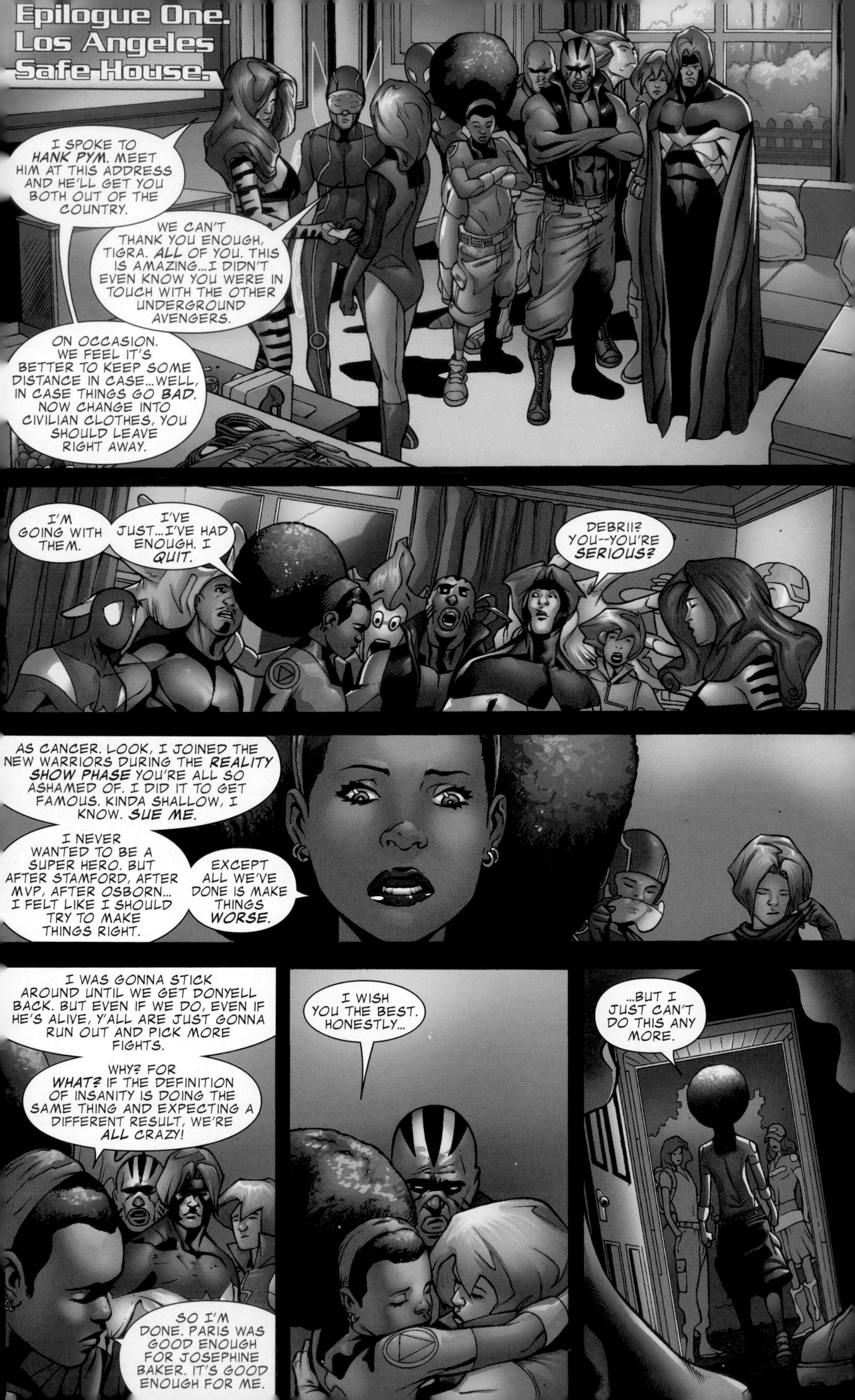
Epilogue One. Los Angeles Safe House.
I SPOKE TO HANK PYM. MEET HIM AT THIS ADDRESS AND HE'LL GET YOU BOTH OUT OF THE COUNTRY.
WE CAN'T THANK YOU ENOUGH, TIGRA. ALL OF YOU. THIS IS AMAZING...I DIDN'T EVEN KNOW YOU WERE IN TOUCH WITH THE OTHER UNDERGROUND AVENGERS.
ON OCCASION. WE FEEL IT'S BETTER TO KEEP SOME DISTANCE IN CASE...WELL, IN CASE THINGS GO BAD. NOW CHANGE INTO CIVILIAN CLOTHES, YOU SHOULD LEAVE RIGHT AWAY.
I'M GOING WITH THEM.
I'VE JUST...I'VE HAD ENOUGH. I QUIT.
DEBRII? YOU--YOU'RE SERIOUS?
AS CANCER. LOOK, I JOINED THE NEW WARRIORS DURING THE REALITY SHOW PHASE YOU'RE ALL SO ASHAMED OF. I DID IT TO GET FAMOUS. KINDA SHALLOW, I KNOW. SUE ME.
I NEVER WANTED TO BE A SUPER HERO. BUT AFTER STAMFORD, AFTER MVP, AFTER OSBORN... I FELT LIKE I SHOULD TRY TO MAKE THINGS RIGHT.
EXCEPT ALL WE'VE DONE IS MAKE THINGS WORSE.
I WAS GONNA STICK AROUND UNTIL WE GET DONYELL BACK. BUT EVEN IF WE DO, EVEN IF HE'S ALIVE, Y'ALL ARE JUST GONNA RUN OUT AND PICK MORE FIGHTS.
WHY? FOR WHAT? IF THE DEFINITION OF INSANITY IS DOING THE SAME THING AND EXPECTING A DIFFERENT RESULT, WE'RE ALL CRAZY!
SO I'M DONE. PARIS WAS GOOD ENOUGH FOR JOSEPHINE BAKER. IT'S GOOD ENOUGH FOR ME.
I WISH YOU THE BEST. HONESTLY...
...BUT I JUST CAN'T DO THIS ANY MORE.

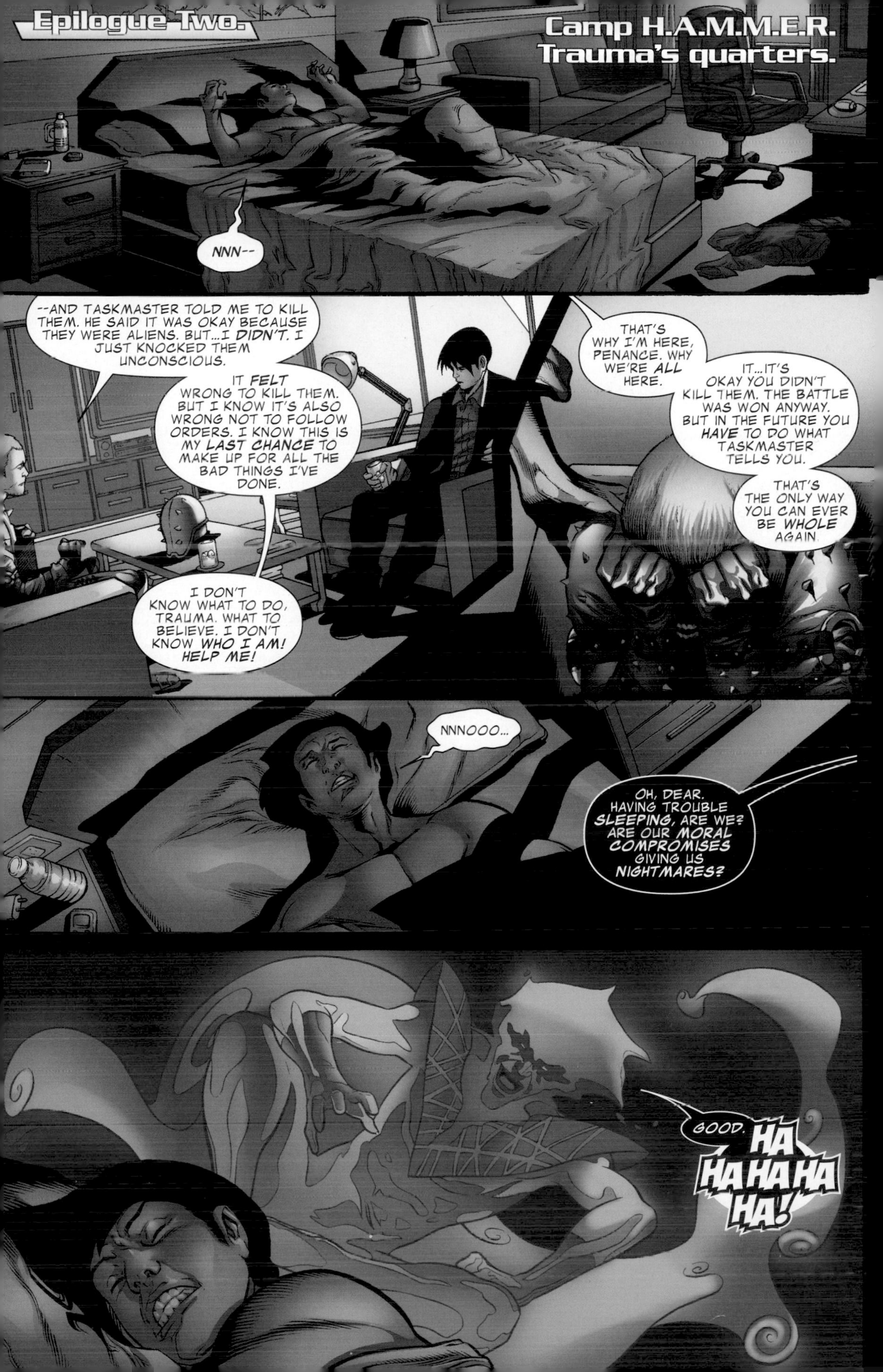

Epilogue Two.
Camp H.A.M.M.E.R. Trauma's quarters.
NNN--
--AND TASKMASTER TOLD ME TO KILL THEM. HE SAID IT WAS OKAY BECAUSE THEY WERE ALIENS. BUT...I DIDN'T. I JUST KNOCKED THEM UNCONSCIOUS.
IT FELT WRONG TO KILL THEM. BUT I KNOW IT'S ALSO WRONG NOT TO FOLLOW ORDERS. I KNOW THIS IS MY LAST CHANCE TO MAKE UP FOR ALL THE BAD THINGS I'VE DONE.
I DON'T KNOW WHAT TO DO, TRAUMA. WHAT TO BELIEVE. I DON'T KNOW WHO I AM! HELP ME!
THAT'S WHY I'M HERE, PENANCE. WHY WE'RE ALL HERE.
IT...IT'S OKAY YOU DIDN'T KILL THEM. THE BATTLE WAS WON ANYWAY. BUT IN THE FUTURE YOU HAVE TO DO WHAT TASKMASTER TELLS YOU.
THAT'S THE ONLY WAY YOU CAN EVER BE WHOLE AGAIN.
NNNOOO...
OH, DEAR. HAVING TROUBLE SLEEPING, ARE WE? ARE OUR MORAL COMPROMISES GIVING US NIGHTMARES?
GOOD.
HA HA HA HA HA!

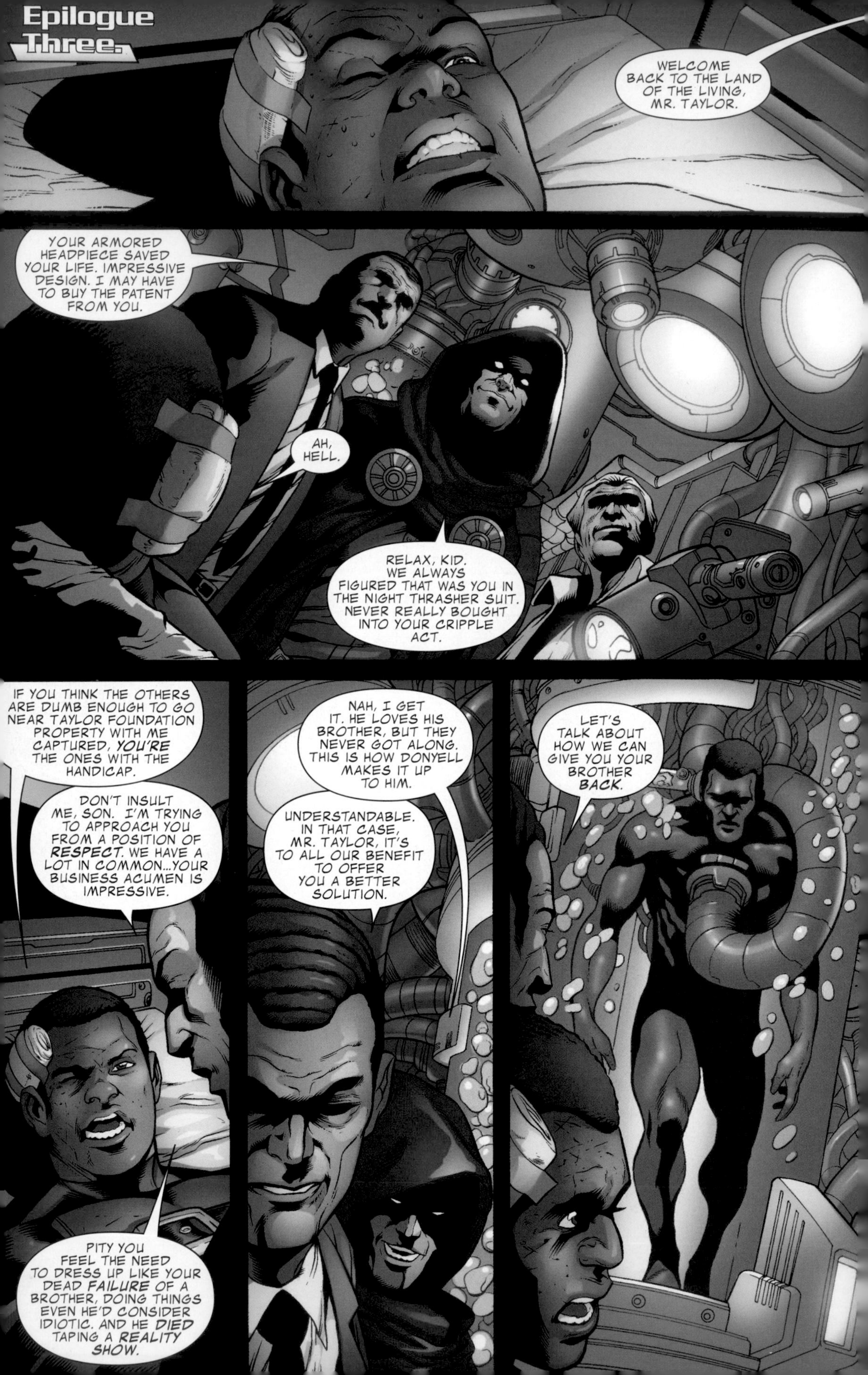
Epilogue Three.
WELCOME BACK TO THE LAND OF THE LIVING, MR. TAYLOR.
YOUR ARMORED HEADPIECE SAVED YOUR LIFE. IMPRESSIVE DESIGN. I MAY HAVE TO BUY THE PATENT FROM YOU.
AH, HELL.
RELAX, KID. WE ALWAYS FIGURED THAT WAS YOU IN THE NIGHT THRASHER SUIT. NEVER REALLY BOUGHT INTO YOUR CRIPPLE ACT.
IF YOU THINK THE OTHERS ARE DUMB ENOUGH TO GO NEAR TAYLOR FOUNDATION PROPERTY WITH ME CAPTURED, YOU'RE THE ONES WITH THE HANDICAP.
DON'T INSULT ME, SON. I'M TRYING TO APPROACH YOU FROM A POSITION OF RESPECT. WE HAVE A LOT IN COMMON...YOUR BUSINESS ACUMEN IS IMPRESSIVE.
PITY YOU FEEL THE NEED TO DRESS UP LIKE YOUR DEAD FAILURE OF A BROTHER, DOING THINGS EVEN HE'D CONSIDER IDIOTIC. AND HE DIED TAPING A REALITY SHOW.
NAH, I GET IT. HE LOVES HIS BROTHER, BUT THEY NEVER GOT ALONG. THIS IS HOW DONYELL MAKES IT UP TO HIM.
UNDERSTANDABLE. IN THAT CASE, MR. TAYLOR, IT'S TO ALL OUR BENEFIT TO OFFER YOU A BETTER SOLUTION.
LET'S TALK ABOUT HOW WE CAN GIVE YOU YOUR BROTHER BACK.

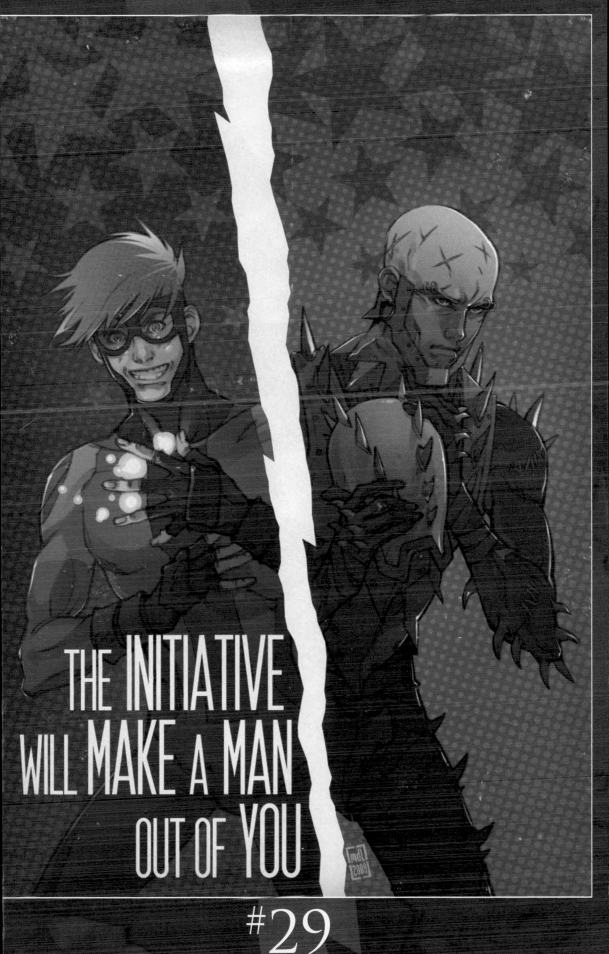

THE INITIATIVE
will MAKE a MAN
OUT OF YOU

#29

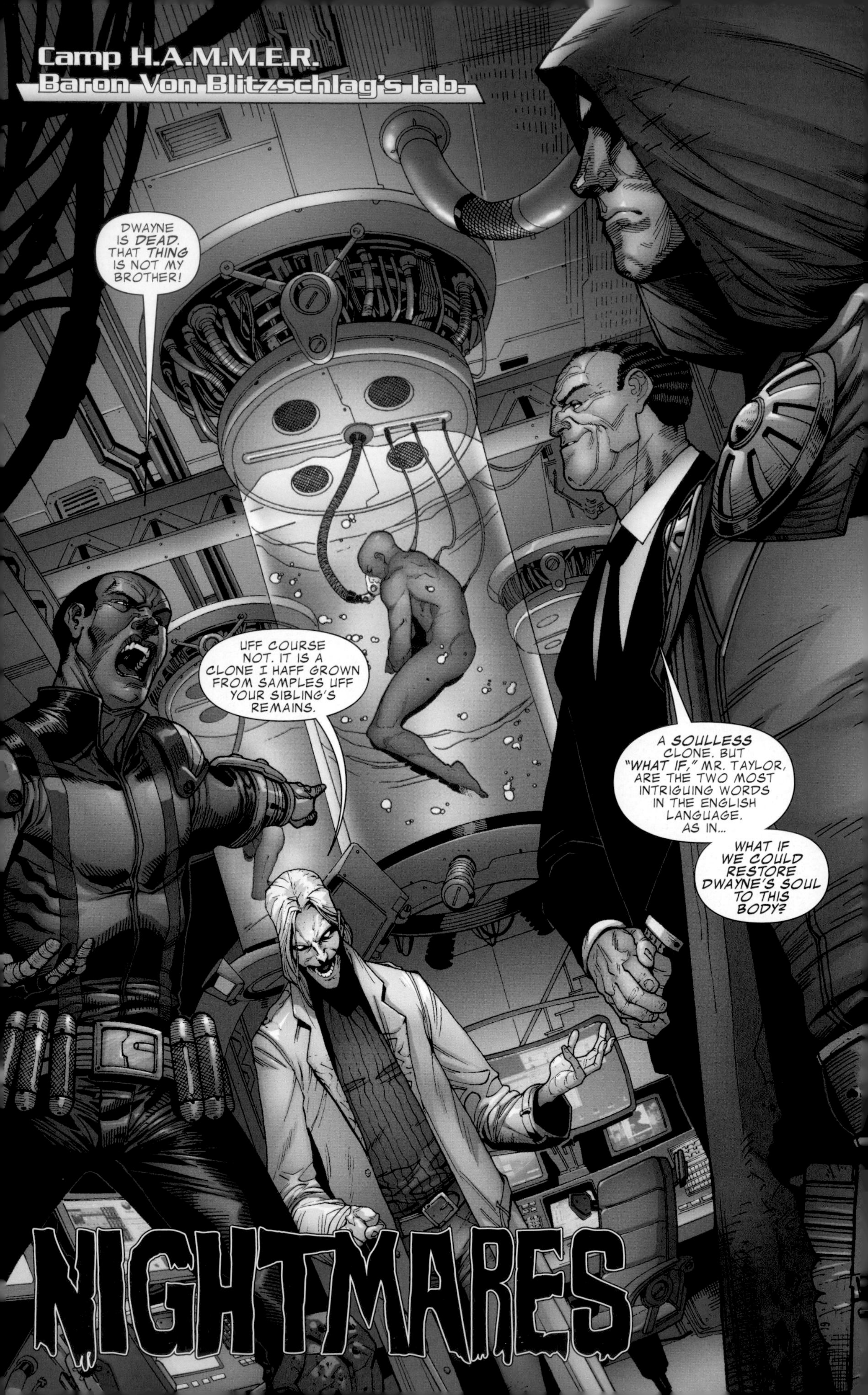
Camp H.A.M.M.E.R.
Baron Von Blitzschlag's lab.
DWAYNE IS DEAD. THAT THING IS NOT MY BROTHER!
UFF COURSE NOT. IT IS A CLONE I HAFF GROWN FROM SAMPLES UFF YOUR SIBLING'S REMAINS.
A SOULLESS CLONE. BUT "WHAT IF," MR. TAYLOR, ARE THE TWO MOST INTRIGUING WORDS IN THE ENGLISH LANGUAGE. AS IN...
WHAT IF WE COULD RESTORE DWAYNE'S SOUL TO THIS BODY?
NIGHTMARES

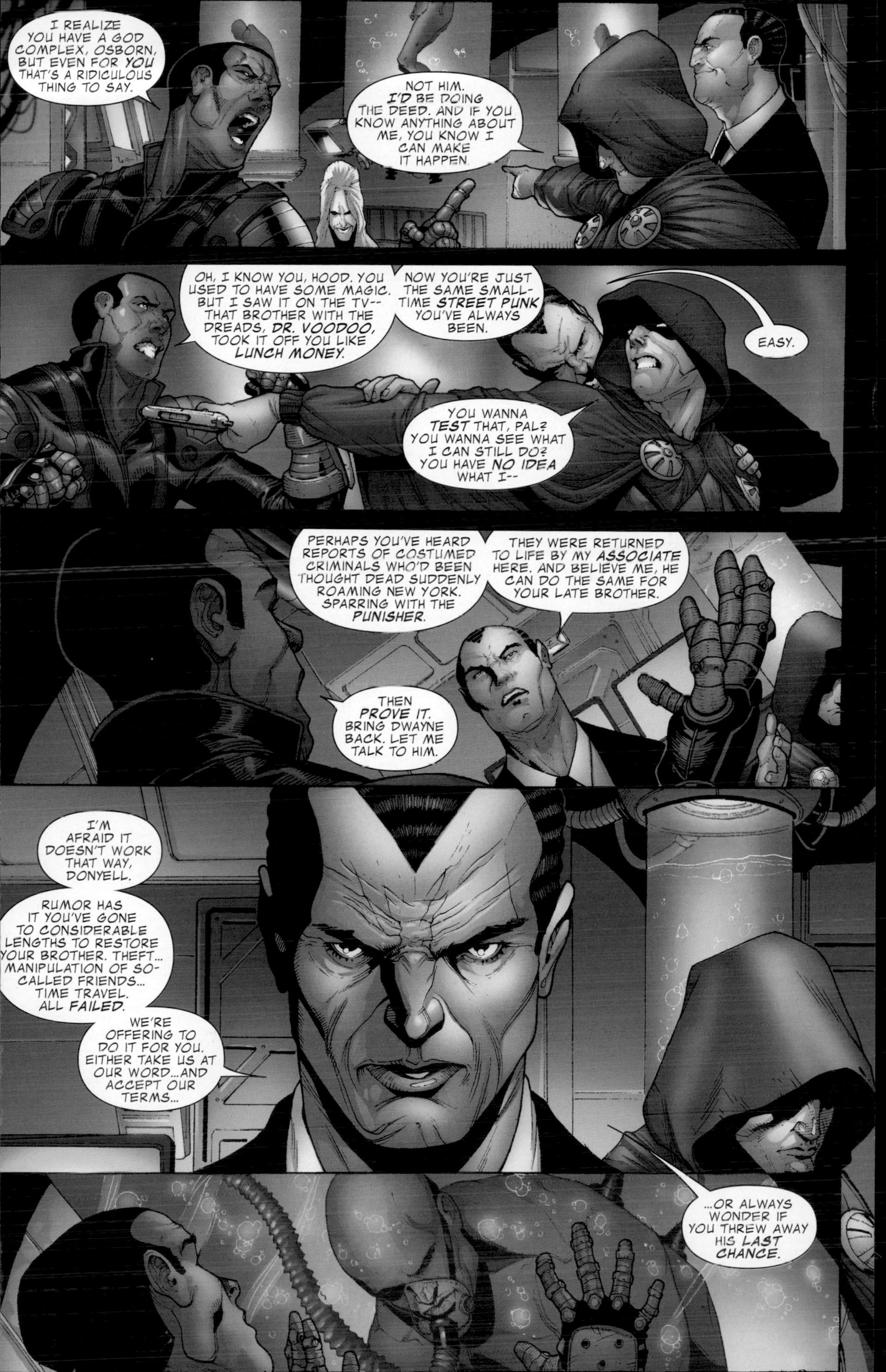
I REALIZE YOU HAVE A GOD COMPLEX, OSBORN, BUT EVEN FOR YOU THAT'S A RIDICULOUS THING TO SAY.
NOT HIM. I'D BE DOING THE DEED. AND IF YOU KNOW ANYTHING ABOUT ME, YOU KNOW I CAN MAKE IT HAPPEN.
OH, I KNOW YOU, HOOD. YOU USED TO HAVE SOME MAGIC. BUT I SAW IT ON THE TV-- THAT BROTHER WITH THE DREADS, DR. VOODOO, TOOK IT OFF YOU LIKE LUNCH MONEY.
NOW YOU'RE JUST THE SAME SMALL-TIME STREET PUNK YOU'VE ALWAYS BEEN.
EASY.
YOU WANNA TEST THAT, PAL? YOU WANNA SEE WHAT I CAN STILL DO? YOU HAVE NO IDEA WHAT I--
PERHAPS YOU'VE HEARD REPORTS OF COSTUMED CRIMINALS WHO'D BEEN THOUGHT DEAD SUDDENLY ROAMING NEW YORK. SPARRING WITH THE PUNISHER.
THEY WERE RETURNED TO LIFE BY MY ASSOCIATE HERE. AND BELIEVE ME, HE CAN DO THE SAME FOR YOUR LATE BROTHER.
THEN PROVE IT. BRING DWAYNE BACK. LET ME TALK TO HIM.
I'M AFRAID IT DOESN'T WORK THAT WAY, DONYELL.
RUMOR HAS IT YOU'VE GONE TO CONSIDERABLE LENGTHS TO RESTORE YOUR BROTHER. THEFT... MANIPULATION OF SO-CALLED FRIENDS... TIME TRAVEL. ALL FAILED.
WE'RE OFFERING TO DO IT FOR YOU. EITHER TAKE US AT OUR WORD...AND ACCEPT OUR TERMS...
...OR ALWAYS WONDER IF YOU THREW AWAY HIS LAST CHANCE.

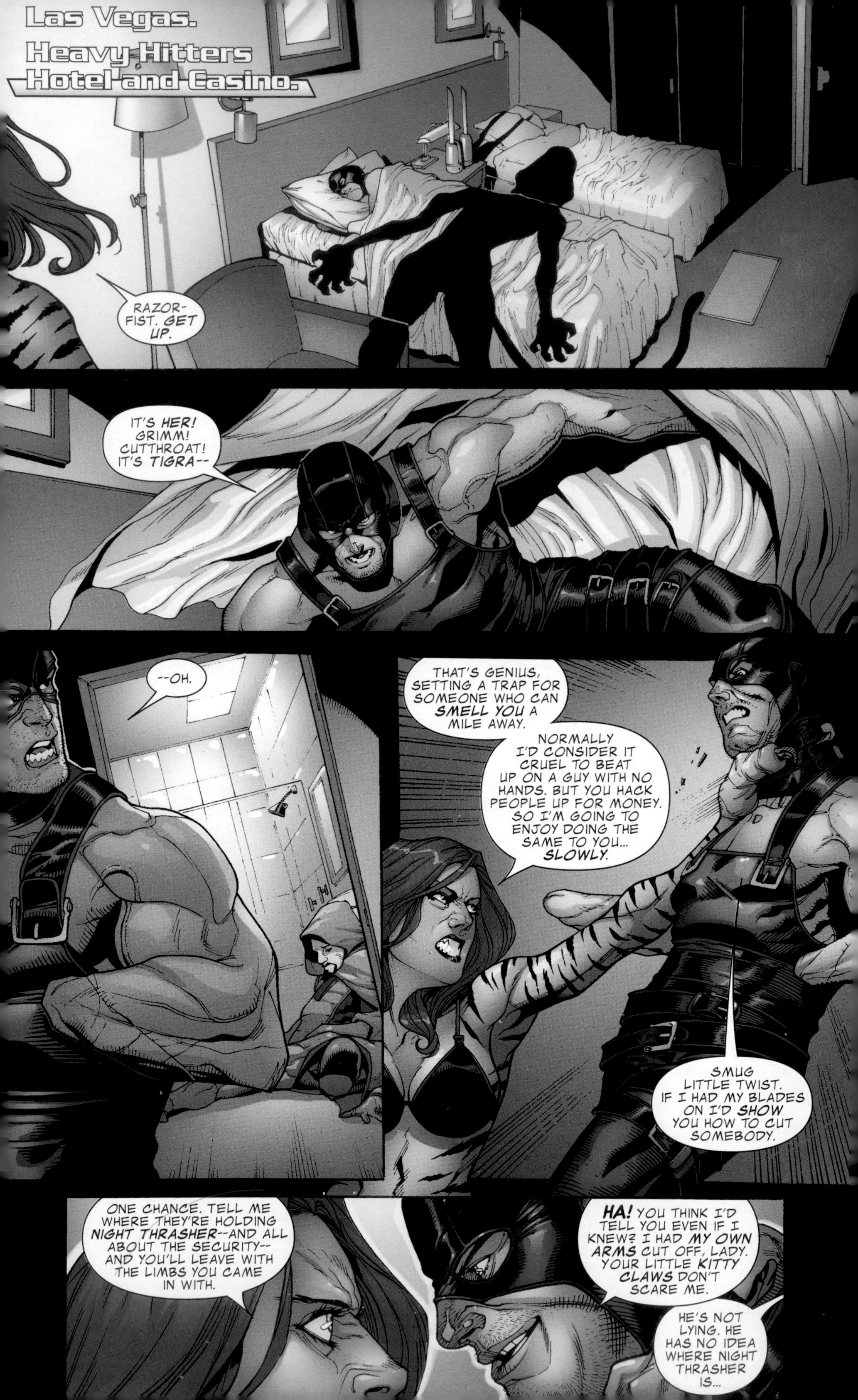
Las Vegas.
Heavy Hitters Hotel and Casino.
RAZOR-FIST. GET UP.
IT'S HER! GRIMM! CUTTHROAT! IT'S TIGRA--
--OH.
THAT'S GENIUS, SETTING A TRAP FOR SOMEONE WHO CAN SMELL YOU A MILE AWAY.
NORMALLY I'D CONSIDER IT CRUEL TO BEAT UP ON A GUY WITH NO HANDS. BUT YOU HACK PEOPLE UP FOR MONEY. SO I'M GOING TO ENJOY DOING THE SAME TO YOU... SLOWLY.
SMUG LITTLE TWIST. IF I HAD MY BLADES ON I'D SHOW YOU HOW TO CUT SOMEBODY.
ONE CHANCE. TELL ME WHERE THEY'RE HOLDING NIGHT THRASHER--AND ALL ABOUT THE SECURITY--AND YOU'LL LEAVE WITH THE LIMBS YOU CAME IN WITH.
HA! YOU THINK I'D TELL YOU EVEN IF I KNEW? I HAD MY OWN ARMS CUT OFF, LADY. YOUR LITTLE KITTY CLAWS DON'T SCARE ME.
HE'S NOT LYING. HE HAS NO IDEA WHERE NIGHT THRASHER IS...

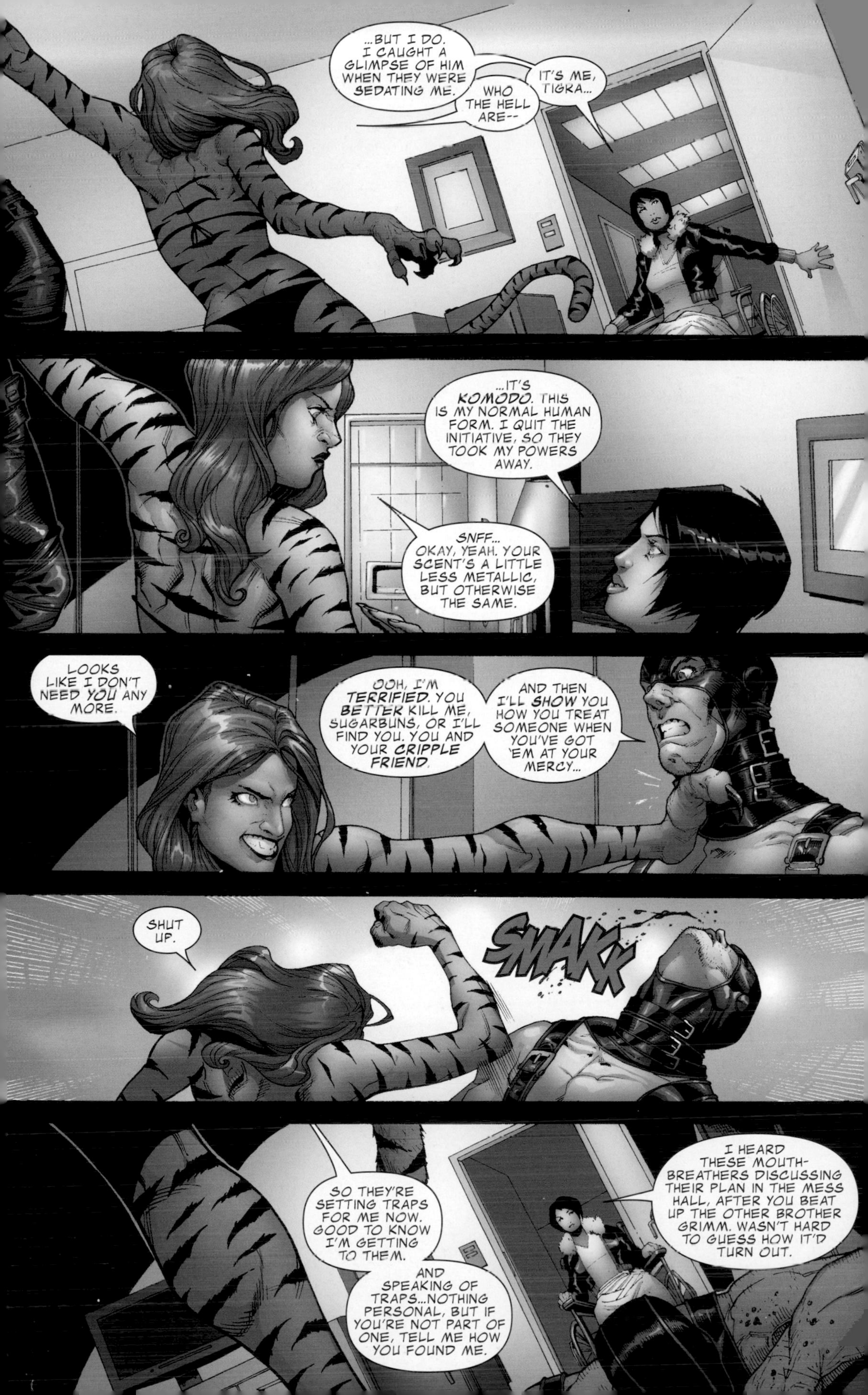

...BUT I DO. I CAUGHT A GLIMPSE OF HIM WHEN THEY WERE SEDATING ME.
WHO THE HELL ARE--
IT'S ME, TIGRA...
...IT'S KOMODO. THIS IS MY NORMAL HUMAN FORM. I QUIT THE INITIATIVE, SO THEY TOOK MY POWERS AWAY.
SNFF... OKAY, YEAH. YOUR SCENT'S A LITTLE LESS METALLIC, BUT OTHERWISE THE SAME.
LOOKS LIKE I DON'T NEED YOU ANY MORE.
OOH, I'M TERRIFIED. YOU BETTER KILL ME, SUGARBUNS, OR I'LL FIND YOU. YOU AND YOUR CRIPPLE FRIEND.
AND THEN I'LL SHOW YOU HOW YOU TREAT SOMEONE WHEN YOU'VE GOT 'EM AT YOUR MERCY...
SHUT UP.
SMAKK
SO THEY'RE SETTING TRAPS FOR ME NOW. GOOD TO KNOW I'M GETTING TO THEM.
AND SPEAKING OF TRAPS...NOTHING PERSONAL, BUT IF YOU'RE NOT PART OF ONE, TELL ME HOW YOU FOUND ME.
I HEARD THESE MOUTH-BREATHERS DISCUSSING THEIR PLAN IN THE MESS HALL, AFTER YOU BEAT UP THE OTHER BROTHER GRIMM. WASN'T HARD TO GUESS HOW IT'D TURN OUT.

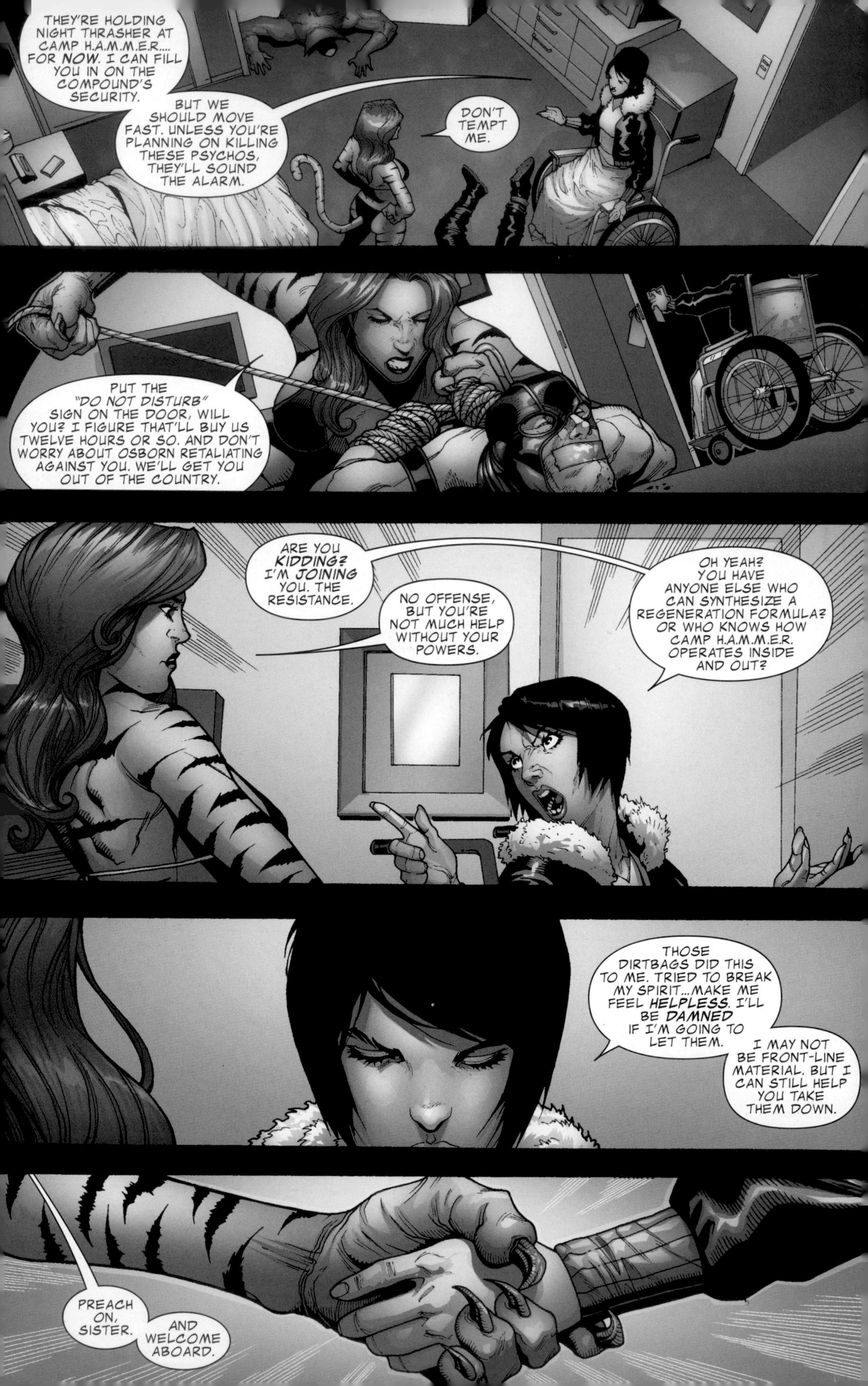
THEY'RE HOLDING NIGHT THRASHER AT CAMP H.A.M.M.E.R.... FOR NOW. I CAN FILL YOU IN ON THE COMPOUND'S SECURITY.
BUT WE SHOULD MOVE FAST. UNLESS YOU'RE PLANNING ON KILLING THESE PSYCHOS, THEY'LL SOUND THE ALARM.
DON'T TEMPT ME.
PUT THE "DO NOT DISTURB" SIGN ON THE DOOR, WILL YOU? I FIGURE THAT'LL BUY US TWELVE HOURS OR SO. AND DON'T WORRY ABOUT OSBORN RETALIATING AGAINST YOU. WE'LL GET YOU OUT OF THE COUNTRY.
ARE YOU KIDDING? I'M JOINING YOU. THE RESISTANCE.
NO OFFENSE, BUT YOU'RE NOT MUCH HELP WITHOUT YOUR POWERS.
OH YEAH? YOU HAVE ANYONE ELSE WHO CAN SYNTHESIZE A REGENERATION FORMULA? OR WHO KNOWS HOW CAMP H.A.M.M.E.R. OPERATES INSIDE AND OUT?
THOSE DIRTBAGS DID THIS TO ME. TRIED TO BREAK MY SPIRIT...MAKE ME FEEL HELPLESS. I'LL BE DAMNED IF I'M GOING TO LET THEM.
I MAY NOT BE FRONT-LINE MATERIAL. BUT I CAN STILL HELP YOU TAKE THEM DOWN.
PREACH ON, SISTER.
AND WELCOME ABOARD.

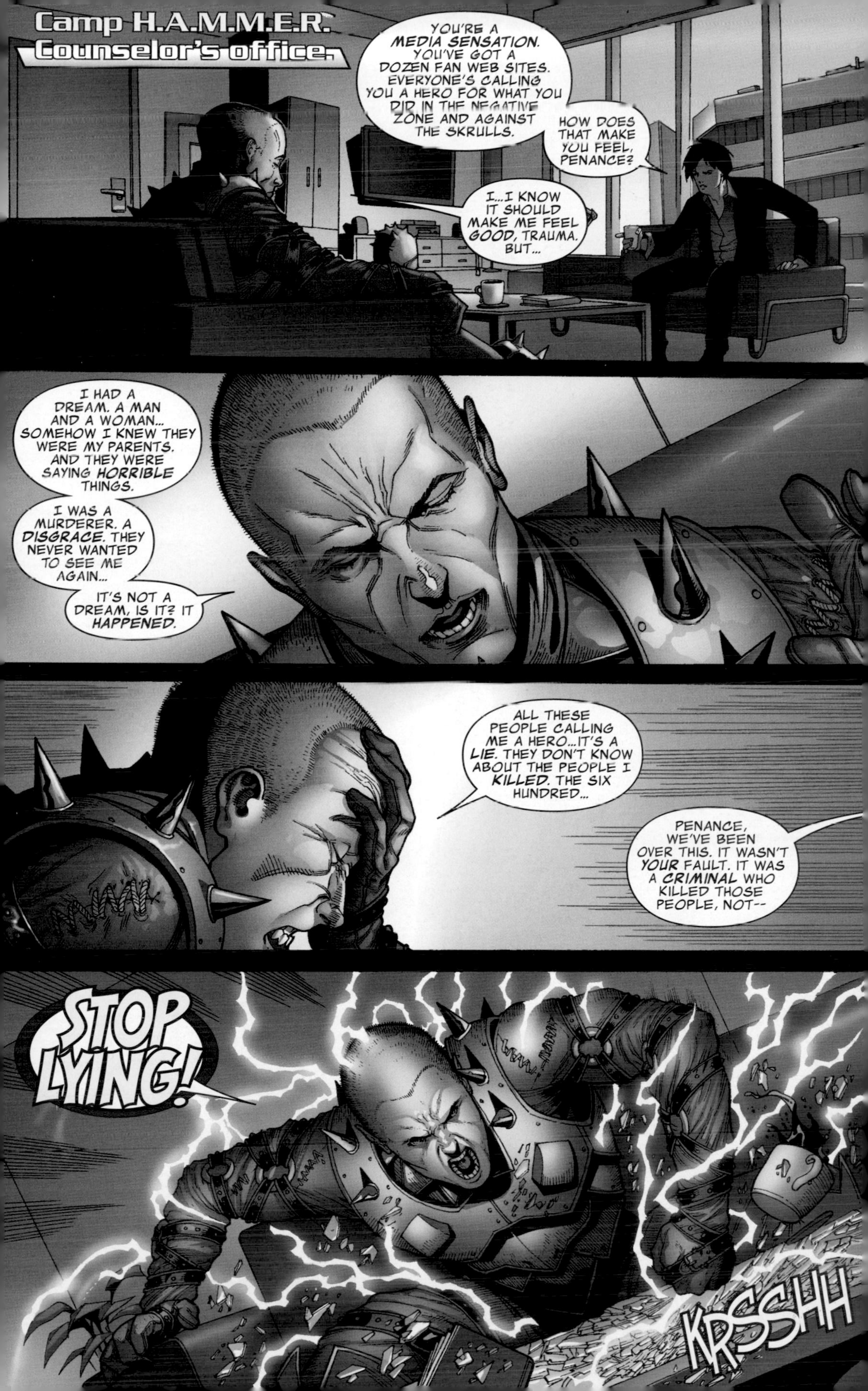
Camp H.A.M.M.E.R. Counselor's office.
YOU'RE A MEDIA SENSATION. YOU'VE GOT A DOZEN FAN WEB SITES. EVERYONE'S CALLING YOU A HERO FOR WHAT YOU DID IN THE NEGATIVE ZONE AND AGAINST THE SKRULLS.
HOW DOES THAT MAKE YOU FEEL, PENANCE?
I...I KNOW IT SHOULD MAKE ME FEEL GOOD, TRAUMA. BUT...
I HAD A DREAM. A MAN AND A WOMAN... SOMEHOW I KNEW THEY WERE MY PARENTS. AND THEY WERE SAYING HORRIBLE THINGS.
I WAS A MURDERER. A DISGRACE. THEY NEVER WANTED TO SEE ME AGAIN...
IT'S NOT A DREAM, IS IT? IT HAPPENED.
ALL THESE PEOPLE CALLING ME A HERO...IT'S A LIE. THEY DON'T KNOW ABOUT THE PEOPLE I KILLED. THE SIX HUNDRED...
PENANCE, WE'VE BEEN OVER THIS. IT WASN'T YOUR FAULT. IT WAS A CRIMINAL WHO KILLED THOSE PEOPLE, NOT--
STOP LYING!
KRSSHH

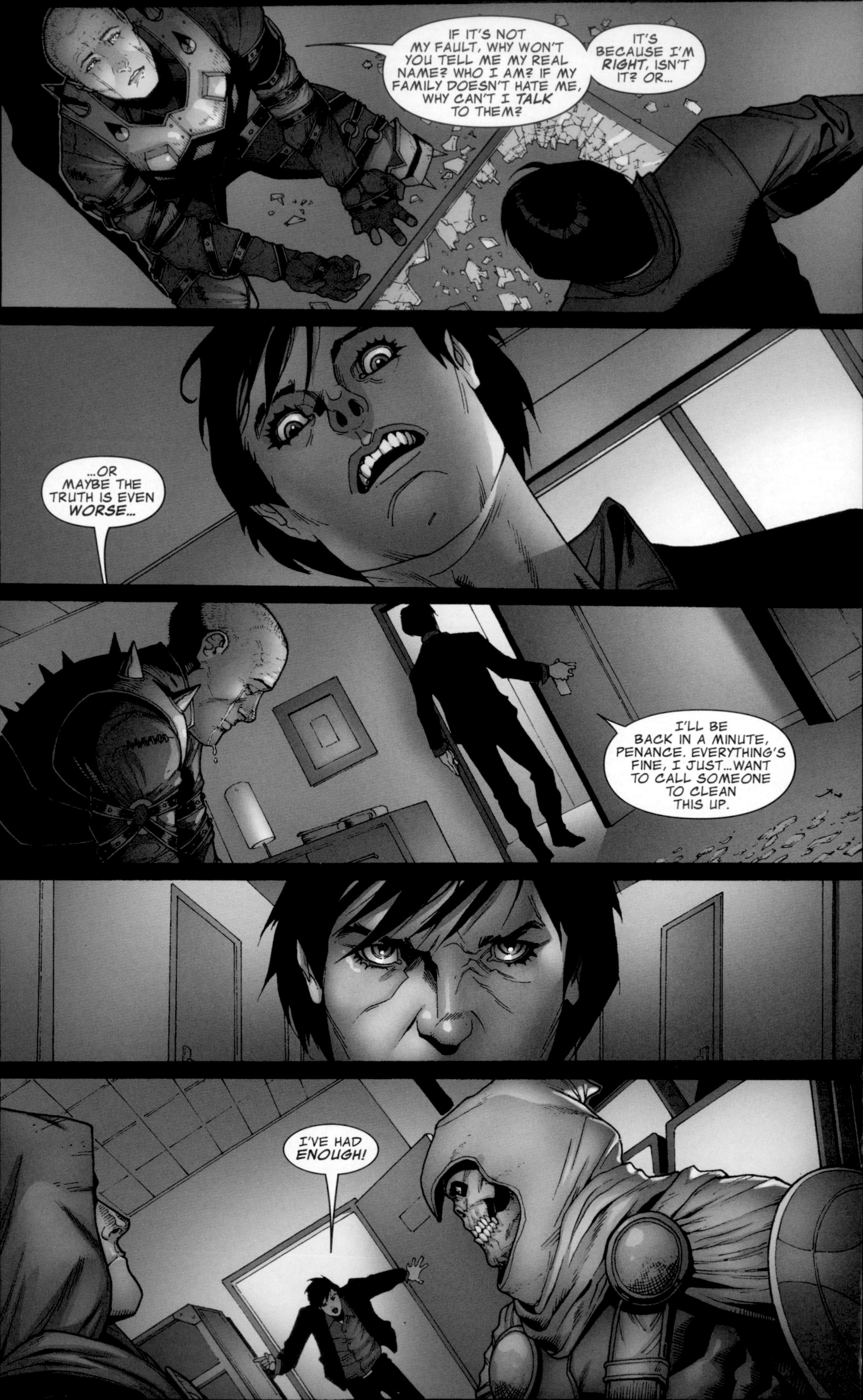
IF IT'S NOT MY FAULT, WHY WON'T YOU TELL ME MY REAL NAME? WHO I AM? IF MY FAMILY DOESN'T HATE ME, WHY CAN'T I TALK TO THEM?
IT'S BECAUSE I'M RIGHT, ISN'T IT? OR...
...OR MAYBE THE TRUTH IS EVEN WORSE...
I'LL BE BACK IN A MINUTE, PENANCE. EVERYTHING'S FINE, I JUST...WANT TO CALL SOMEONE TO CLEAN THIS UP.
I'VE HAD ENOUGH!

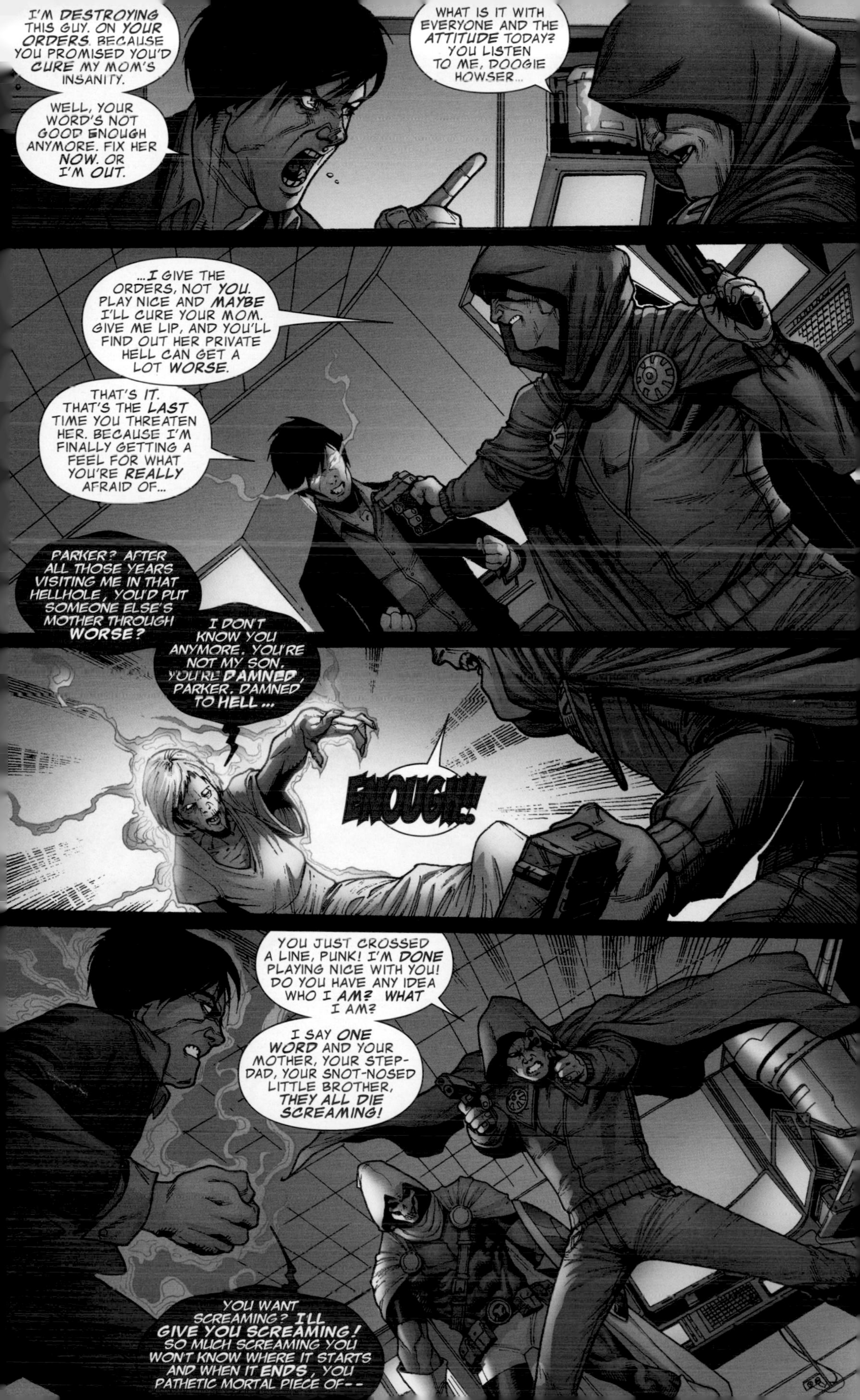
I'M DESTROYING THIS GUY. ON YOUR ORDERS. BECAUSE YOU PROMISED YOU'D CURE MY MOM'S INSANITY.
WELL, YOUR WORD'S NOT GOOD ENOUGH ANYMORE. FIX HER NOW. OR I'M OUT.
WHAT IS IT WITH EVERYONE AND THE ATTITUDE TODAY? YOU LISTEN TO ME, DOOGIE HOWSER...
...I GIVE THE ORDERS, NOT YOU. PLAY NICE AND MAYBE I'LL CURE YOUR MOM. GIVE ME LIP, AND YOU'LL FIND OUT HER PRIVATE HELL CAN GET A LOT WORSE.
THAT'S IT. THAT'S THE LAST TIME YOU THREATEN HER. BECAUSE I'M FINALLY GETTING A FEEL FOR WHAT YOU'RE REALLY AFRAID OF...
PARKER? AFTER ALL THOSE YEARS VISITING ME IN THAT HELLHOLE, YOU'D PUT SOMEONE ELSE'S MOTHER THROUGH WORSE?
I DON'T KNOW YOU ANYMORE. YOU'RE NOT MY SON. YOU'RE DAMNED, PARKER. DAMNED TO HELL...
ENOUGH!!
YOU JUST CROSSED A LINE, PUNK! I'M DONE PLAYING NICE WITH YOU! DO YOU HAVE ANY IDEA WHO I AM? WHAT I AM?
I SAY ONE WORD AND YOUR MOTHER, YOUR STEP-DAD, YOUR SNOT-NOSED LITTLE BROTHER, THEY ALL DIE SCREAMING!
YOU WANT SCREAMING? I'LL GIVE YOU SCREAMING! SO MUCH SCREAMING YOU WON'T KNOW WHERE IT STARTS AND WHEN IT ENDS, YOU PATHETIC MORTAL PIECE OF--

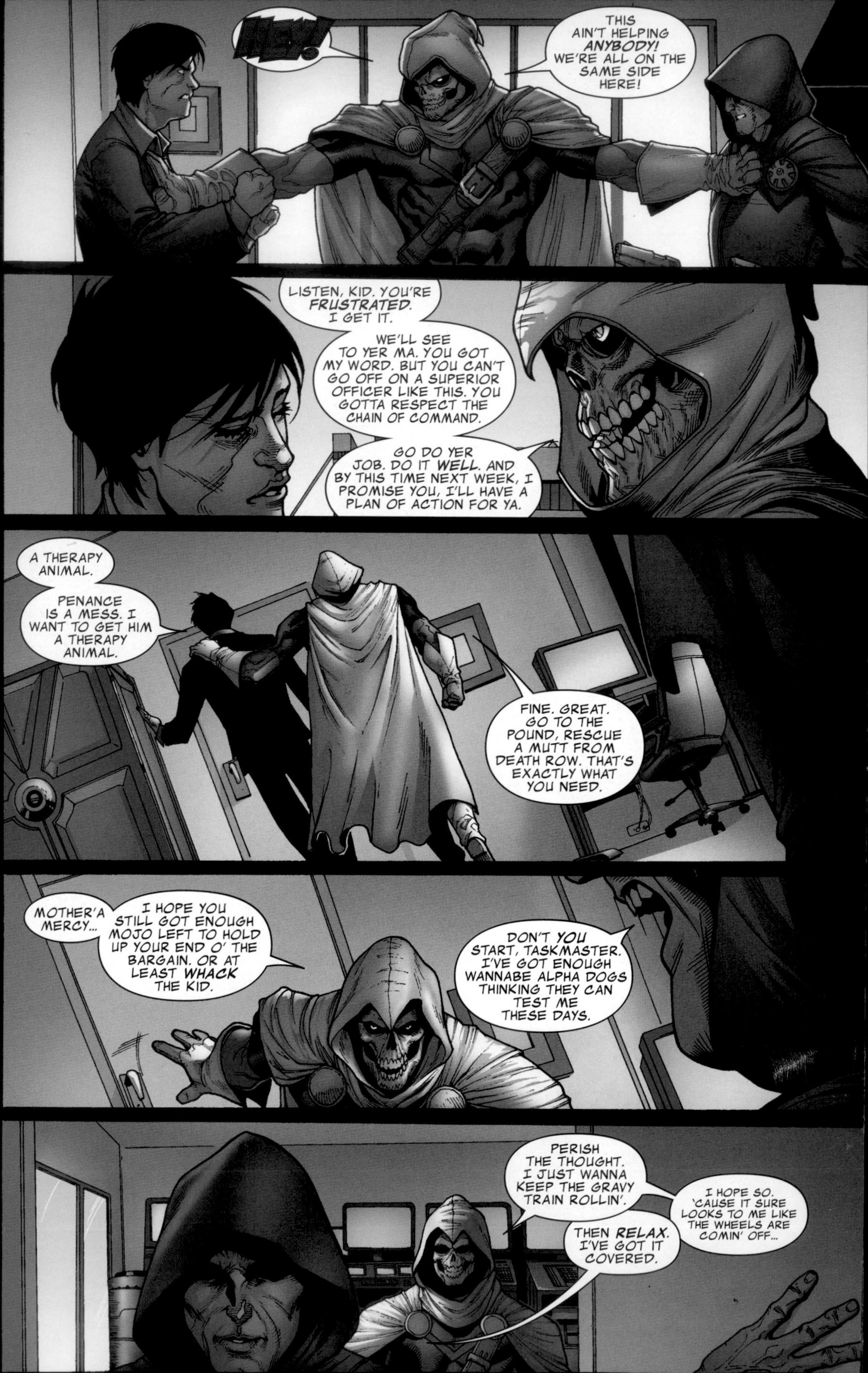
HEY!
THIS AIN'T HELPING ANYBODY! WE'RE ALL ON THE SAME SIDE HERE!
LISTEN, KID. YOU'RE FRUSTRATED. I GET IT.
WE'LL SEE TO YER MA. YOU GOT MY WORD. BUT YOU CAN'T GO OFF ON A SUPERIOR OFFICER LIKE THIS. YOU GOTTA RESPECT THE CHAIN OF COMMAND.
GO DO YER JOB. DO IT WELL. AND BY THIS TIME NEXT WEEK, I PROMISE YOU, I'LL HAVE A PLAN OF ACTION FOR YA.
A THERAPY ANIMAL.
PENANCE IS A MESS. I WANT TO GET HIM A THERAPY ANIMAL.
FINE. GREAT. GO TO THE POUND, RESCUE A MUTT FROM DEATH ROW. THAT'S EXACTLY WHAT YOU NEED.
MOTHER'A MERCY...
I HOPE YOU STILL GOT ENOUGH MOJO LEFT TO HOLD UP YOUR END O' THE BARGAIN. OR AT LEAST WHACK THE KID.
DON'T YOU START, TASKMASTER. I'VE GOT ENOUGH WANNABE ALPHA DOGS THINKING THEY CAN TEST ME THESE DAYS.
PERISH THE THOUGHT. I JUST WANNA KEEP THE GRAVY TRAIN ROLLIN'.
THEN RELAX. I'VE GOT IT COVERED.
I HOPE SO. 'CAUSE IT SURE LOOKS TO ME LIKE THE WHEELS ARE COMIN' OFF...

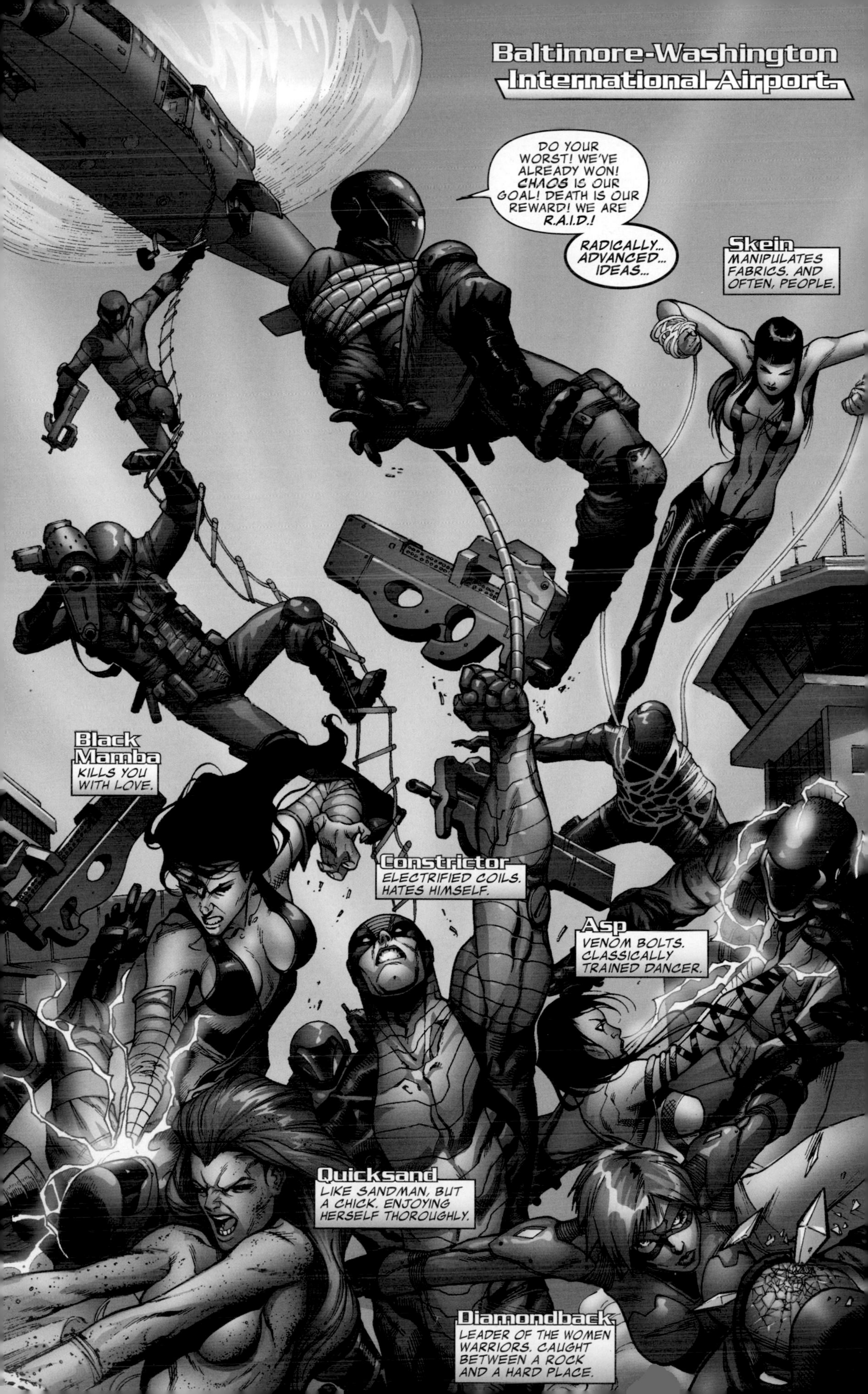
Baltimore-Washington International Airport.
DO YOUR WORST! WE'VE ALREADY WON! CHAOS IS OUR GOAL! DEATH IS OUR REWARD! WE ARE R.A.I.D.!
RADICALLY... ADVANCED... IDEAS...
Skein
MANIPULATES FABRICS. AND OFTEN, PEOPLE.
Black Mamba
KILLS YOU WITH LOVE.
Constrictor
ELECTRIFIED COILS. HATES HIMSELF.
Asp
VENOM BOLTS. CLASSICALLY TRAINED DANCER.
Quicksand
LIKE SANDMAN, BUT A CHICK. ENJOYING HERSELF THOROUGHLY.
Diamondback
LEADER OF THE WOMEN WARRIORS. CAUGHT BETWEEN A ROCK AND A HARD PLACE.

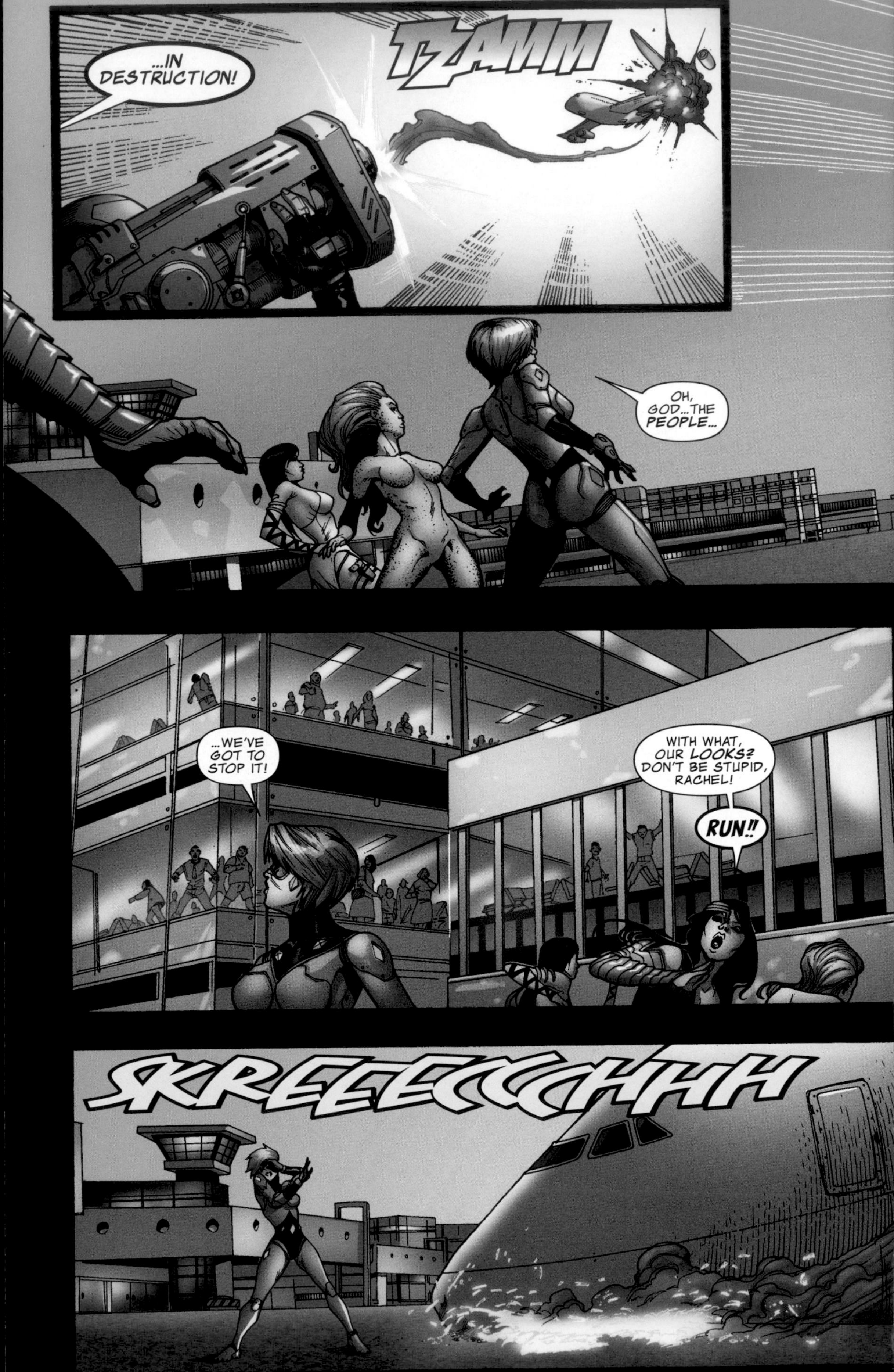
...IN DESTRUCTION!
TZAMM
OH, GOD...THE PEOPLE...
...WE'VE GOT TO STOP IT!
WITH WHAT, OUR LOOKS? DON'T BE STUPID, RACHEL!
RUN!!
SKREEEECCHHHH

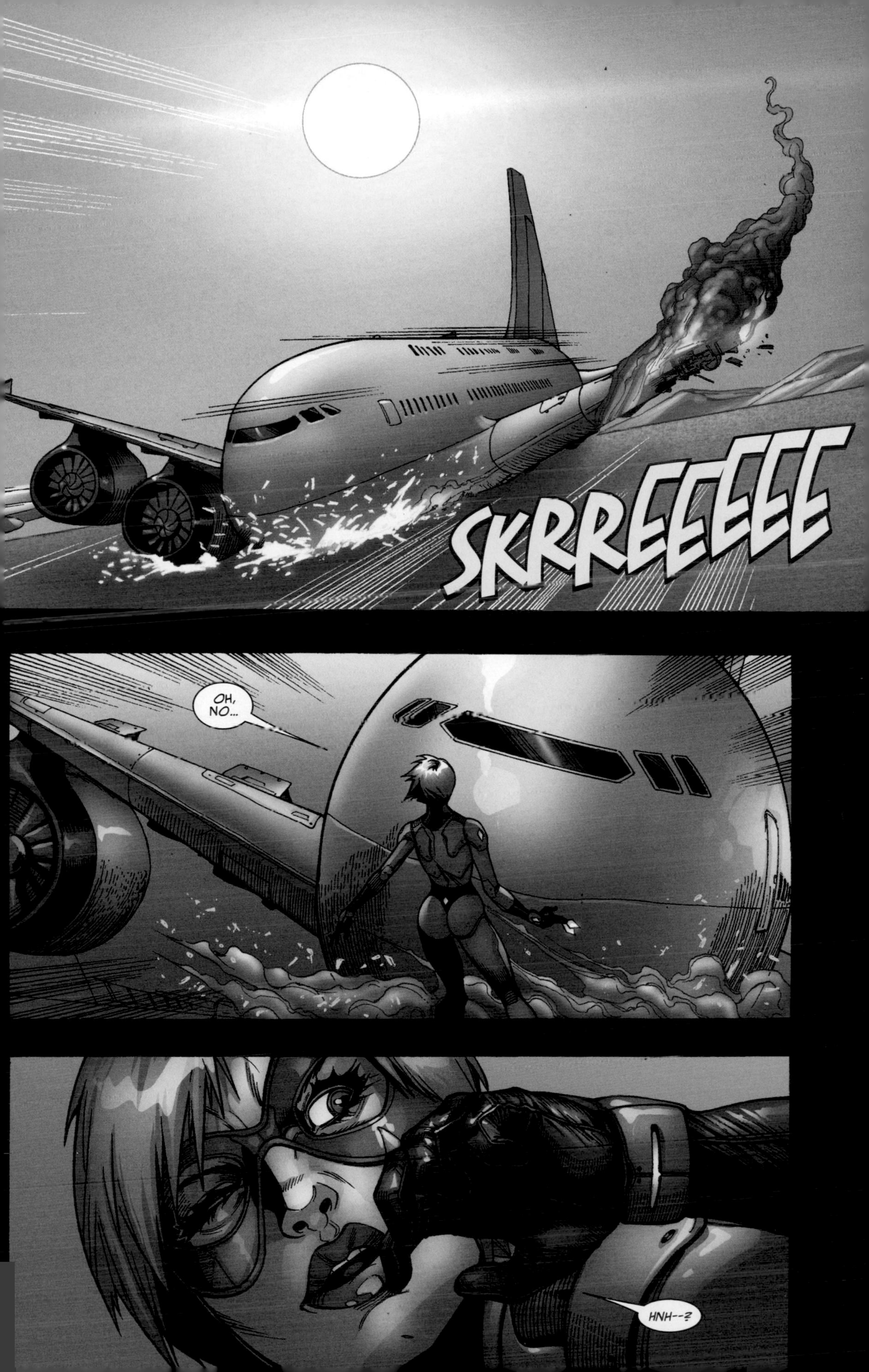
SKRREEEEEE
OH, NO...
HNH--?

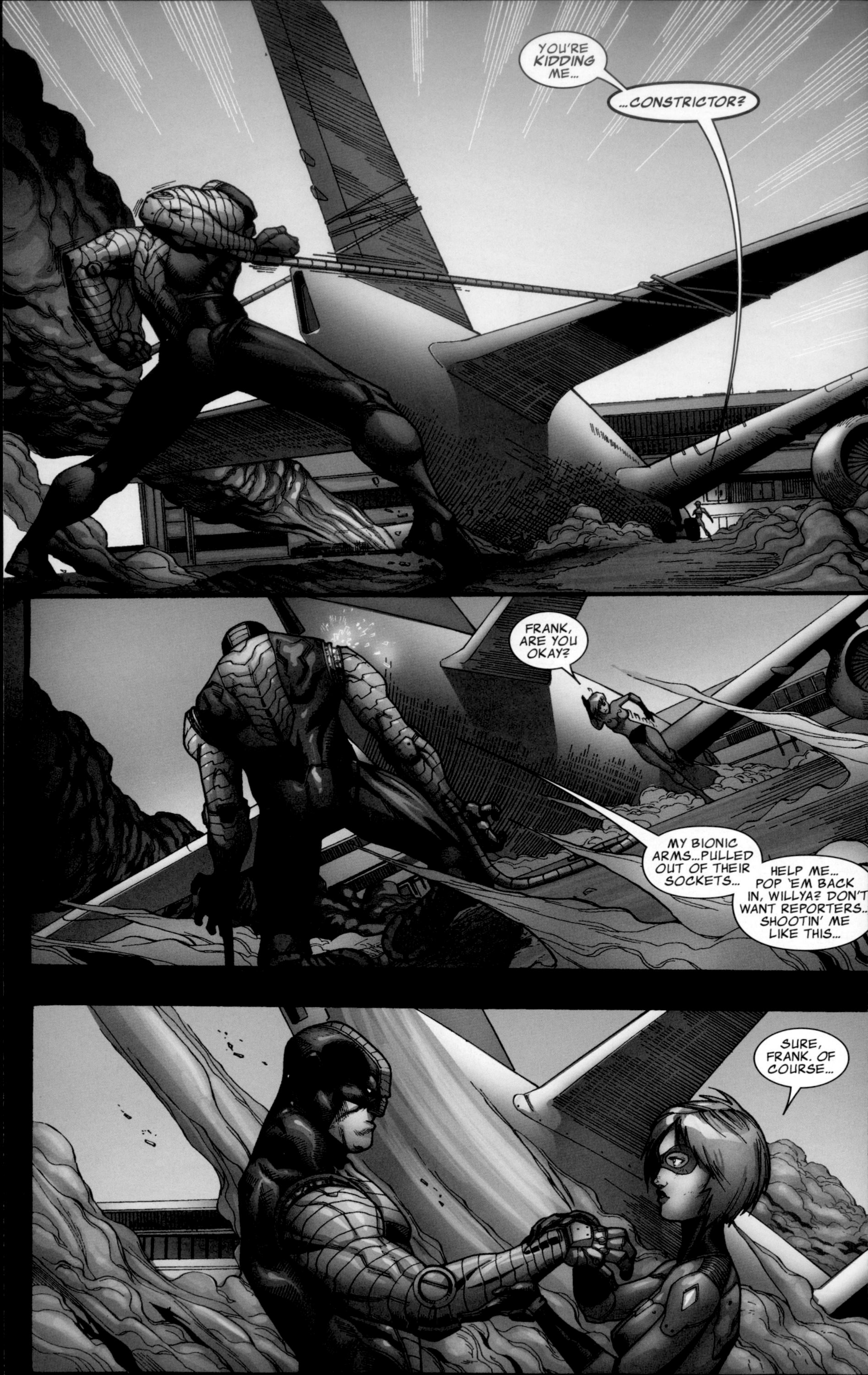
YOU'RE KIDDING ME...
...CONSTRICTOR?
FRANK, ARE YOU OKAY?
MY BIONIC ARMS...PULLED OUT OF THEIR SOCKETS...
HELP ME... POP 'EM BACK IN, WILLYA? DON'T WANT REPORTERS... SHOOTIN' ME LIKE THIS...
SURE, FRANK. OF COURSE...

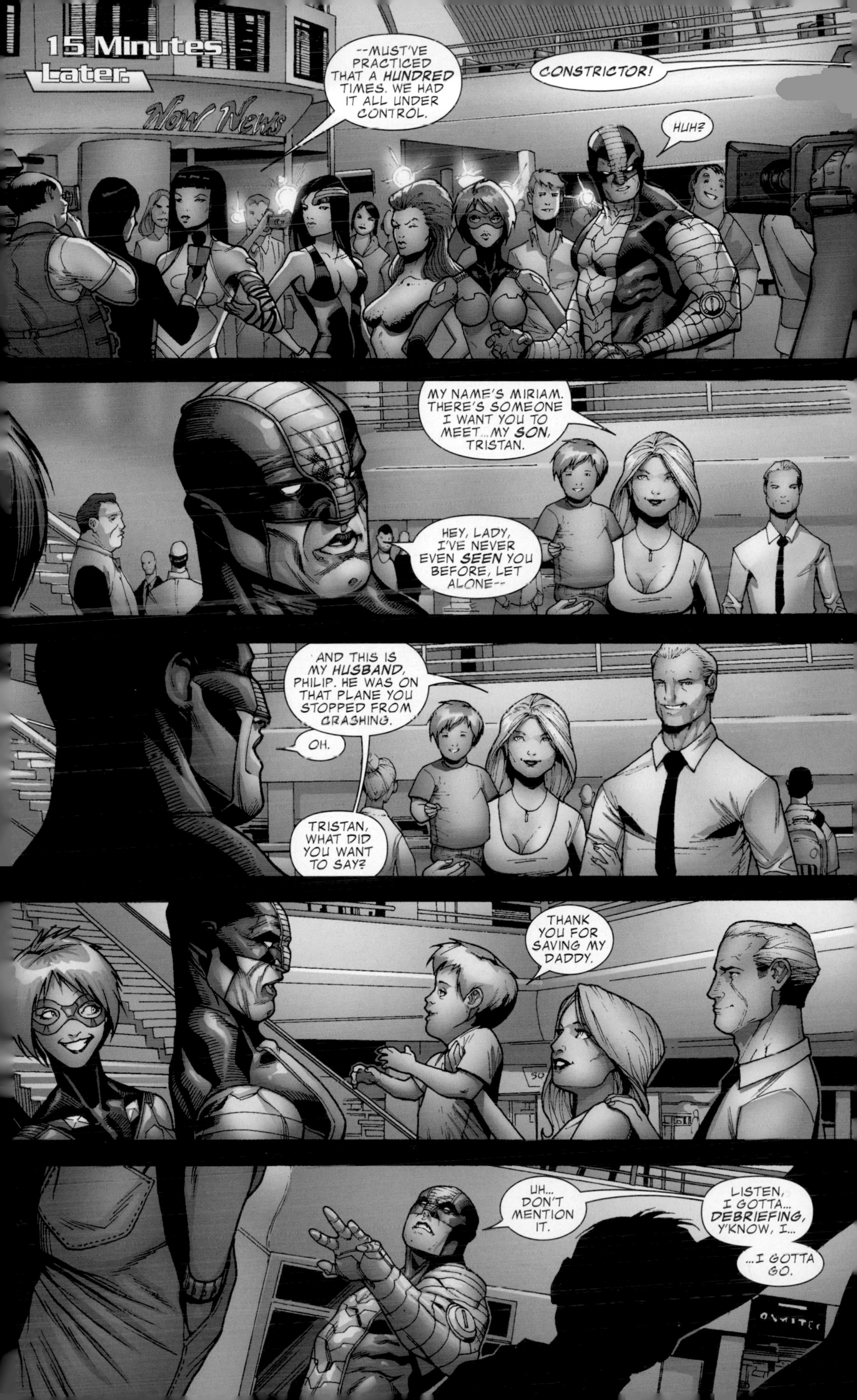
15 Minutes Later.
--MUST'VE PRACTICED THAT A HUNDRED TIMES. WE HAD IT ALL UNDER CONTROL.
Now News
CONSTRICTOR!
HUH?
MY NAME'S MIRIAM. THERE'S SOMEONE I WANT YOU TO MEET...MY SON, TRISTAN.
HEY, LADY, I'VE NEVER EVEN SEEN YOU BEFORE, LET ALONE--
AND THIS IS MY HUSBAND, PHILIP. HE WAS ON THAT PLANE YOU STOPPED FROM CRASHING.
OH.
TRISTAN, WHAT DID YOU WANT TO SAY?
THANK YOU FOR SAVING MY DADDY.
UH... DON'T MENTION IT.
LISTEN, I GOTTA... DEBRIEFING, Y'KNOW, I...
...I GOTTA GO.

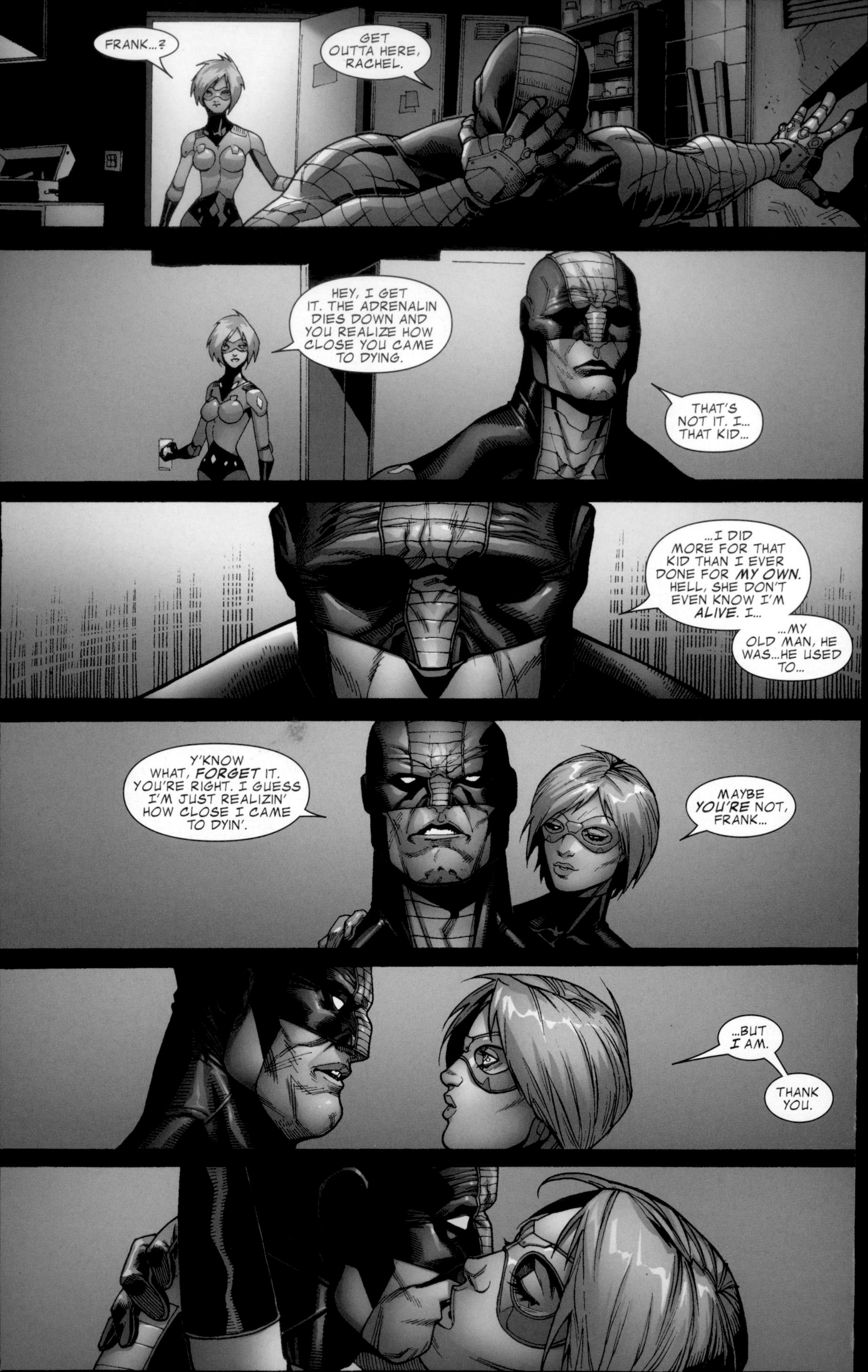
FRANK...?
GET OUTTA HERE, RACHEL.
HEY, I GET IT. THE ADRENALIN DIES DOWN AND YOU REALIZE HOW CLOSE YOU CAME TO DYING.
THAT'S NOT IT. I... THAT KID...
...I DID MORE FOR THAT KID THAN I EVER DONE FOR MY OWN. HELL, SHE DON'T EVEN KNOW I'M ALIVE. I...
...MY OLD MAN, HE WAS...HE USED TO...
Y'KNOW WHAT, FORGET IT. YOU'RE RIGHT. I GUESS I'M JUST REALIZIN' HOW CLOSE I CAME TO DYIN'.
MAYBE YOU'RE NOT, FRANK...
...BUT I AM.
THANK YOU.

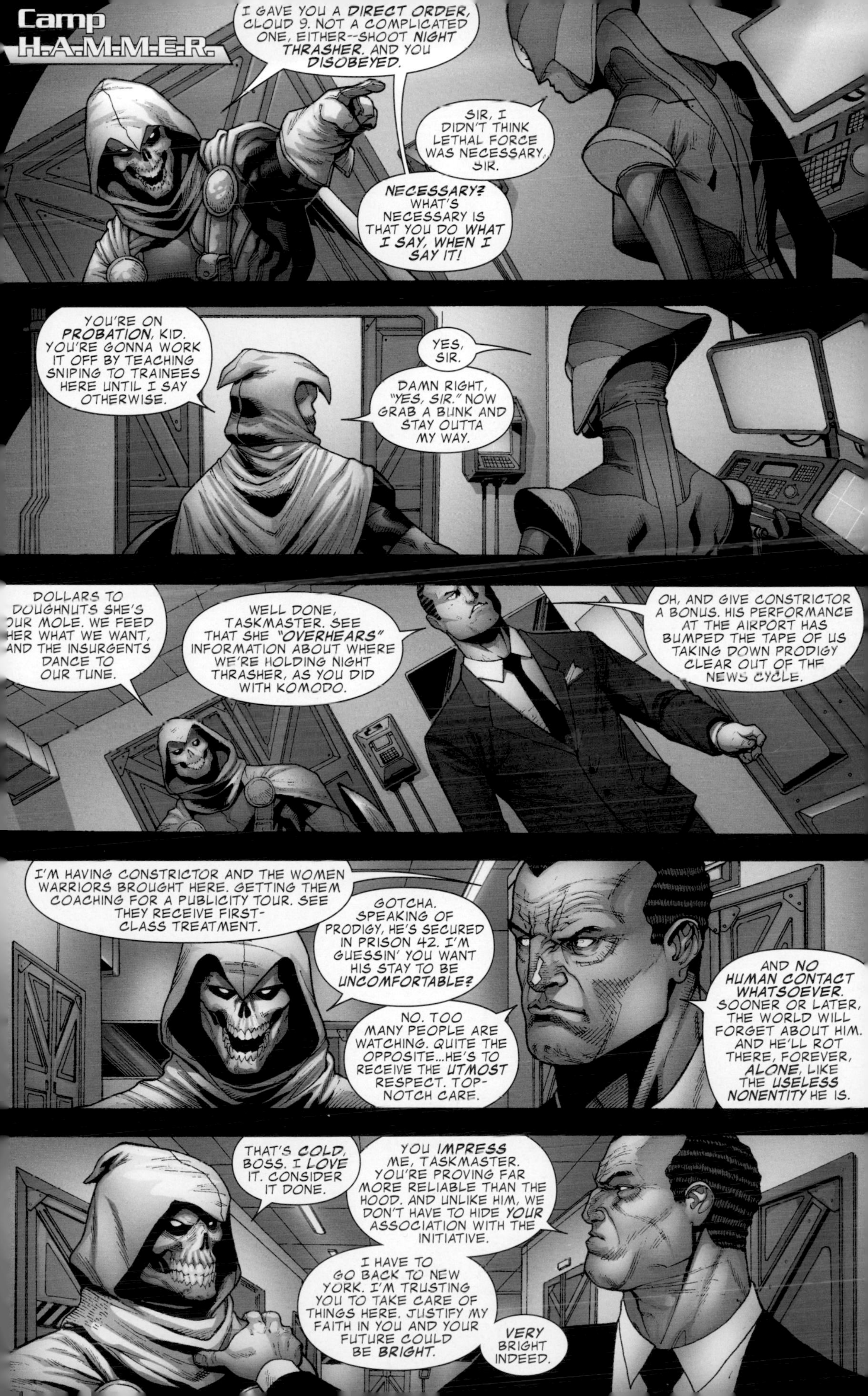
Camp H.A.M.M.E.R.
I GAVE YOU A DIRECT ORDER, CLOUD 9. NOT A COMPLICATED ONE, EITHER--SHOOT NIGHT THRASHER. AND YOU DISOBEYED.
SIR, I DIDN'T THINK LETHAL FORCE WAS NECESSARY, SIR.
NECESSARY? WHAT'S NECESSARY IS THAT YOU DO WHAT I SAY, WHEN I SAY IT!
YOU'RE ON PROBATION, KID. YOU'RE GONNA WORK IT OFF BY TEACHING SNIPING TO TRAINEES HERE UNTIL I SAY OTHERWISE.
YES, SIR.
DAMN RIGHT, "YES, SIR." NOW GRAB A BUNK AND STAY OUTTA MY WAY.
DOLLARS TO DOUGHNUTS SHE'S OUR MOLE. WE FEED HER WHAT WE WANT, AND THE INSURGENTS DANCE TO OUR TUNE.
WELL DONE, TASKMASTER. SEE THAT SHE "OVERHEARS" INFORMATION ABOUT WHERE WE'RE HOLDING NIGHT THRASHER, AS YOU DID WITH KOMODO.
OH, AND GIVE CONSTRICTOR A BONUS. HIS PERFORMANCE AT THE AIRPORT HAS BUMPED THE TAPE OF US TAKING DOWN PRODIGY CLEAR OUT OF THE NEWS CYCLE.
I'M HAVING CONSTRICTOR AND THE WOMEN WARRIORS BROUGHT HERE. GETTING THEM COACHING FOR A PUBLICITY TOUR. SEE THEY RECEIVE FIRST-CLASS TREATMENT.
GOTCHA. SPEAKING OF PRODIGY, HE'S SECURED IN PRISON 42. I'M GUESSIN' YOU WANT HIS STAY TO BE UNCOMFORTABLE?
NO. TOO MANY PEOPLE ARE WATCHING. QUITE THE OPPOSITE...HE'S TO RECEIVE THE UTMOST RESPECT. TOP-NOTCH CARE.
AND NO HUMAN CONTACT WHATSOEVER. SOONER OR LATER, THE WORLD WILL FORGET ABOUT HIM. AND HE'LL ROT THERE, FOREVER, ALONE, LIKE THE USELESS NONENTITY HE IS.
THAT'S COLD, BOSS. I LOVE IT. CONSIDER IT DONE.
YOU IMPRESS ME, TASKMASTER. YOU'RE PROVING FAR MORE RELIABLE THAN THE HOOD. AND UNLIKE HIM, WE DON'T HAVE TO HIDE YOUR ASSOCIATION WITH THE INITIATIVE.
I HAVE TO GO BACK TO NEW YORK. I'M TRUSTING YOU TO TAKE CARE OF THINGS HERE. JUSTIFY MY FAITH IN YOU AND YOUR FUTURE COULD BE BRIGHT.
VERY BRIGHT INDEED.

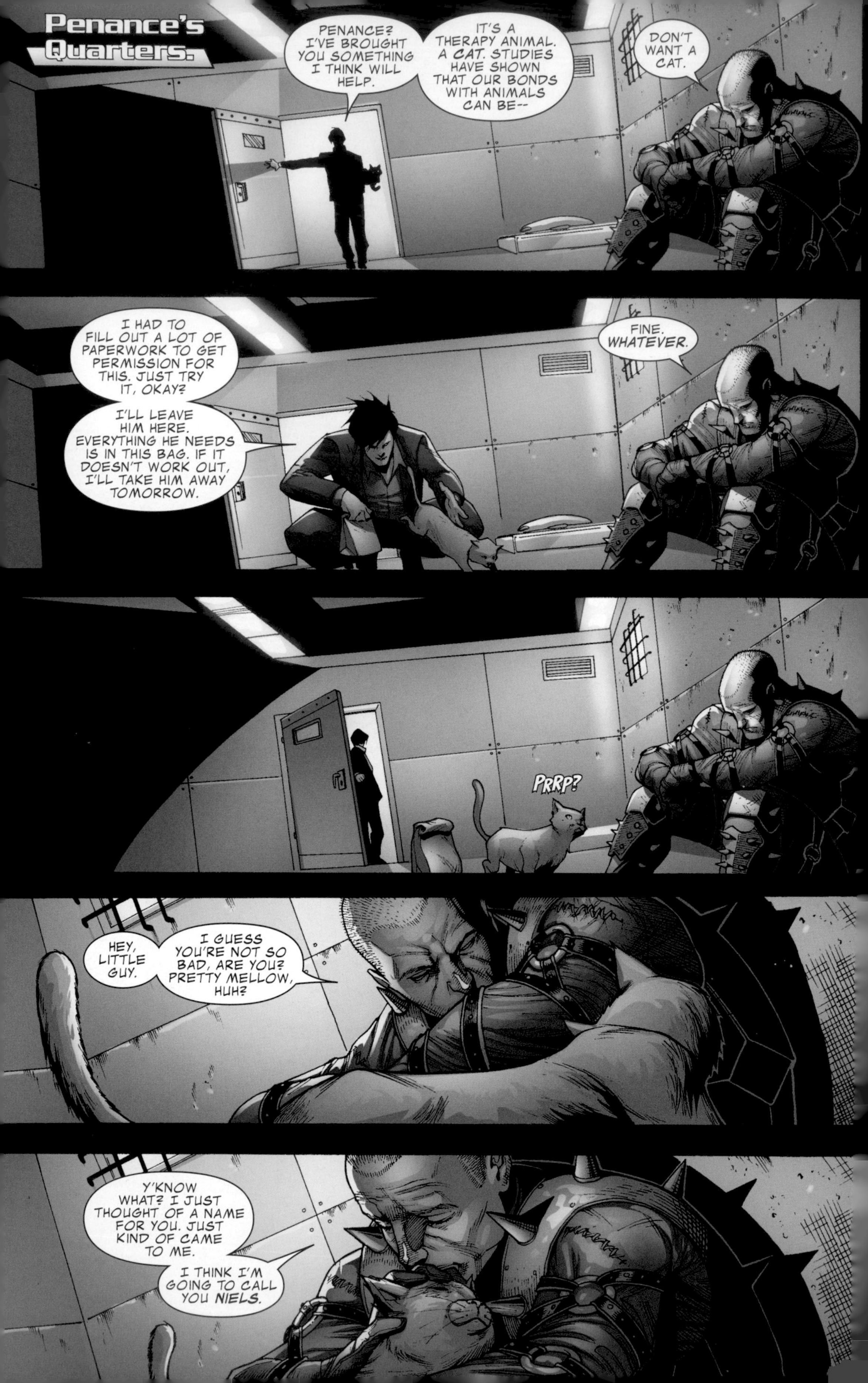
Penance's Quarters.
PENANCE? I'VE BROUGHT YOU SOMETHING I THINK WILL HELP.
IT'S A THERAPY ANIMAL. A CAT. STUDIES HAVE SHOWN THAT OUR BONDS WITH ANIMALS CAN BE--
DON'T WANT A CAT.
I HAD TO FILL OUT A LOT OF PAPERWORK TO GET PERMISSION FOR THIS. JUST TRY IT, OKAY?
I'LL LEAVE HIM HERE. EVERYTHING HE NEEDS IS IN THIS BAG. IF IT DOESN'T WORK OUT, I'LL TAKE HIM AWAY TOMORROW.
FINE. WHATEVER.
PRRP?
HEY, LITTLE GUY.
I GUESS YOU'RE NOT SO BAD, ARE YOU? PRETTY MELLOW, HUH?
Y'KNOW WHAT? I JUST THOUGHT OF A NAME FOR YOU. JUST KIND OF CAME TO ME.
I THINK I'M GOING TO CALL YOU NIELS.

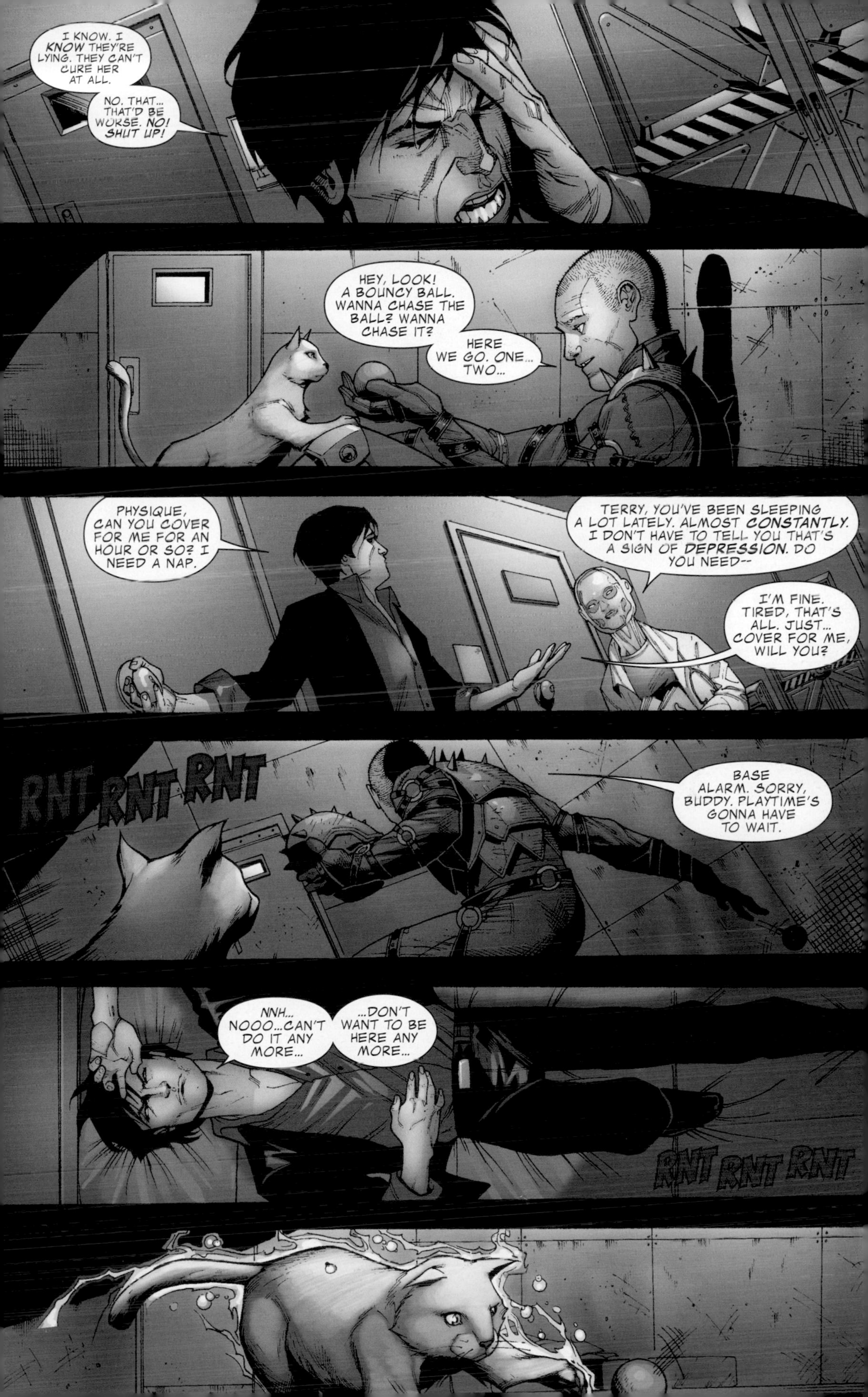

I KNOW. I KNOW THEY'RE LYING. THEY CAN'T CURE HER AT ALL.
NO. THAT... THAT'D BE WORSE. NO! SHUT UP!
HEY, LOOK! A BOUNCY BALL. WANNA CHASE THE BALL? WANNA CHASE IT?
HERE WE GO. ONE... TWO...
PHYSIQUE, CAN YOU COVER FOR ME FOR AN HOUR OR SO? I NEED A NAP.
TERRY, YOU'VE BEEN SLEEPING A LOT LATELY. ALMOST CONSTANTLY. I DON'T HAVE TO TELL YOU THAT'S A SIGN OF DEPRESSION. DO YOU NEED--
I'M FINE. TIRED, THAT'S ALL. JUST... COVER FOR ME, WILL YOU?
RNT RNT RNT
BASE ALARM. SORRY, BUDDY. PLAYTIME'S GONNA HAVE TO WAIT.
NNH... NOOO...CAN'T DO IT ANY MORE...
...DON'T WANT TO BE HERE ANY MORE...
RNT RNT RNT

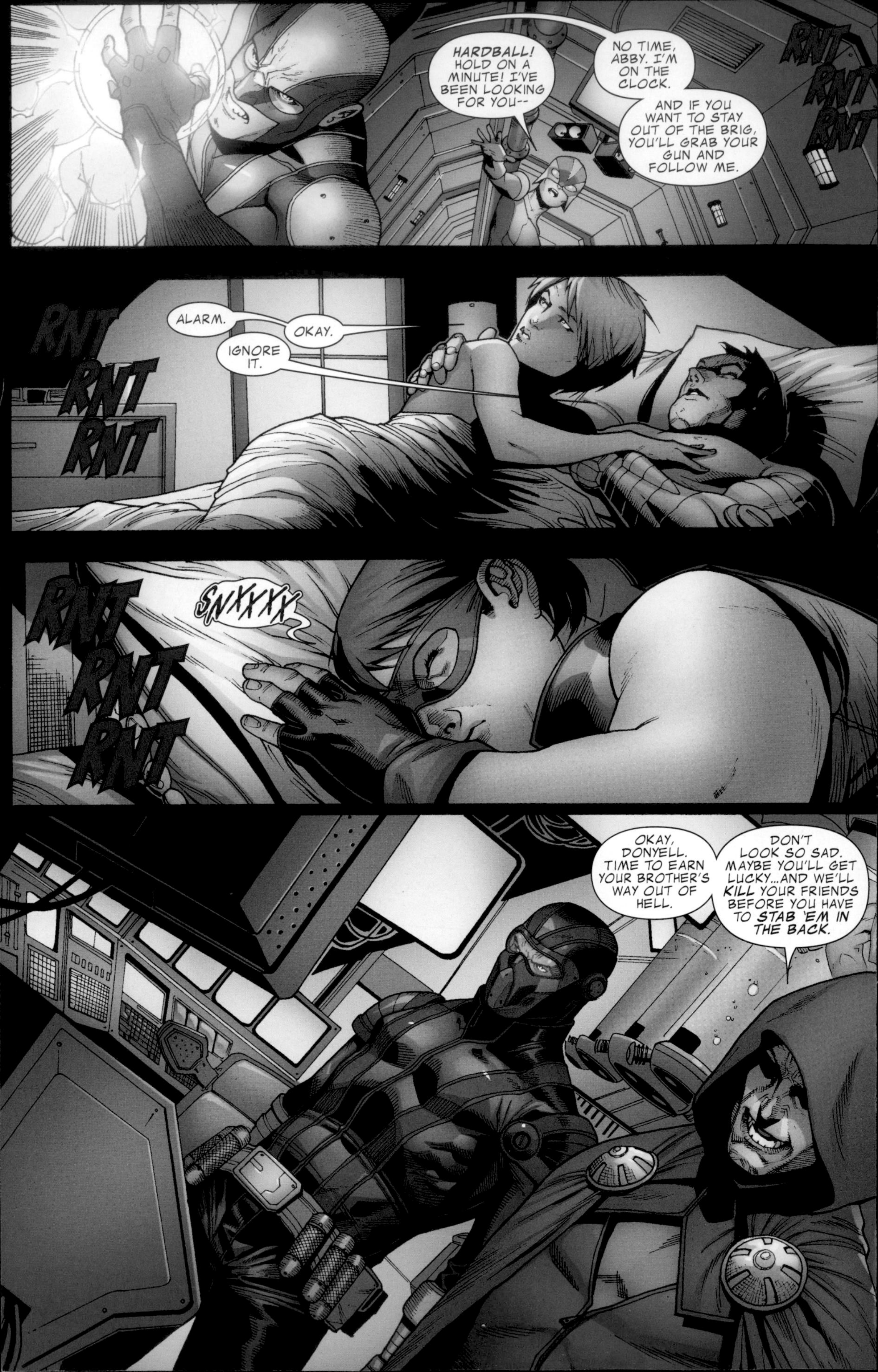
HARDBALL! HOLD ON A MINUTE! I'VE BEEN LOOKING FOR YOU--
NO TIME, ABBY. I'M ON THE CLOCK.
AND IF YOU WANT TO STAY OUT OF THE BRIG, YOU'LL GRAB YOUR GUN AND FOLLOW ME.
RNT RNT RNT
RNT RNT RNT
ALARM.
OKAY.
IGNORE IT.
RNT RNT RNT
SNXXXX
OKAY, DONYELL. TIME TO EARN YOUR BROTHER'S WAY OUT OF HELL.
DON'T LOOK SO SAD. MAYBE YOU'LL GET LUCKY...AND WE'LL KILL YOUR FRIENDS BEFORE YOU HAVE TO STAB 'EM IN THE BACK.

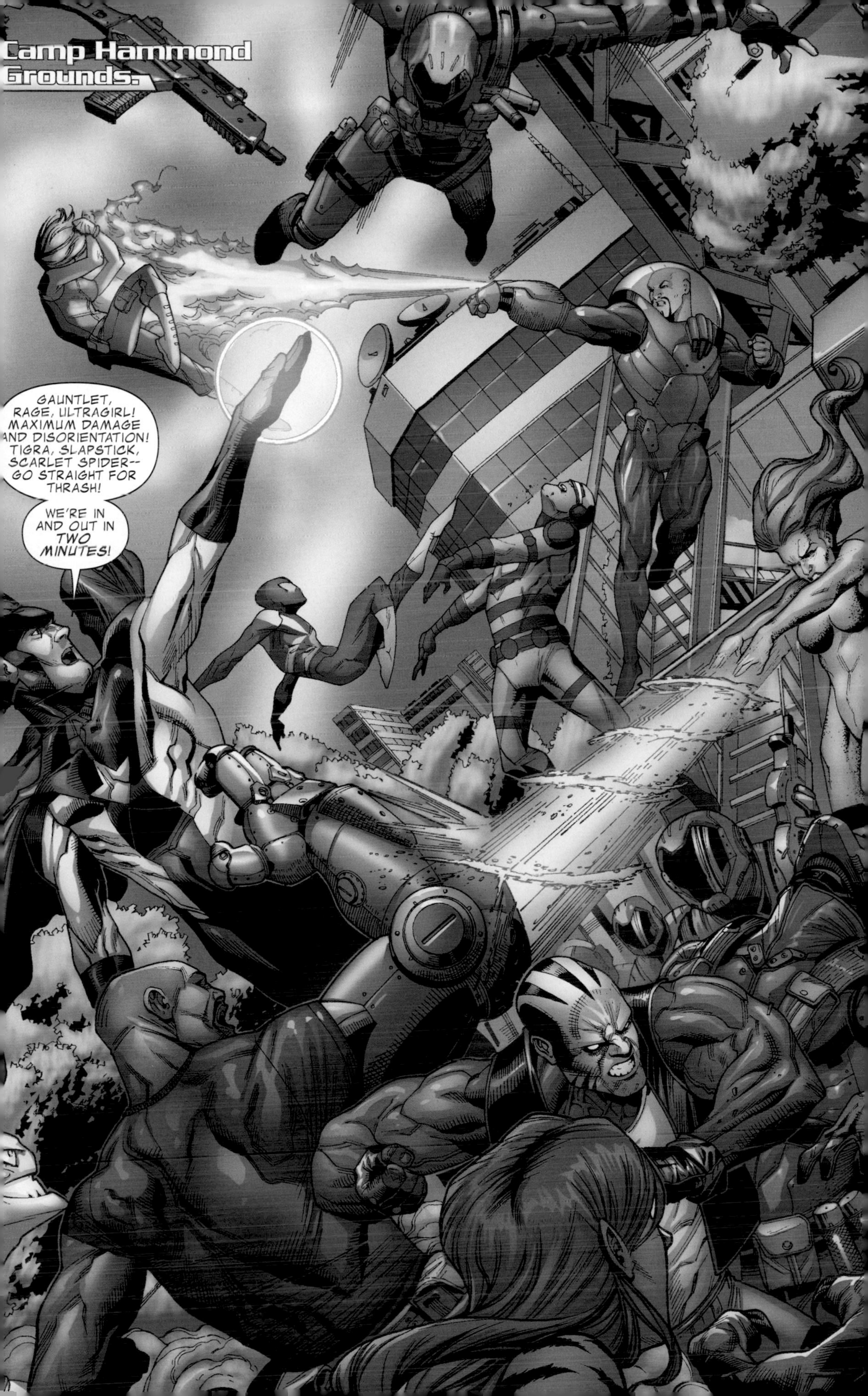
Camp Hammond Grounds.
GAUNTLET, RAGE, ULTRAGIRL! MAXIMUM DAMAGE AND DISORIENTATION! TIGRA, SLAPSTICK, SCARLET SPIDER--GO STRAIGHT FOR THRASH!
WE'RE IN AND OUT IN TWO MINUTES!

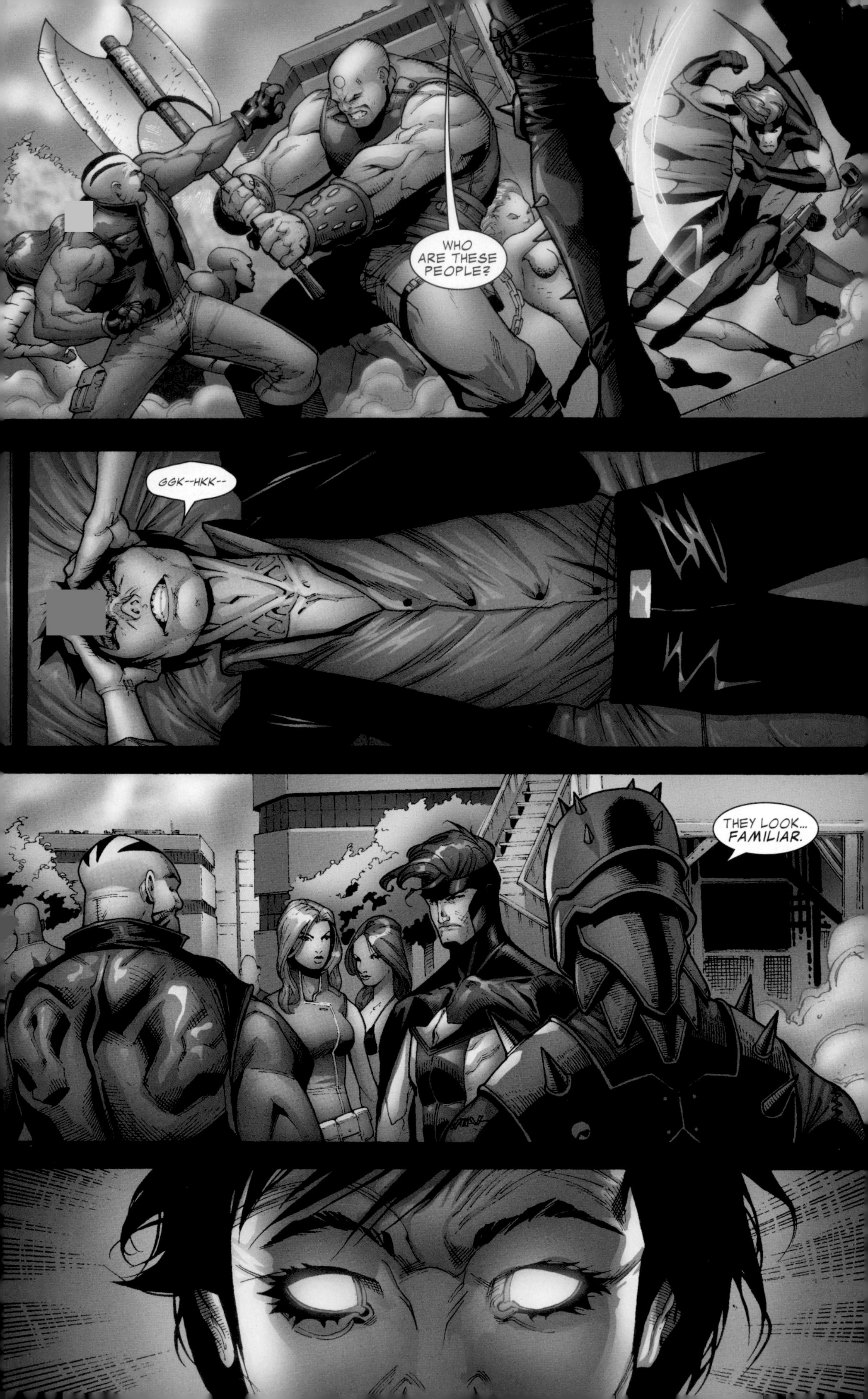
WHO ARE THESE PEOPLE?
GGK--HKK--
THEY LOOK... FAMILIAR.

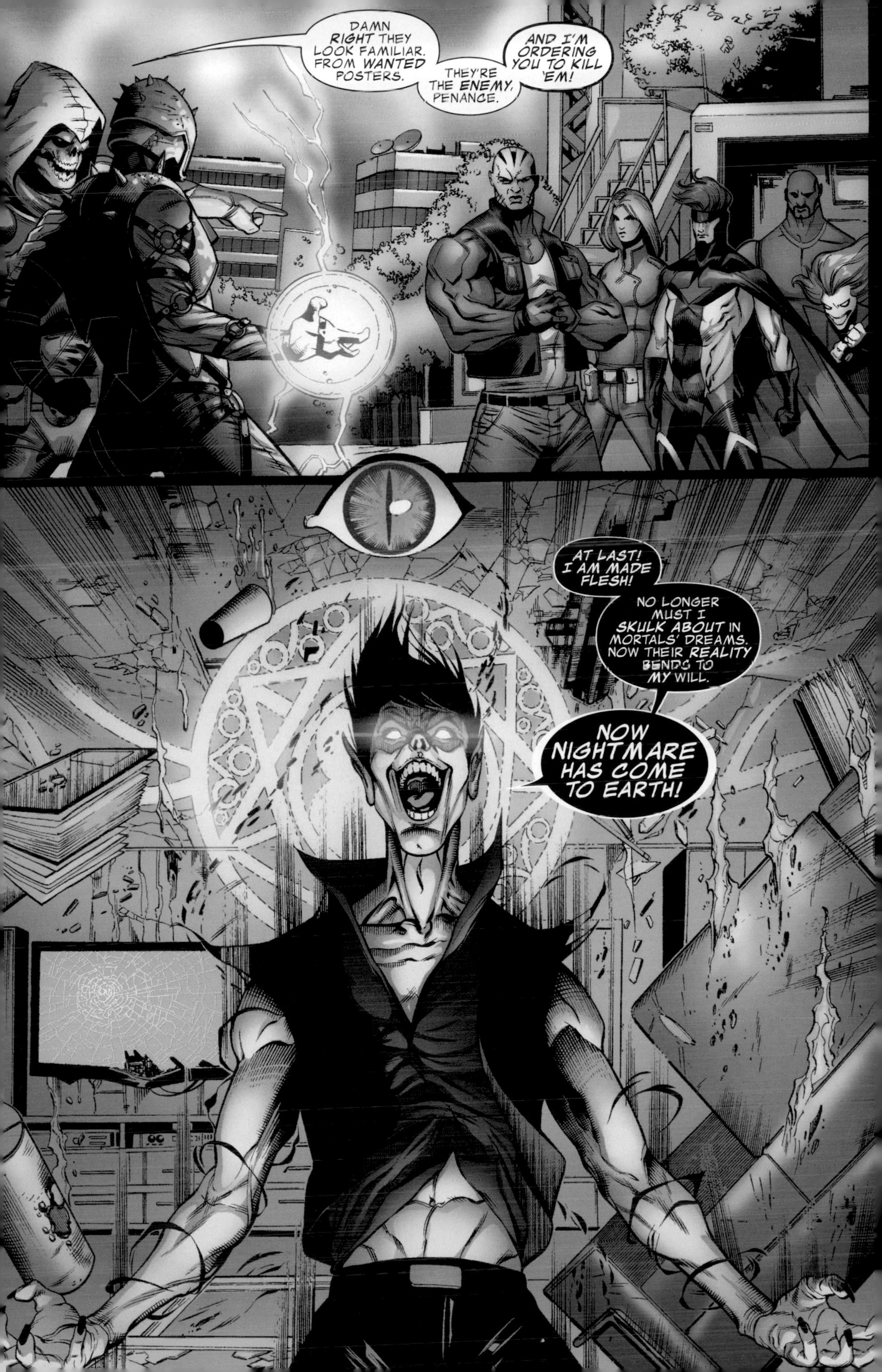
DAMN RIGHT THEY LOOK FAMILIAR. FROM WANTED POSTERS.
THEY'RE THE ENEMY, PENANCE.
AND I'M ORDERING YOU TO KILL 'EM!
AT LAST! I AM MADE FLESH!
NO LONGER MUST I SKULK ABOUT IN MORTALS' DREAMS. NOW THEIR REALITY BENDS TO MY WILL.
NOW NIGHTMARE HAS COME TO EARTH!

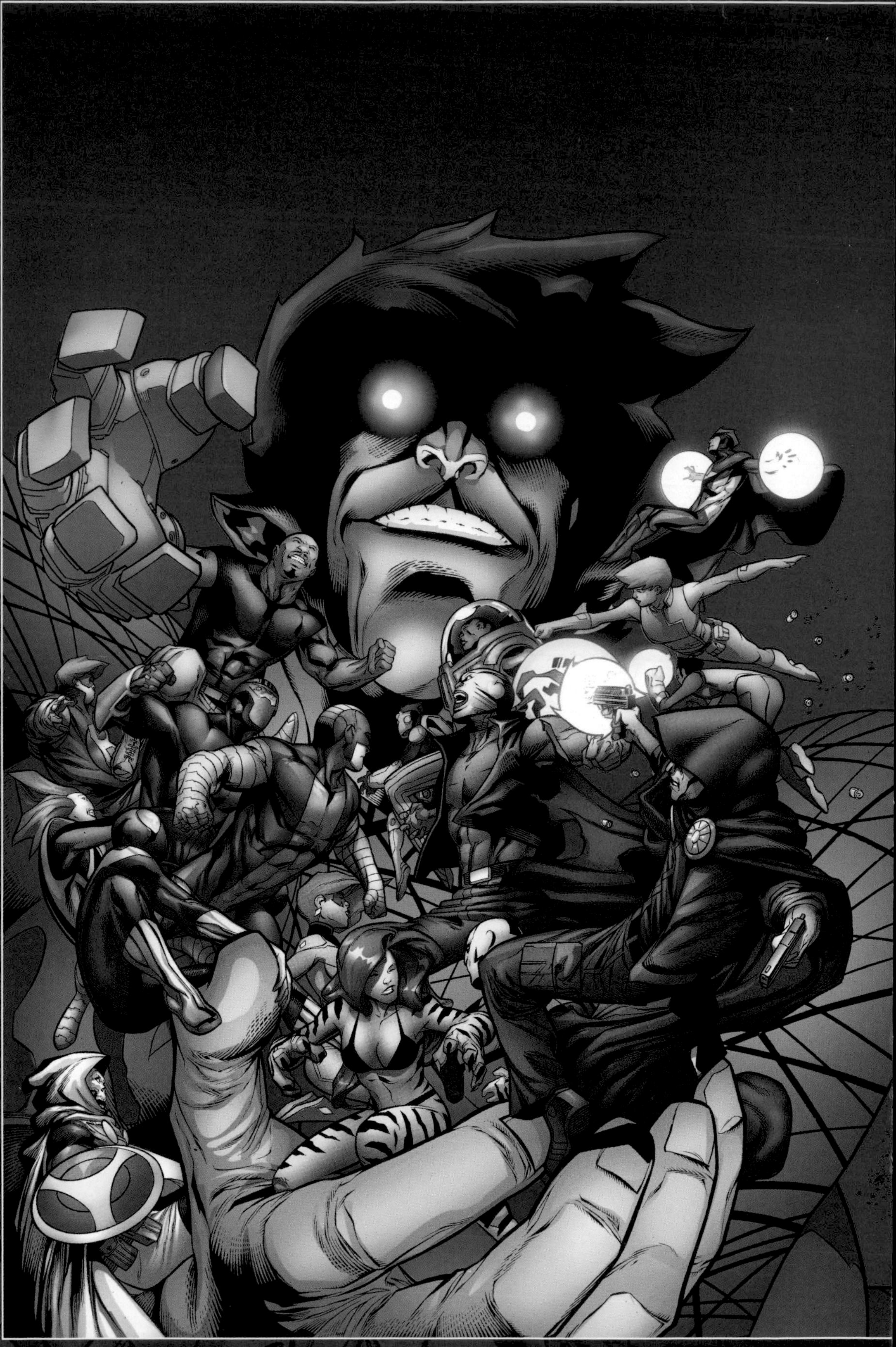

#30

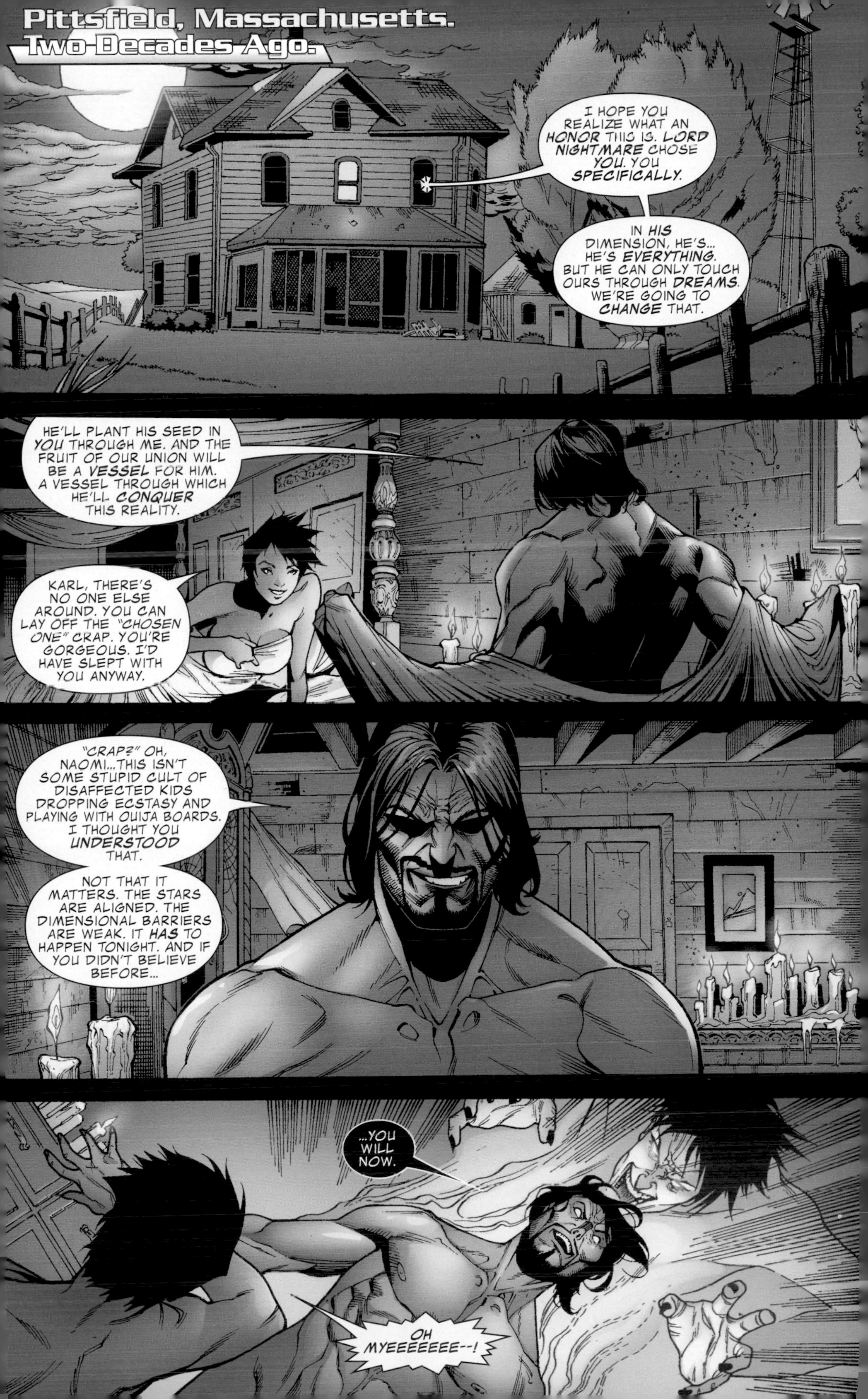

Pittsfield, Massachusetts.
Two Decades Ago.
I HOPE YOU REALIZE WHAT AN HONOR THIS IS. LORD NIGHTMARE CHOSE YOU. YOU SPECIFICALLY.
IN HIS DIMENSION, HE'S... HE'S EVERYTHING. BUT HE CAN ONLY TOUCH OURS THROUGH DREAMS. WE'RE GOING TO CHANGE THAT.
HE'LL PLANT HIS SEED IN YOU THROUGH ME. AND THE FRUIT OF OUR UNION WILL BE A VESSEL FOR HIM. A VESSEL THROUGH WHICH HE'LL CONQUER THIS REALITY.
KARL, THERE'S NO ONE ELSE AROUND. YOU CAN LAY OFF THE "CHOSEN ONE" CRAP. YOU'RE GORGEOUS. I'D HAVE SLEPT WITH YOU ANYWAY.
"CRAP?" OH, NAOMI...THIS ISN'T SOME STUPID CULT OF DISAFFECTED KIDS DROPPING ECSTASY AND PLAYING WITH OUIJA BOARDS. I THOUGHT YOU UNDERSTOOD THAT.
NOT THAT IT MATTERS. THE STARS ARE ALIGNED. THE DIMENSIONAL BARRIERS ARE WEAK. IT HAS TO HAPPEN TONIGHT. AND IF YOU DIDN'T BELIEVE BEFORE...
...YOU WILL NOW.
OH MYEEEEEEEE--!

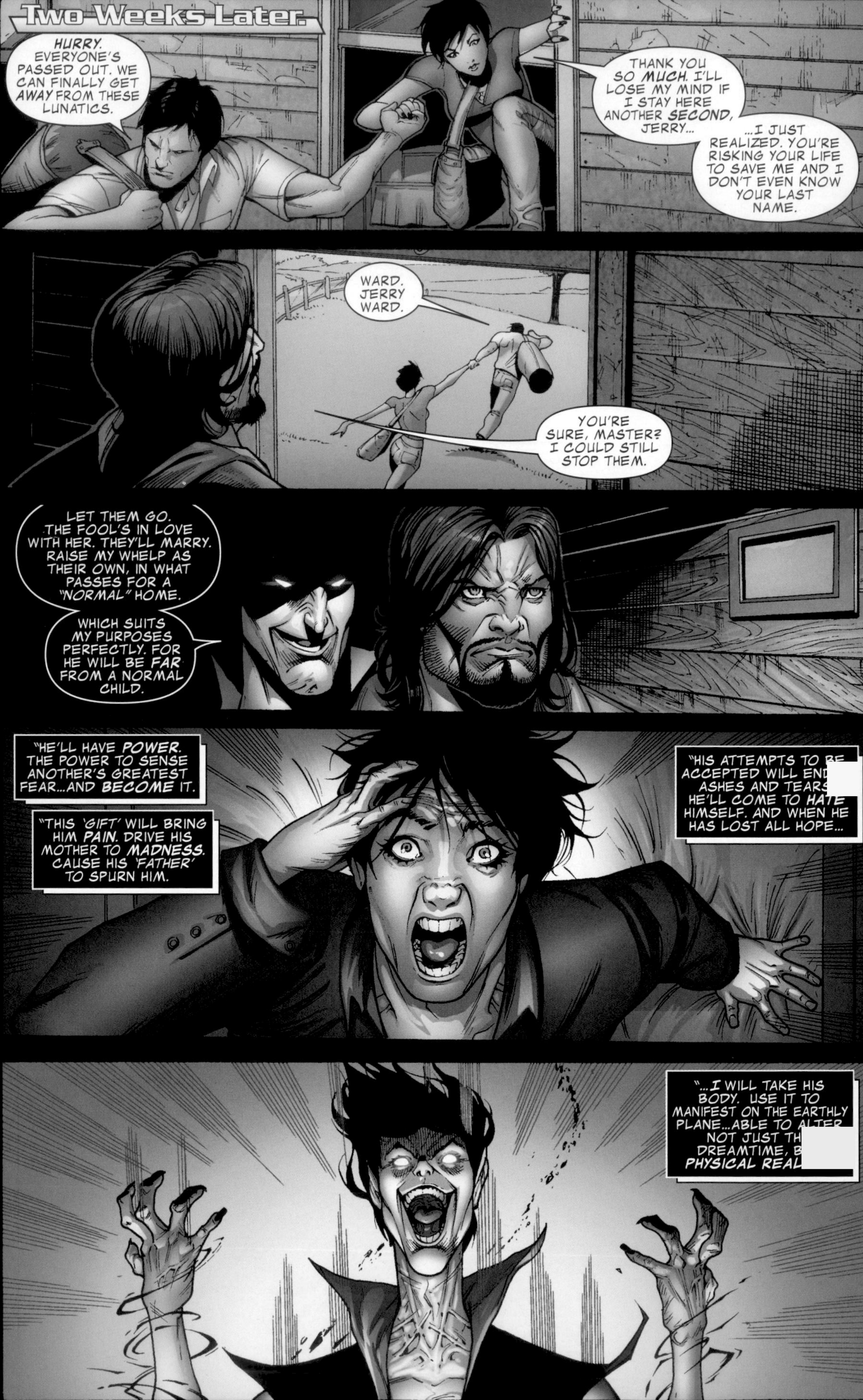
Two Weeks Later.
HURRY. EVERYONE'S PASSED OUT. WE CAN FINALLY GET AWAY FROM THESE LUNATICS.
THANK YOU SO MUCH. I'LL LOSE MY MIND IF I STAY HERE ANOTHER SECOND, JERRY...
...I JUST REALIZED. YOU'RE RISKING YOUR LIFE TO SAVE ME AND I DON'T EVEN KNOW YOUR LAST NAME.
WARD. JERRY WARD.
YOU'RE SURE, MASTER? I COULD STILL STOP THEM.
LET THEM GO. THE FOOL'S IN LOVE WITH HER. THEY'LL MARRY. RAISE MY WHELP AS THEIR OWN, IN WHAT PASSES FOR A "NORMAL" HOME.
WHICH SUITS MY PURPOSES PERFECTLY. FOR HE WILL BE FAR FROM A NORMAL CHILD.
"HE'LL HAVE POWER. THE POWER TO SENSE ANOTHER'S GREATEST FEAR...AND BECOME IT.
"THIS 'GIFT' WILL BRING HIM PAIN. DRIVE HIS MOTHER TO MADNESS. CAUSE HIS 'FATHER' TO SPURN HIM.
"HIS ATTEMPTS TO ACCEPTED WILL END ASHES AND TEARS HE'LL COME TO HATE HIMSELF. AND WHEN HE HAS LOST ALL HOPE...
"...I WILL TAKE HIS BODY. USE IT TO MANIFEST ON THE EARTHLY PLANE...ABLE TO NOT JUST TH DREAMTIME, PHYSICAL REAL

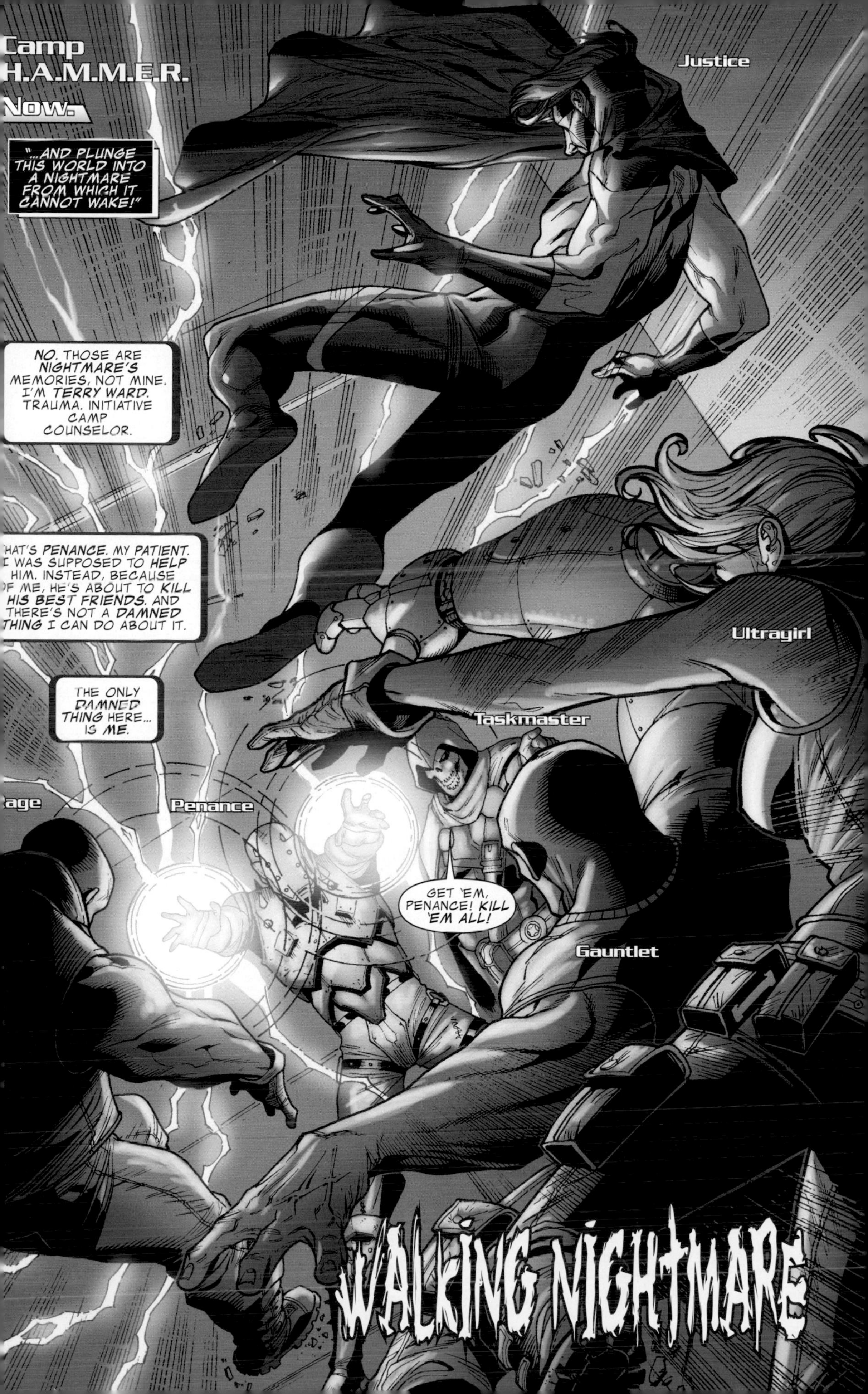
Camp H.A.M.M.E.R.
Now.
"...AND PLUNGE THIS WORLD INTO A NIGHTMARE FROM WHICH IT CANNOT WAKE!"
Justice
NO. THOSE ARE NIGHTMARE'S MEMORIES, NOT MINE. I'M TERRY WARD. TRAUMA. INITIATIVE CAMP COUNSELOR.
HAT'S PENANCE. MY PATIENT. I WAS SUPPOSED TO HELP HIM. INSTEAD, BECAUSE OF ME, HE'S ABOUT TO KILL HIS BEST FRIENDS. AND THERE'S NOT A DAMNED THING I CAN DO ABOUT IT.
Ultragirl
THE ONLY DAMNED THING HERE... IS ME.
Taskmaster
age
Penance
GET 'EM, PENANCE! KILL 'EM ALL!
Gauntlet
WALKING NIGHTMARE

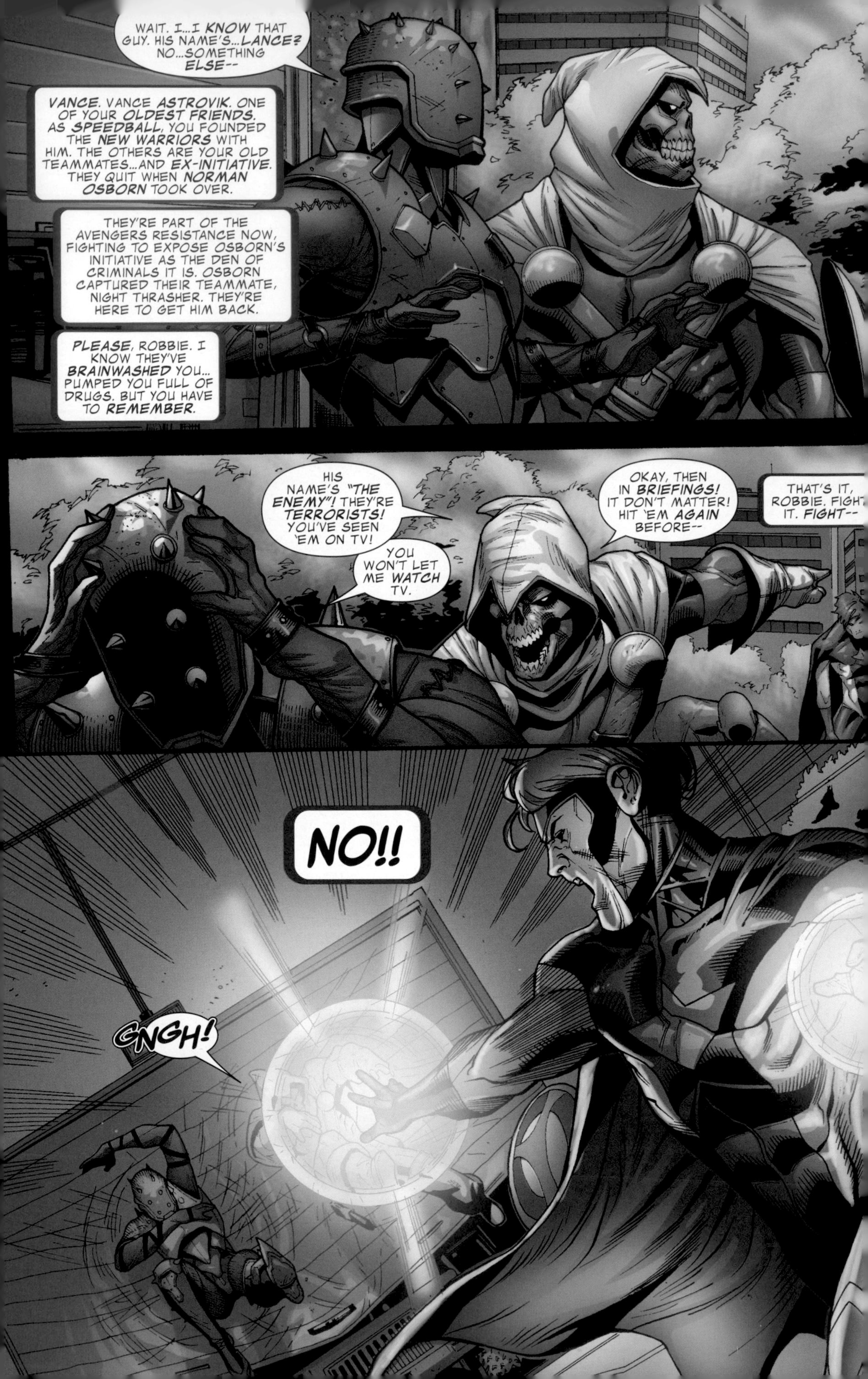
WAIT. I...I KNOW THAT GUY. HIS NAME'S...LANCE? NO...SOMETHING ELSE--
VANCE. VANCE ASTROVIK. ONE OF YOUR OLDEST FRIENDS. AS SPEEDBALL, YOU FOUNDED THE NEW WARRIORS WITH HIM. THE OTHERS ARE YOUR OLD TEAMMATES...AND EX-INITIATIVE. THEY QUIT WHEN NORMAN OSBORN TOOK OVER.
THEY'RE PART OF THE AVENGERS RESISTANCE NOW, FIGHTING TO EXPOSE OSBORN'S INITIATIVE AS THE DEN OF CRIMINALS IT IS. OSBORN CAPTURED THEIR TEAMMATE, NIGHT THRASHER. THEY'RE HERE TO GET HIM BACK.
PLEASE, ROBBIE. I KNOW THEY'VE BRAINWASHED YOU... PUMPED YOU FULL OF DRUGS. BUT YOU HAVE TO REMEMBER.
HIS NAME'S "THE ENEMY"! THEY'RE TERRORISTS! YOU'VE SEEN 'EM ON TV!
YOU WON'T LET ME WATCH TV.
OKAY, THEN IN BRIEFINGS! IT DON'T MATTER! HIT 'EM AGAIN BEFORE--
THAT'S IT, ROBBIE. FIGHT IT. FIGHT--
NO!!
GNGH!

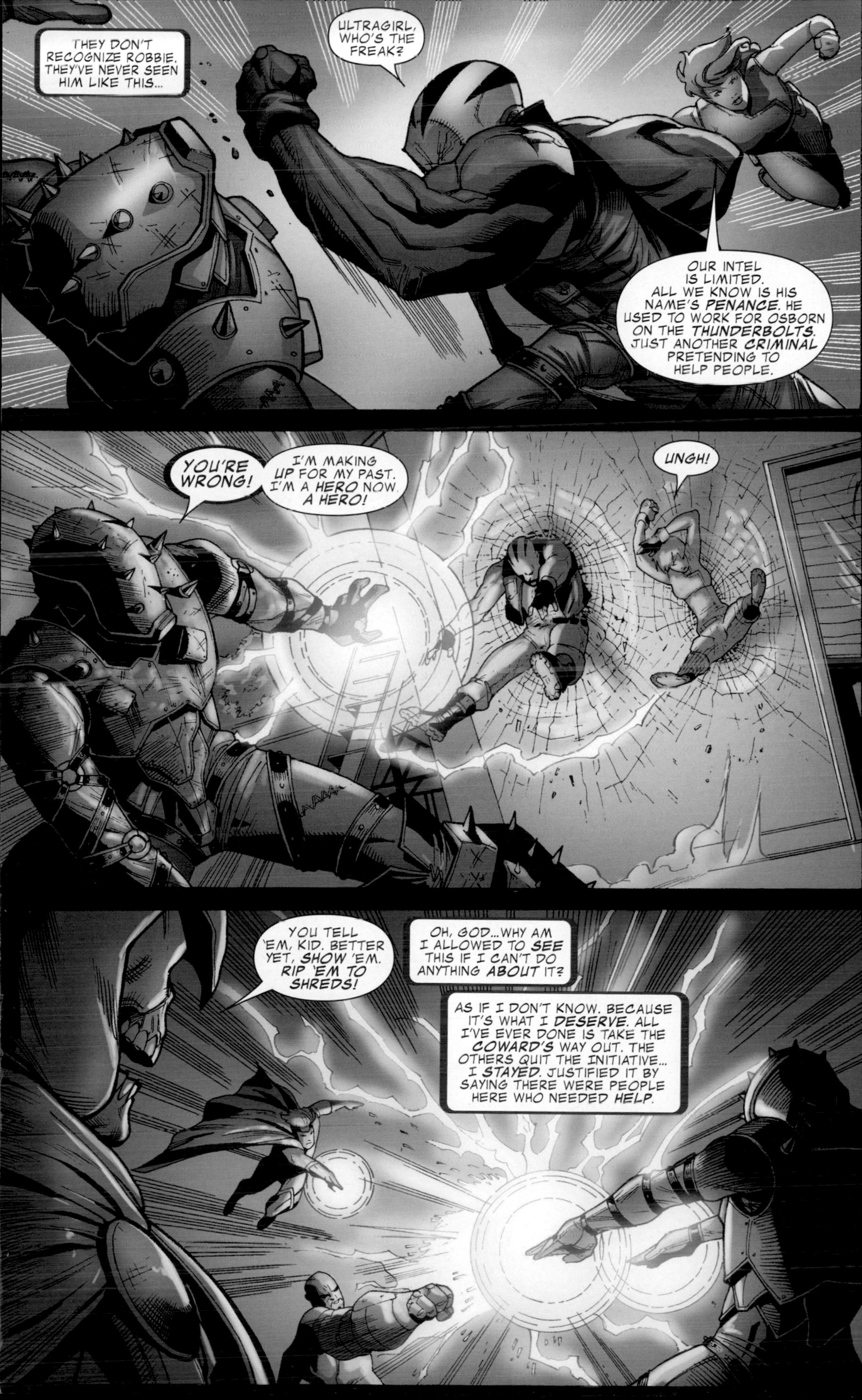
THEY DON'T RECOGNIZE ROBBIE. THEY'VE NEVER SEEN HIM LIKE THIS...
ULTRAGIRL, WHO'S THE FREAK?
OUR INTEL IS LIMITED. ALL WE KNOW IS HIS NAME'S PENANCE. HE USED TO WORK FOR OSBORN ON THE THUNDERBOLTS. JUST ANOTHER CRIMINAL PRETENDING TO HELP PEOPLE.
YOU'RE WRONG!
I'M MAKING UP FOR MY PAST. I'M A HERO NOW. A HERO!
UNGH!
YOU TELL 'EM, KID. BETTER YET, SHOW 'EM. RIP 'EM TO SHREDS!
OH, GOD...WHY AM I ALLOWED TO SEE THIS IF I CAN'T DO ANYTHING ABOUT IT?
AS IF I DON'T KNOW. BECAUSE IT'S WHAT I DESERVE. ALL I'VE EVER DONE IS TAKE THE COWARD'S WAY OUT. THE OTHERS QUIT THE INITIATIVE... I STAYED. JUSTIFIED IT BY SAYING THERE WERE PEOPLE HERE WHO NEEDED HELP.

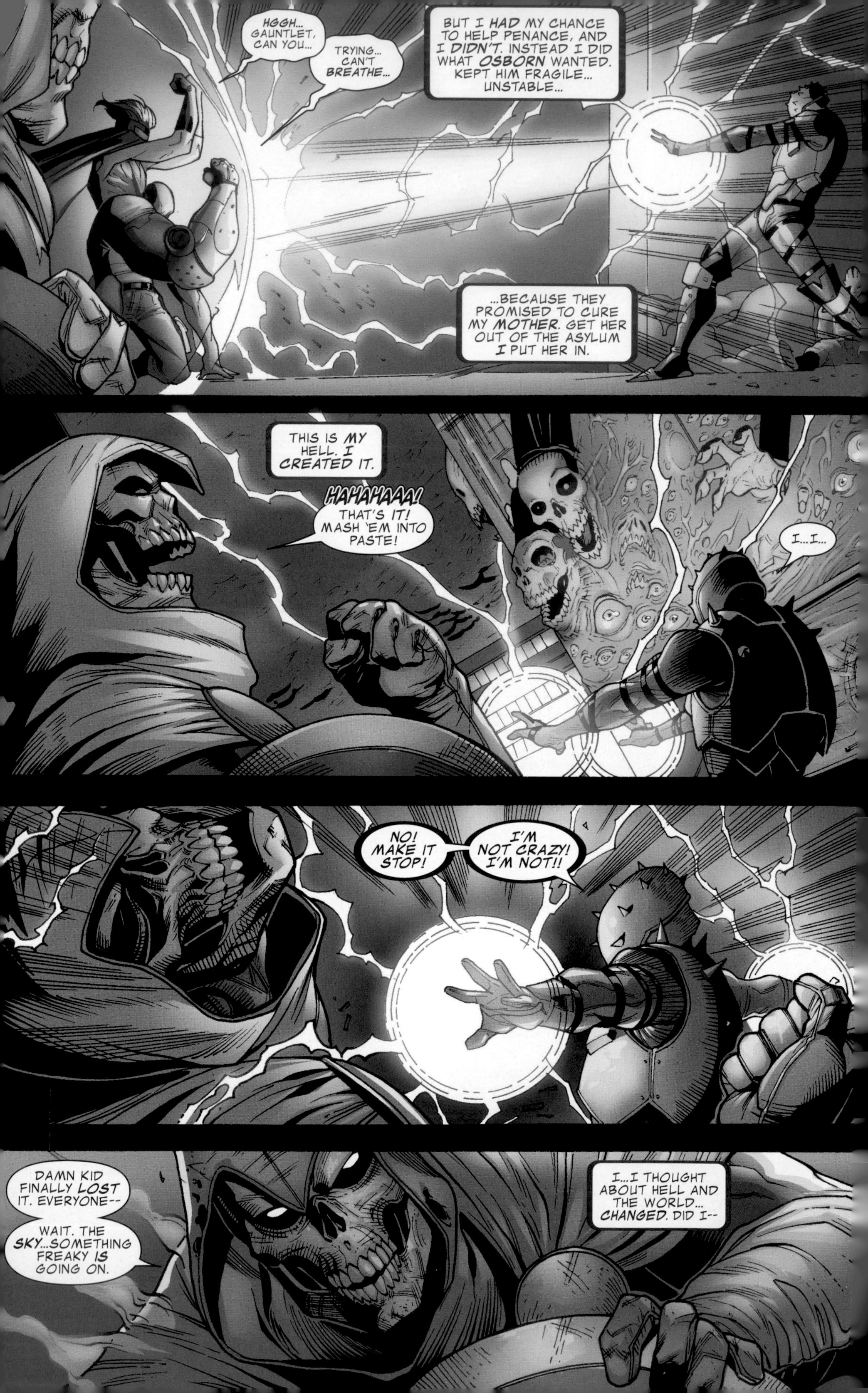
HGGH... GAUNTLET, CAN YOU...
TRYING... CAN'T BREATHE...
BUT I HAD MY CHANCE TO HELP PENANCE, AND I DIDN'T. INSTEAD I DID WHAT OSBORN WANTED. KEPT HIM FRAGILE... UNSTABLE...
...BECAUSE THEY PROMISED TO CURE MY MOTHER. GET HER OUT OF THE ASYLUM I PUT HER IN.
THIS IS MY HELL. I CREATED IT.
HAHAHAAA! THAT'S IT! MASH 'EM INTO PASTE!
I...I...
NO! MAKE IT STOP!
I'M NOT CRAZY! I'M NOT!!
DAMN KID FINALLY LOST IT. EVERYONE--
WAIT. THE SKY...SOMETHING FREAKY IS GOING ON.
I...I THOUGHT ABOUT HELL AND THE WORLD... CHANGED. DID I--

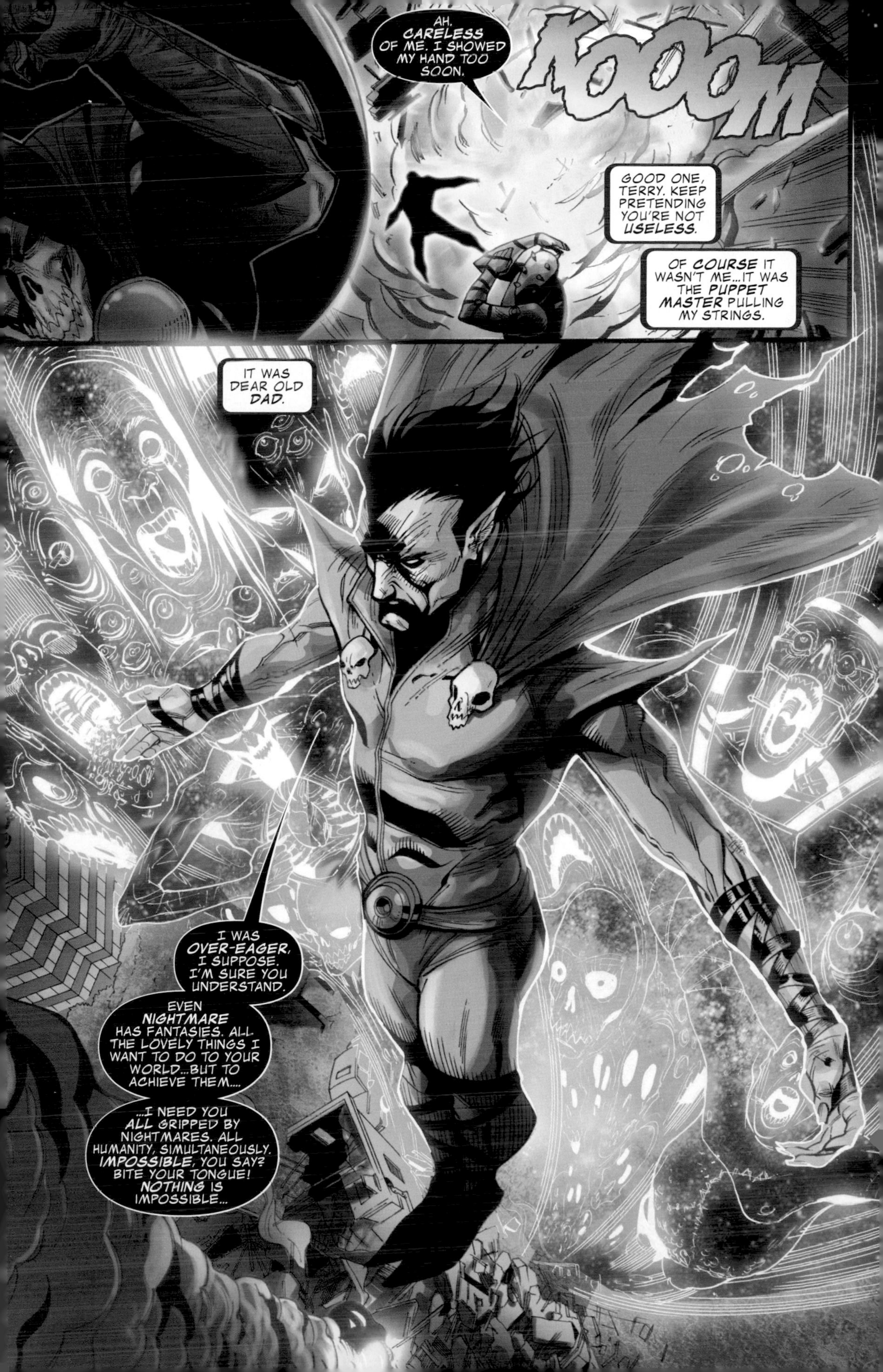
AH, CARELESS OF ME. I SHOWED MY HAND TOO SOON.
KOOOM
GOOD ONE, TERRY. KEEP PRETENDING YOU'RE NOT USELESS.
OF COURSE IT WASN'T ME...IT WAS THE PUPPET MASTER PULLING MY STRINGS.
IT WAS DEAR OLD DAD.
I WAS OVER-EAGER, I SUPPOSE. I'M SURE YOU UNDERSTAND.
EVEN NIGHTMARE HAS FANTASIES. ALL THE LOVELY THINGS I WANT TO DO TO YOUR WORLD...BUT TO ACHIEVE THEM....
...I NEED YOU ALL GRIPPED BY NIGHTMARES. ALL HUMANITY, SIMULTANEOUSLY. IMPOSSIBLE, YOU SAY? BITE YOUR TONGUE! NOTHING IS IMPOSSIBLE...

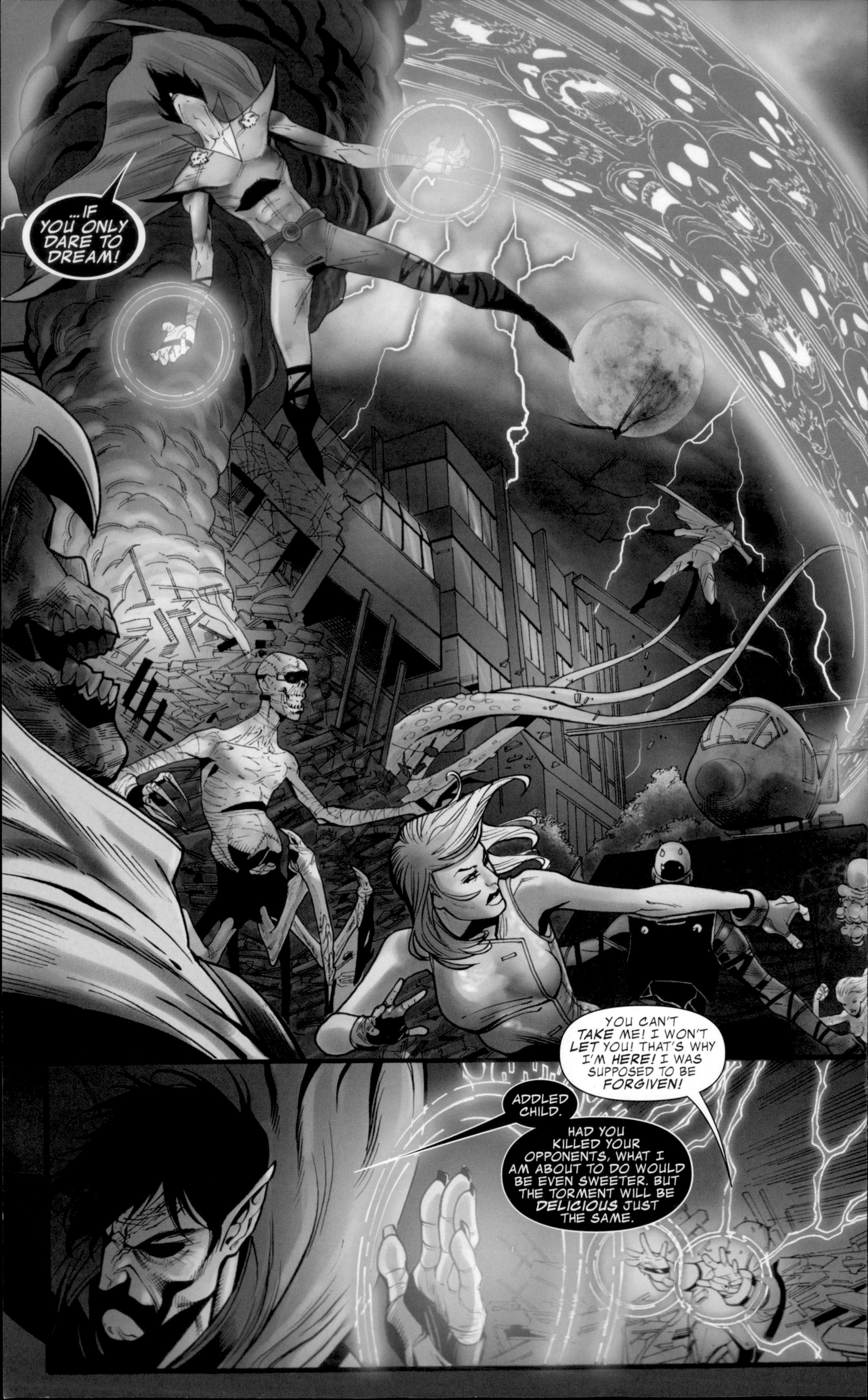
...IF YOU ONLY DARE TO DREAM!
YOU CAN'T TAKE ME! I WON'T LET YOU! THAT'S WHY I'M HERE! I WAS SUPPOSED TO BE FORGIVEN!
ADDLED CHILD.
HAD YOU KILLED YOUR OPPONENTS, WHAT I AM ABOUT TO DO WOULD BE EVEN SWEETER. BUT THE TORMENT WILL BE DELICIOUS JUST THE SAME.

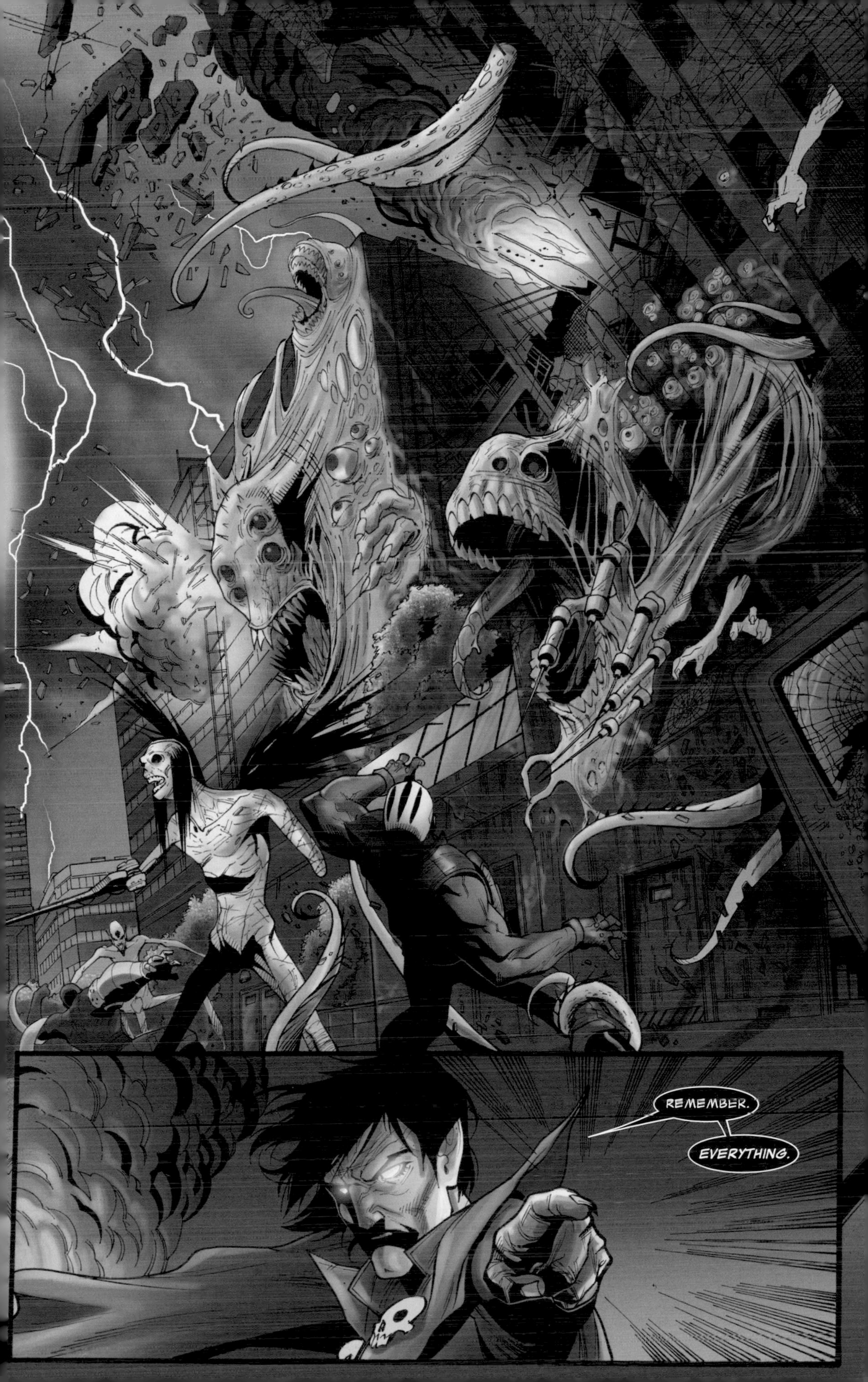
REMEMBER.
EVERYTHING.

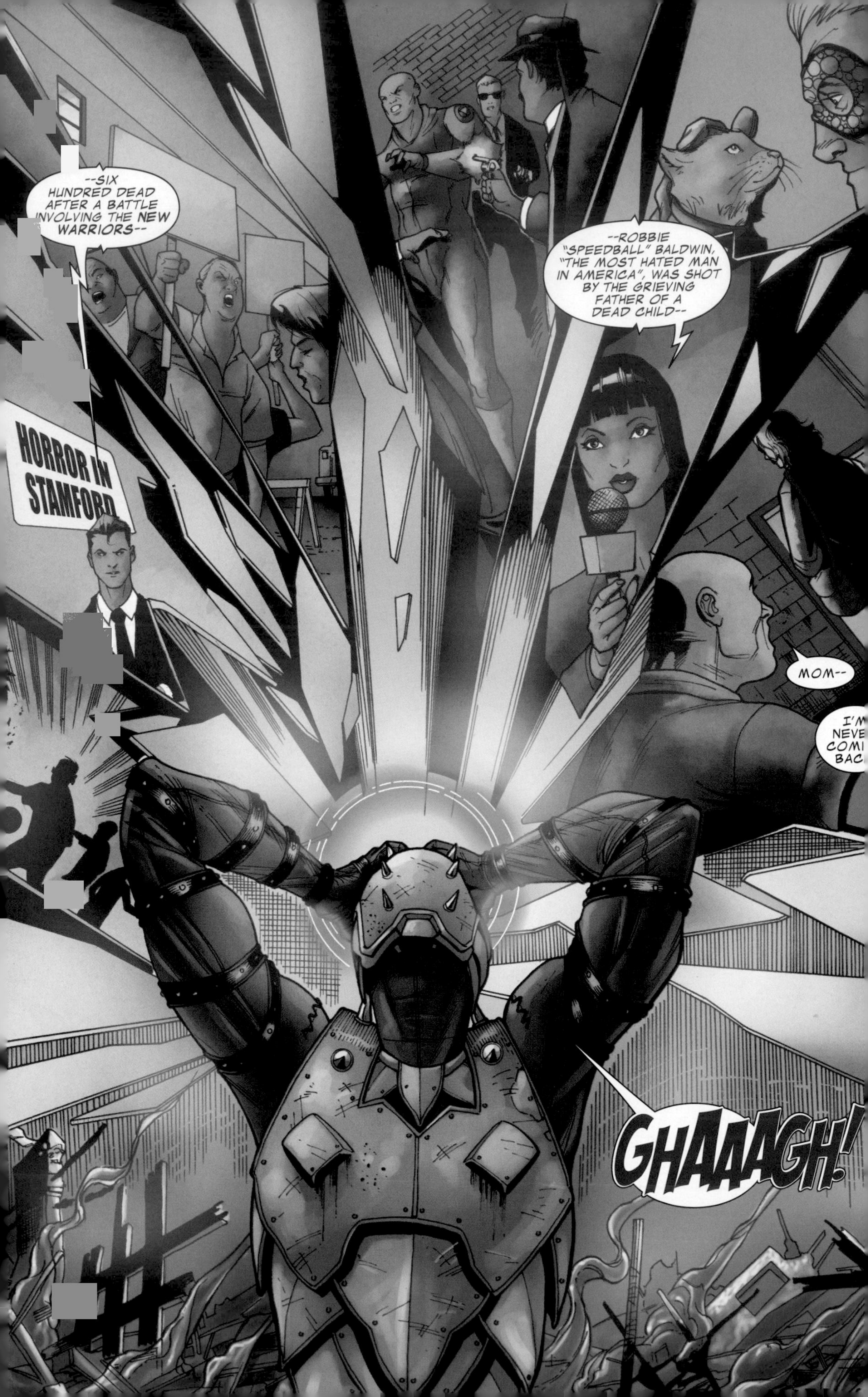
--SIX HUNDRED DEAD AFTER A BATTLE INVOLVING THE NEW WARRIORS--
HORROR IN STAMFORD
--ROBBIE "SPEEDBALL" BALDWIN, "THE MOST HATED MAN IN AMERICA", WAS SHOT BY THE GRIEVING FATHER OF A DEAD CHILD--
MOM--
I'M NEVE COMI BAC
GHAAAGH!

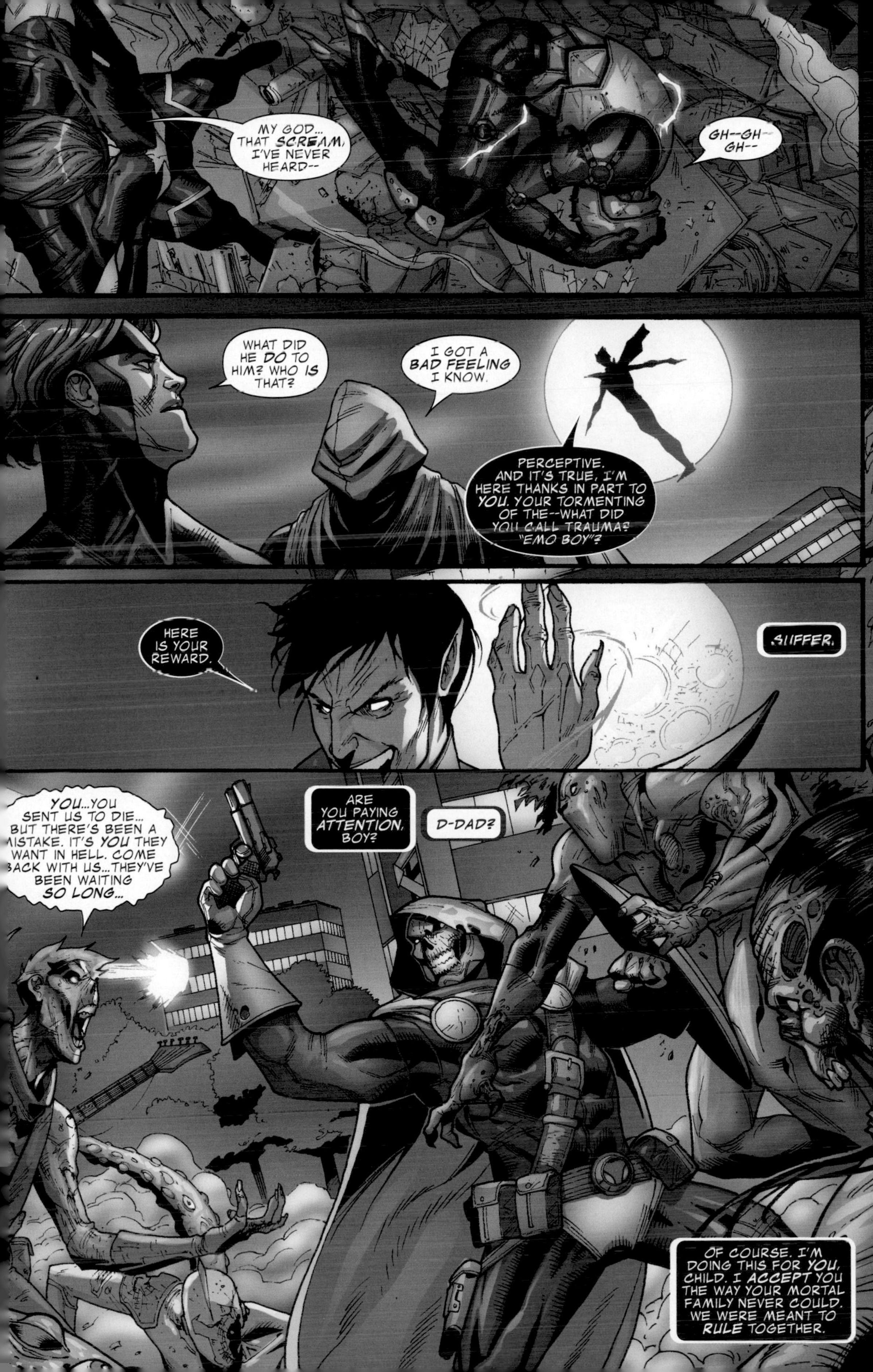

MY GOD... THAT SCREAM, I'VE NEVER HEARD--
GH--GH-GH--
WHAT DID HE DO TO HIM? WHO IS THAT?
I GOT A BAD FEELING I KNOW.
PERCEPTIVE. AND IT'S TRUE, I'M HERE THANKS IN PART TO YOU. YOUR TORMENTING OF THE--WHAT DID YOU CALL TRAUMA? "EMO BOY"?
HERE IS YOUR REWARD.
SUFFER.
YOU...YOU SENT US TO DIE... BUT THERE'S BEEN A MISTAKE. IT'S YOU THEY WANT IN HELL. COME BACK WITH US...THEY'VE BEEN WAITING SO LONG...
ARE YOU PAYING ATTENTION, BOY?
D-DAD?
OF COURSE. I'M DOING THIS FOR YOU, CHILD. I ACCEPT YOU THE WAY YOUR MORTAL FAMILY NEVER COULD. WE WERE MEANT TO RULE TOGETHER.

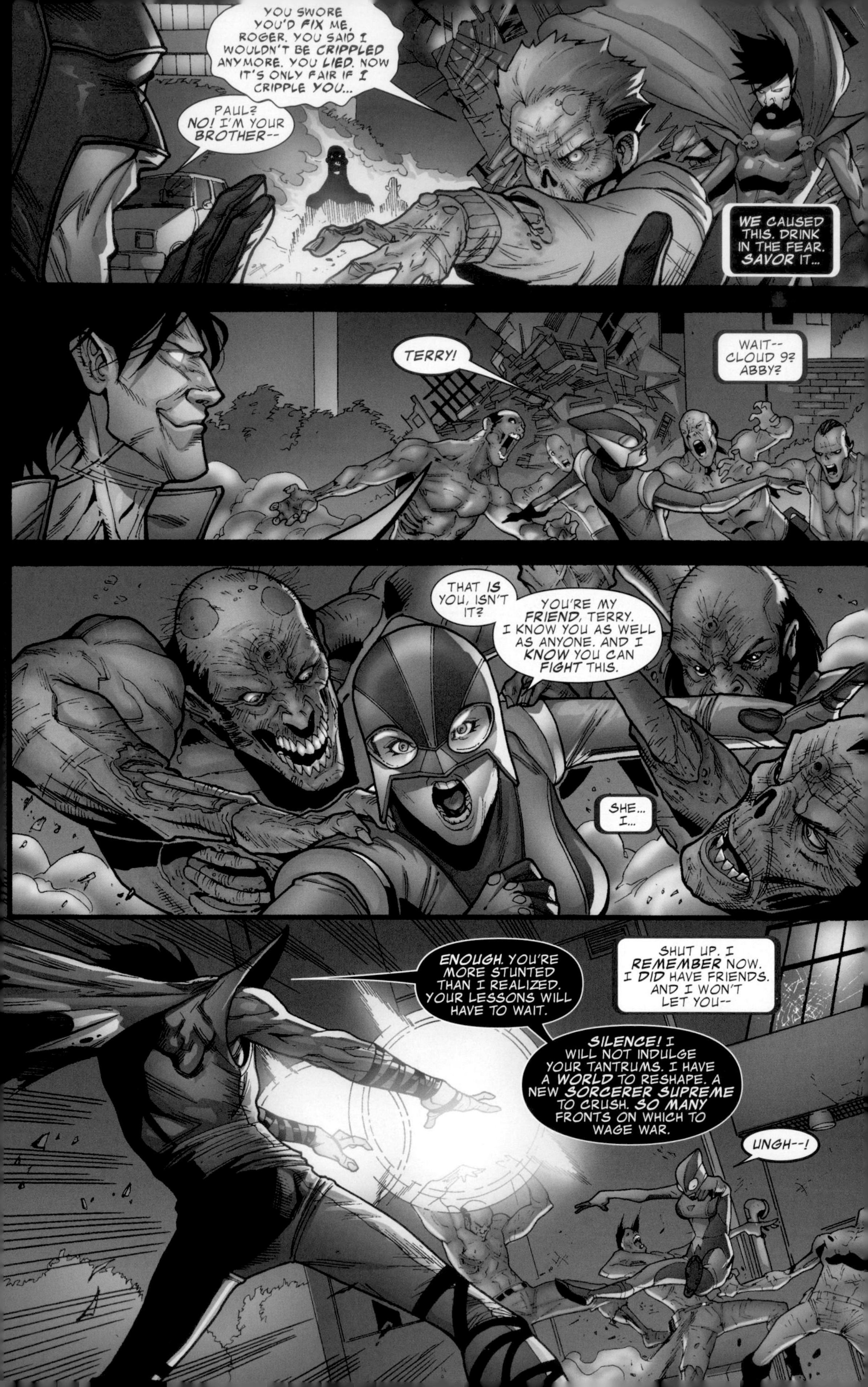
YOU SWORE YOU'D FIX ME, ROGER. YOU SAID I WOULDN'T BE CRIPPLED ANYMORE. YOU LIED. NOW IT'S ONLY FAIR IF I CRIPPLE YOU...
PAUL? NO! I'M YOUR BROTHER--
WE CAUSED THIS. DRINK IN THE FEAR. SAVOR IT...
TERRY!
WAIT-- CLOUD 9? ABBY?
THAT IS YOU, ISN'T IT?
YOU'RE MY FRIEND, TERRY. I KNOW YOU AS WELL AS ANYONE. AND I KNOW YOU CAN FIGHT THIS.
SHE... I...
ENOUGH. YOU'RE MORE STUNTED THAN I REALIZED. YOUR LESSONS WILL HAVE TO WAIT.
SHUT UP. I REMEMBER NOW. I DID HAVE FRIENDS. AND I WON'T LET YOU--
SILENCE! I WILL NOT INDULGE YOUR TANTRUMS. I HAVE A WORLD TO RESHAPE. A NEW SORCERER SUPREME TO CRUSH. SO MANY FRONTS ON WHICH TO WAGE WAR.
UNGH--!

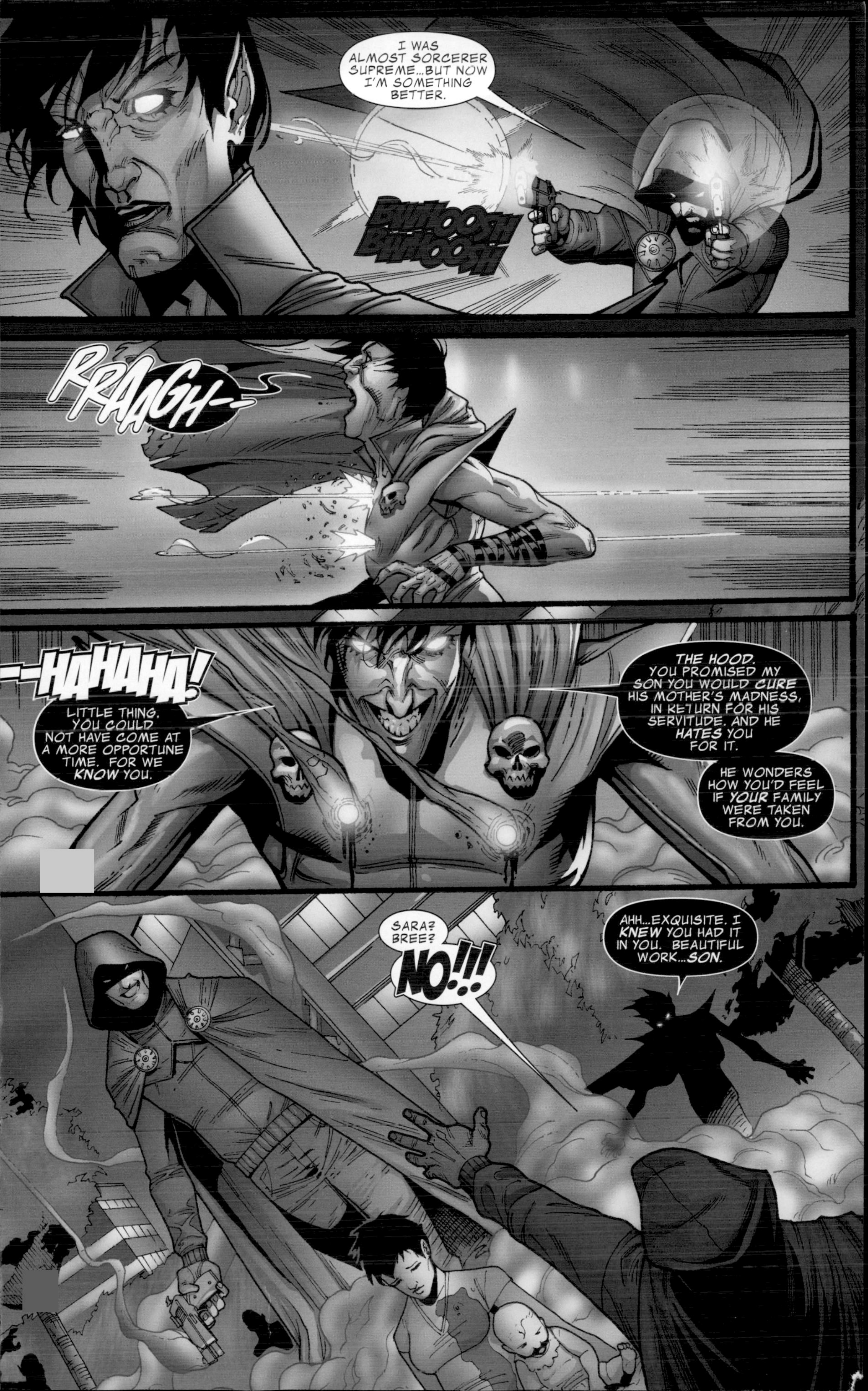
I WAS ALMOST SORCERER SUPREME...BUT NOW I'M SOMETHING BETTER.
BWHOOSH BWHOOSH
RRAAGH--
--HAHAHA!
LITTLE THING. YOU COULD NOT HAVE COME AT A MORE OPPORTUNE TIME. FOR WE KNOW YOU.
THE HOOD. YOU PROMISED MY SON YOU WOULD CURE HIS MOTHER'S MADNESS, IN RETURN FOR HIS SERVITUDE. AND HE HATES YOU FOR IT.
HE WONDERS HOW YOU'D FEEL IF YOUR FAMILY WERE TAKEN FROM YOU.
SARA? BREE?
NO!!!
AHH...EXQUISITE. I KNEW YOU HAD IT IN YOU. BEAUTIFUL WORK...SON.

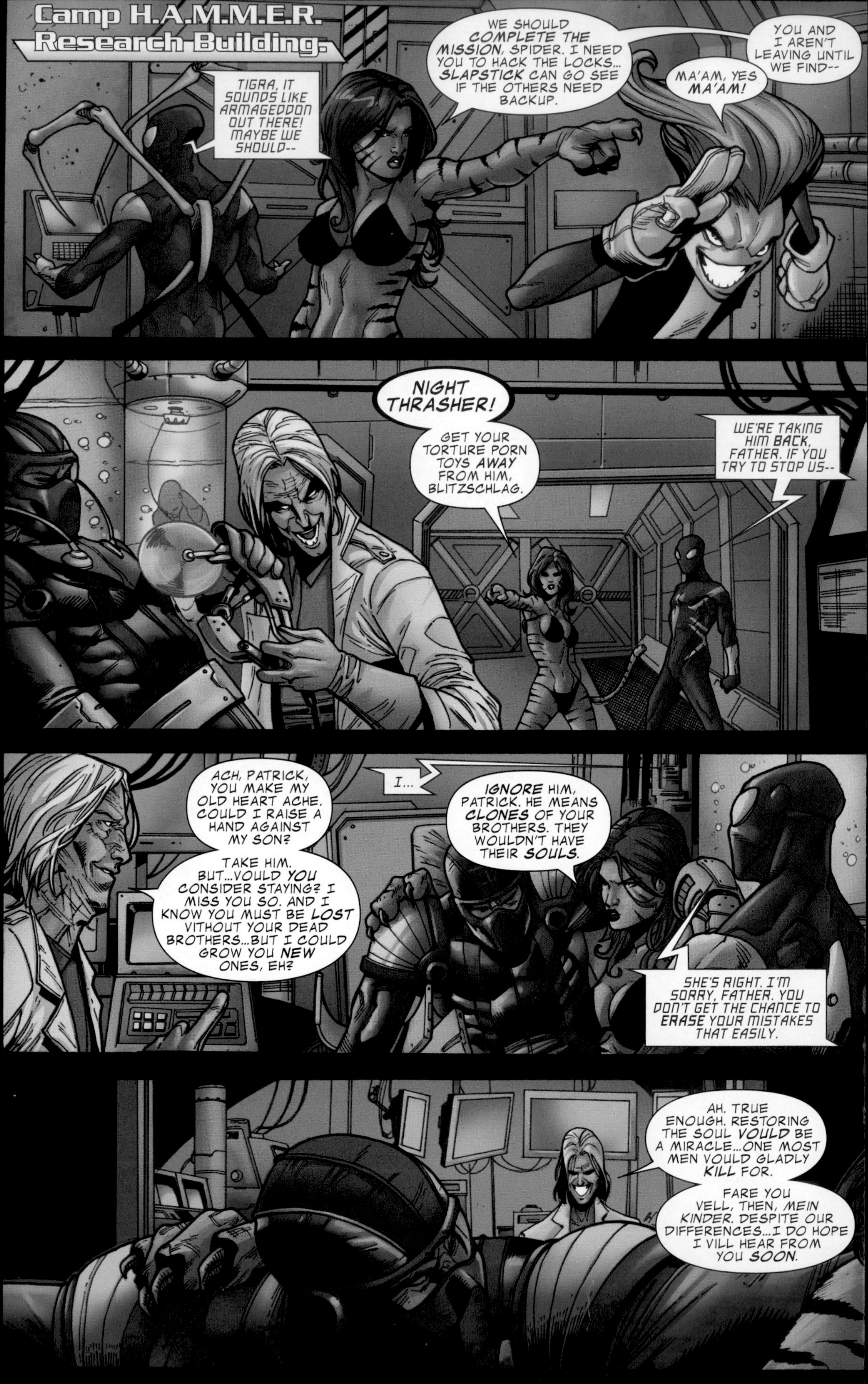
Camp H.A.M.M.E.R. Research Building.
TIGRA, IT SOUNDS LIKE ARMAGEDDON OUT THERE! MAYBE WE SHOULD--
WE SHOULD COMPLETE THE MISSION, SPIDER. I NEED YOU TO HACK THE LOCKS... SLAPSTICK CAN GO SEE IF THE OTHERS NEED BACKUP.
YOU AND I AREN'T LEAVING UNTIL WE FIND--
MA'AM, YES MA'AM!
NIGHT THRASHER!
GET YOUR TORTURE PORN TOYS AWAY FROM HIM, BLITZSCHLAG.
WE'RE TAKING HIM BACK, FATHER. IF YOU TRY TO STOP US--
ACH, PATRICK, YOU MAKE MY OLD HEART ACHE. COULD I RAISE A HAND AGAINST MY SON?
TAKE HIM. BUT...VOULD YOU CONSIDER STAYING? I MISS YOU SO. AND I KNOW YOU MUST BE LOST VITHOUT YOUR DEAD BROTHERS...BUT I COULD GROW YOU NEW ONES, EH?
I...
IGNORE HIM, PATRICK. HE MEANS CLONES OF YOUR BROTHERS. THEY WOULDN'T HAVE THEIR SOULS.
SHE'S RIGHT. I'M SORRY, FATHER. YOU DON'T GET THE CHANCE TO ERASE YOUR MISTAKES THAT EASILY.
AH. TRUE ENOUGH. RESTORING THE SOUL VOULD BE A MIRACLE...ONE MOST MEN VOULD GLADLY KILL FOR.
FARE YOU VELL, THEN, MEIN KINDER. DESPITE OUR DIFFERENCES...I DO HOPE I VILL HEAR FROM YOU SOON.

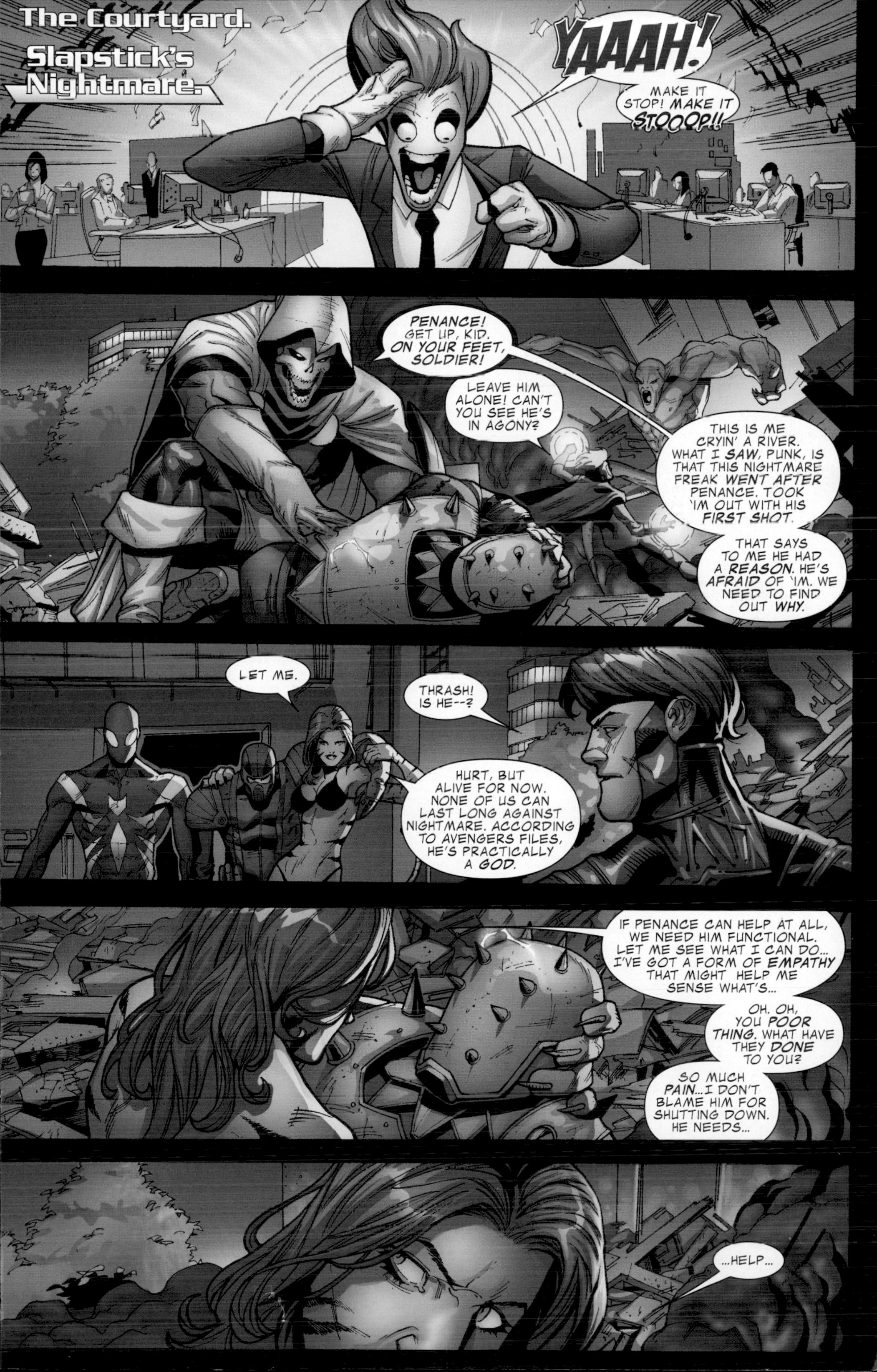
The Courtyard.
Slapstick's Nightmare.
YAAAH!
MAKE IT STOP! MAKE IT STOOOP!!
PENANCE! GET UP, KID. ON YOUR FEET, SOLDIER!
LEAVE HIM ALONE! CAN'T YOU SEE HE'S IN AGONY?
THIS IS ME CRYIN' A RIVER. WHAT I SAW, PUNK, IS THAT THIS NIGHTMARE FREAK WENT AFTER PENANCE. TOOK 'IM OUT WITH HIS FIRST SHOT.
THAT SAYS TO ME HE HAD A REASON. HE'S AFRAID OF 'IM. WE NEED TO FIND OUT WHY.
LET ME.
THRASH! IS HE--?
HURT, BUT ALIVE FOR NOW. NONE OF US CAN LAST LONG AGAINST NIGHTMARE. ACCORDING TO AVENGERS FILES, HE'S PRACTICALLY A GOD.
IF PENANCE CAN HELP AT ALL, WE NEED HIM FUNCTIONAL. LET ME SEE WHAT I CAN DO... I'VE GOT A FORM OF EMPATHY THAT MIGHT HELP ME SENSE WHAT'S...
OH. OH, YOU POOR THING. WHAT HAVE THEY DONE TO YOU?
SO MUCH PAIN...I DON'T BLAME HIM FOR SHUTTING DOWN. HE NEEDS...
...HELP...

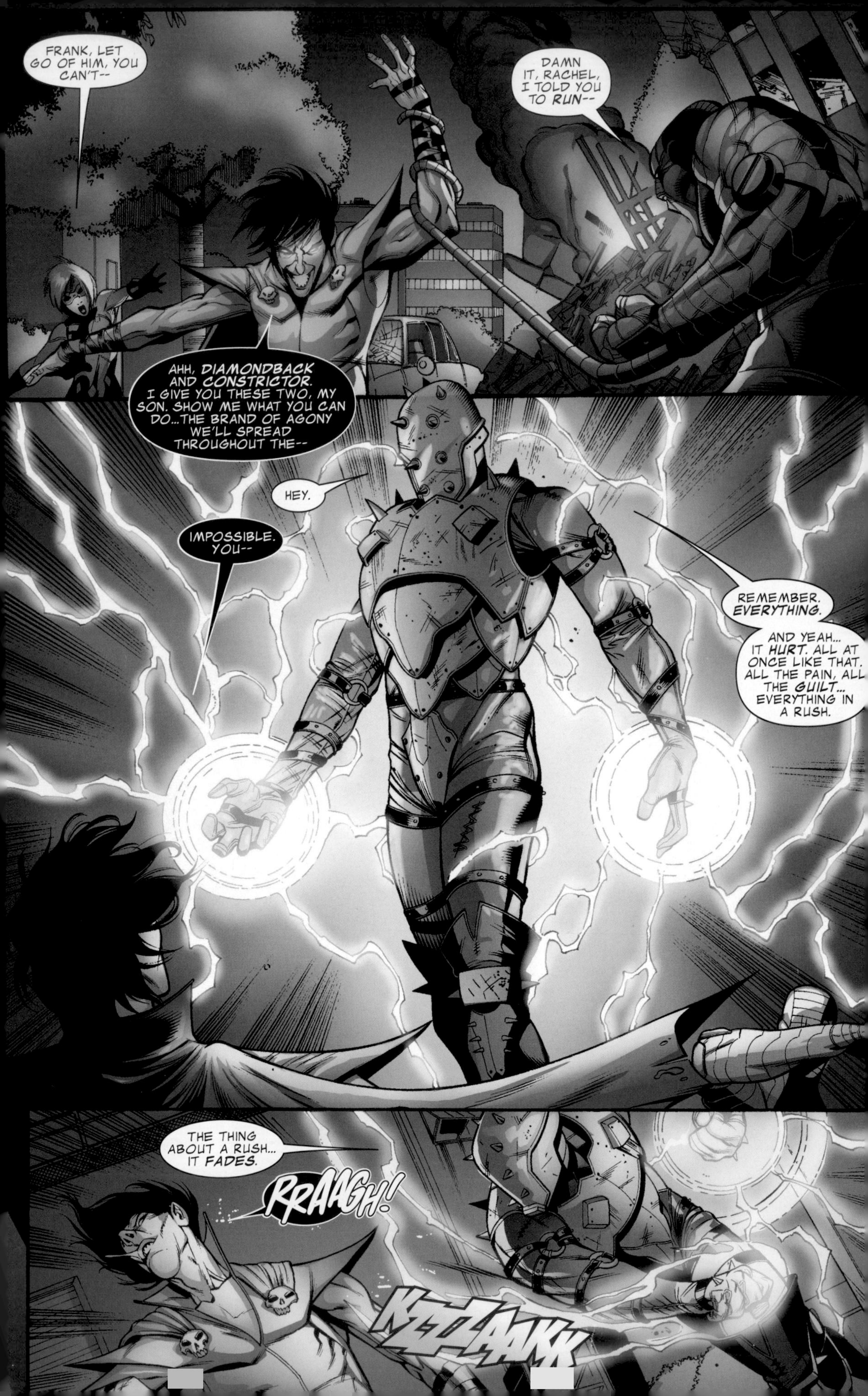

FRANK, LET GO OF HIM, YOU CAN'T--
DAMN IT, RACHEL, I TOLD YOU TO RUN--
AHH, DIAMONDBACK AND CONSTRICTOR. I GIVE YOU THESE TWO, MY SON. SHOW ME WHAT YOU CAN DO...THE BRAND OF AGONY WE'LL SPREAD THROUGHOUT THE--
HEY.
IMPOSSIBLE. YOU--
REMEMBER. EVERYTHING.
AND YEAH... IT HURT. ALL AT ONCE LIKE THAT. ALL THE PAIN, ALL THE GUILT... EVERYTHING IN A RUSH.
THE THING ABOUT A RUSH... IT FADES.
RRAAGH!
KZZZAAKK

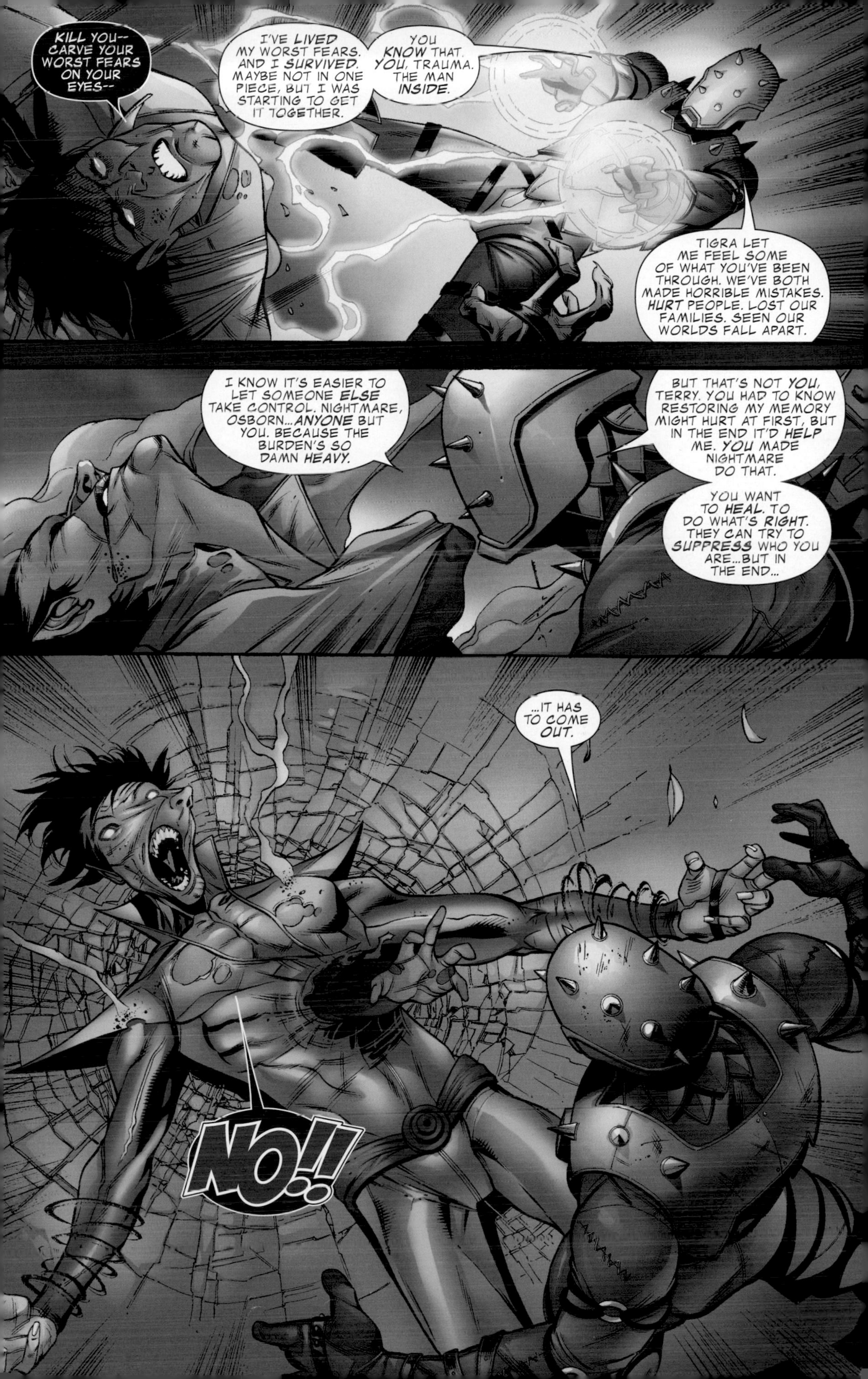
KILL YOU-- CARVE YOUR WORST FEARS ON YOUR EYES--
I'VE LIVED MY WORST FEARS. AND I SURVIVED. MAYBE NOT IN ONE PIECE, BUT I WAS STARTING TO GET IT TOGETHER.
YOU KNOW THAT. YOU, TRAUMA. THE MAN INSIDE.
TIGRA LET ME FEEL SOME OF WHAT YOU'VE BEEN THROUGH. WE'VE BOTH MADE HORRIBLE MISTAKES. HURT PEOPLE. LOST OUR FAMILIES. SEEN OUR WORLDS FALL APART.
I KNOW IT'S EASIER TO LET SOMEONE ELSE TAKE CONTROL. NIGHTMARE, OSBORN...ANYONE BUT YOU. BECAUSE THE BURDEN'S SO DAMN HEAVY.
BUT THAT'S NOT YOU, TERRY. YOU HAD TO KNOW RESTORING MY MEMORY MIGHT HURT AT FIRST, BUT IN THE END IT'D HELP ME. YOU MADE NIGHTMARE DO THAT.
YOU WANT TO HEAL. TO DO WHAT'S RIGHT. THEY CAN TRY TO SUPPRESS WHO YOU ARE...BUT IN THE END...
...IT HAS TO COME OUT.
NO!!

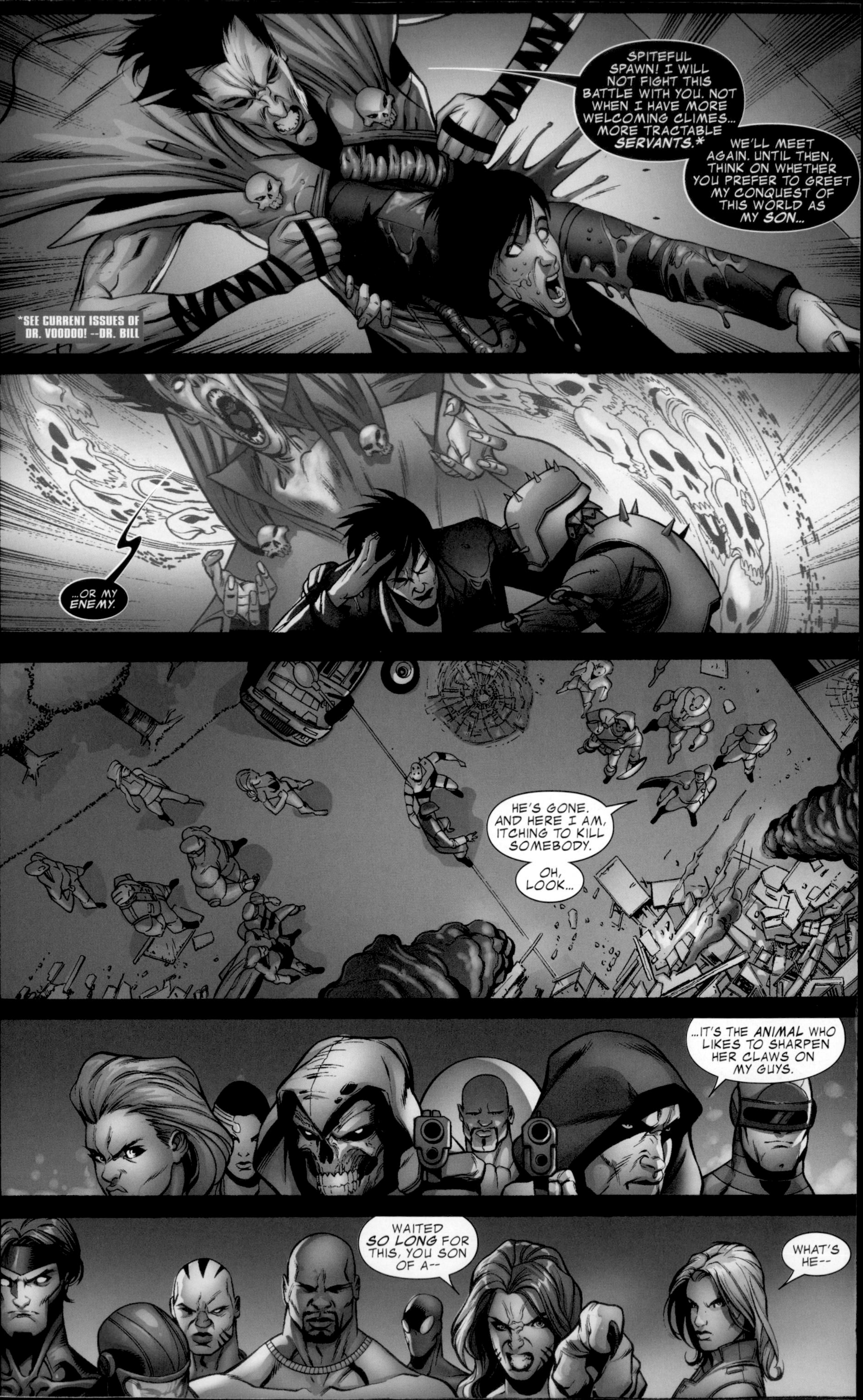
SPITEFUL SPAWN! I WILL NOT FIGHT THIS BATTLE WITH YOU. NOT WHEN I HAVE MORE WELCOMING CLIMES... MORE TRACTABLE SERVANTS.*
WE'LL MEET AGAIN. UNTIL THEN, THINK ON WHETHER YOU PREFER TO GREET MY CONQUEST OF THIS WORLD AS MY SON...
*SEE CURRENT ISSUES OF DR. VOODOO! --DR. BILL
...OR MY ENEMY.
HE'S GONE. AND HERE I AM, ITCHING TO KILL SOMEBODY.
OH, LOOK...
...IT'S THE ANIMAL WHO LIKES TO SHARPEN HER CLAWS ON MY GUYS.
WAITED SO LONG FOR THIS, YOU SON OF A--
WHAT'S HE--

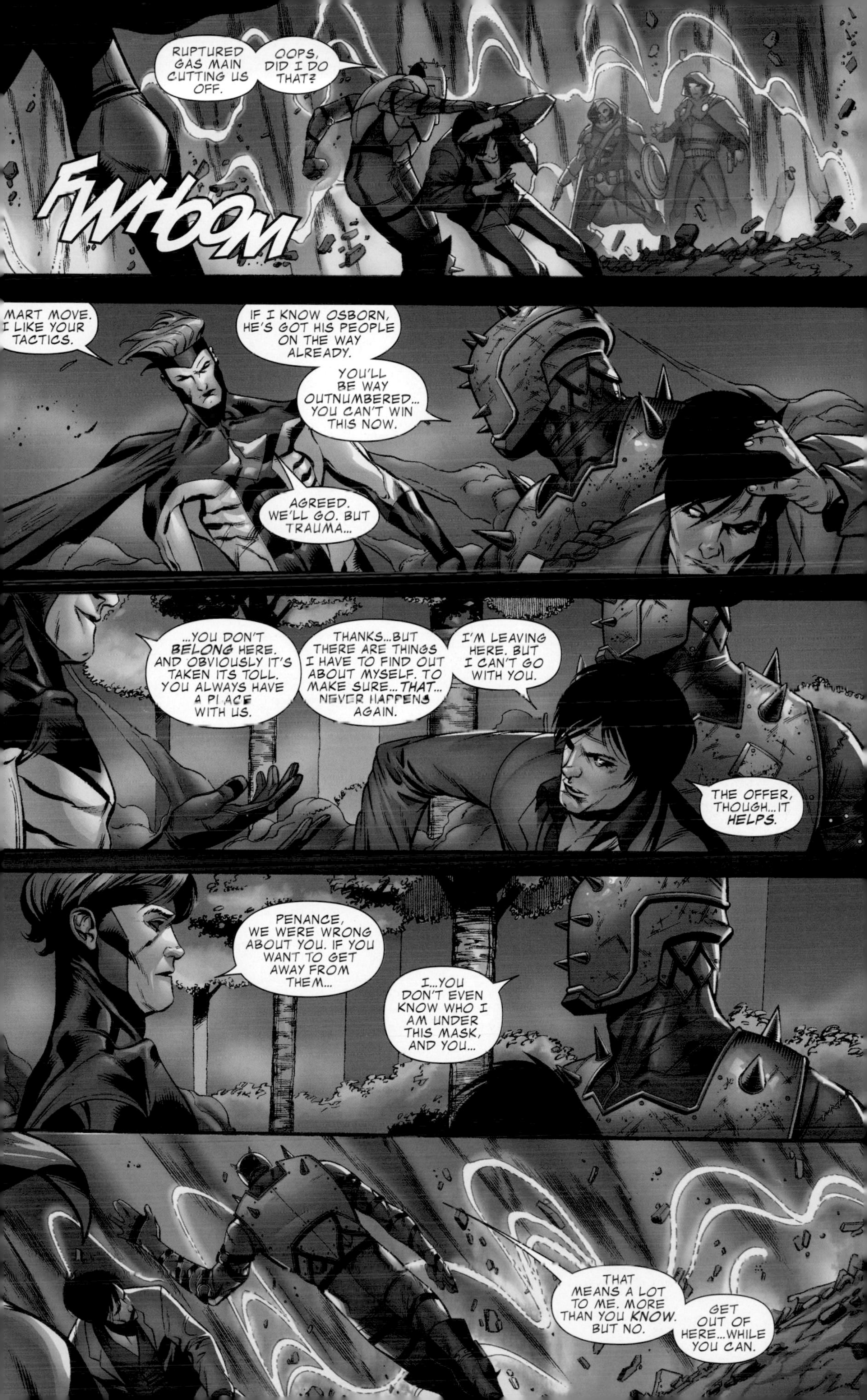
RUPTURED GAS MAIN CUTTING US OFF.
OOPS, DID I DO THAT?
FWHOOM
MART MOVE. I LIKE YOUR TACTICS.
IF I KNOW OSBORN, HE'S GOT HIS PEOPLE ON THE WAY ALREADY.
YOU'LL BE WAY OUTNUMBERED... YOU CAN'T WIN THIS NOW.
AGREED. WE'LL GO. BUT TRAUMA...
...YOU DON'T BELONG HERE. AND OBVIOUSLY IT'S TAKEN ITS TOLL. YOU ALWAYS HAVE A PLACE WITH US.
THANKS...BUT THERE ARE THINGS I HAVE TO FIND OUT ABOUT MYSELF. TO MAKE SURE...THAT... NEVER HAPPENS AGAIN.
I'M LEAVING HERE. BUT I CAN'T GO WITH YOU.
THE OFFER, THOUGH...IT HELPS.
PENANCE, WE WERE WRONG ABOUT YOU. IF YOU WANT TO GET AWAY FROM THEM...
I...YOU DON'T EVEN KNOW WHO I AM UNDER THIS MASK, AND YOU...
THAT MEANS A LOT TO ME. MORE THAN YOU KNOW. BUT NO.
GET OUT OF HERE...WHILE YOU CAN.

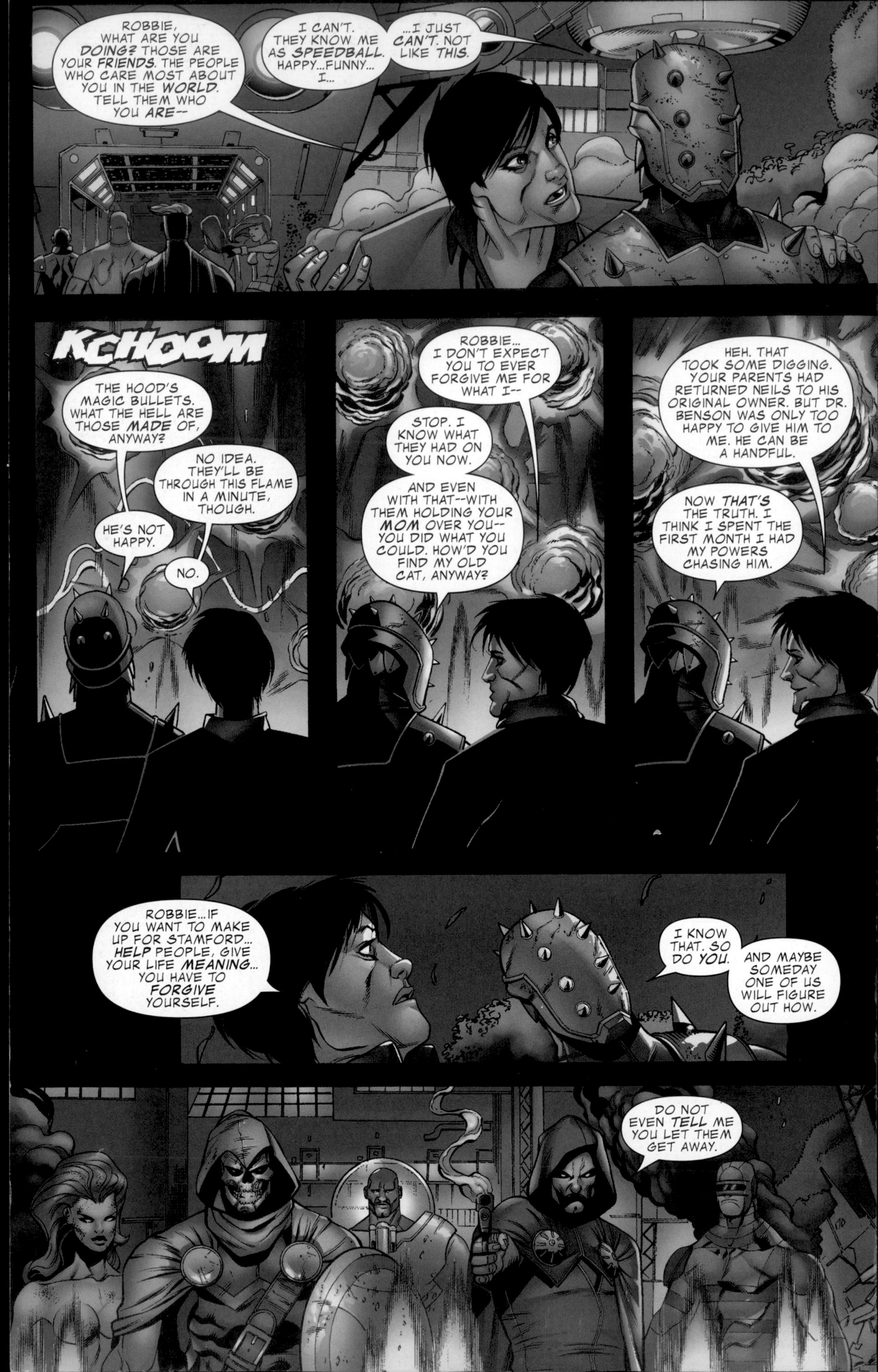
ROBBIE, WHAT ARE YOU DOING? THOSE ARE YOUR FRIENDS. THE PEOPLE WHO CARE MOST ABOUT YOU IN THE WORLD. TELL THEM WHO YOU ARE--
I CAN'T. THEY KNOW ME AS SPEEDBALL. HAPPY...FUNNY... I...
...I JUST CAN'T. NOT LIKE THIS.
KCHOOM
THE HOOD'S MAGIC BULLETS. WHAT THE HELL ARE THOSE MADE OF, ANYWAY?
NO IDEA. THEY'LL BE THROUGH THIS FLAME IN A MINUTE, THOUGH.
HE'S NOT HAPPY.
NO.
ROBBIE... I DON'T EXPECT YOU TO EVER FORGIVE ME FOR WHAT I--
STOP. I KNOW WHAT THEY HAD ON YOU NOW.
AND EVEN WITH THAT--WITH THEM HOLDING YOUR MOM OVER YOU--YOU DID WHAT YOU COULD. HOW'D YOU FIND MY OLD CAT, ANYWAY?
HEH. THAT TOOK SOME DIGGING. YOUR PARENTS HAD RETURNED NEILS TO HIS ORIGINAL OWNER. BUT DR. BENSON WAS ONLY TOO HAPPY TO GIVE HIM TO ME. HE CAN BE A HANDFUL.
NOW THAT'S THE TRUTH. I THINK I SPENT THE FIRST MONTH I HAD MY POWERS CHASING HIM.
ROBBIE...IF YOU WANT TO MAKE UP FOR STAMFORD... HELP PEOPLE, GIVE YOUR LIFE MEANING... YOU HAVE TO FORGIVE YOURSELF.
I KNOW THAT. SO DO YOU.
AND MAYBE SOMEDAY ONE OF US WILL FIGURE OUT HOW.
DO NOT EVEN TELL ME YOU LET THEM GET AWAY.

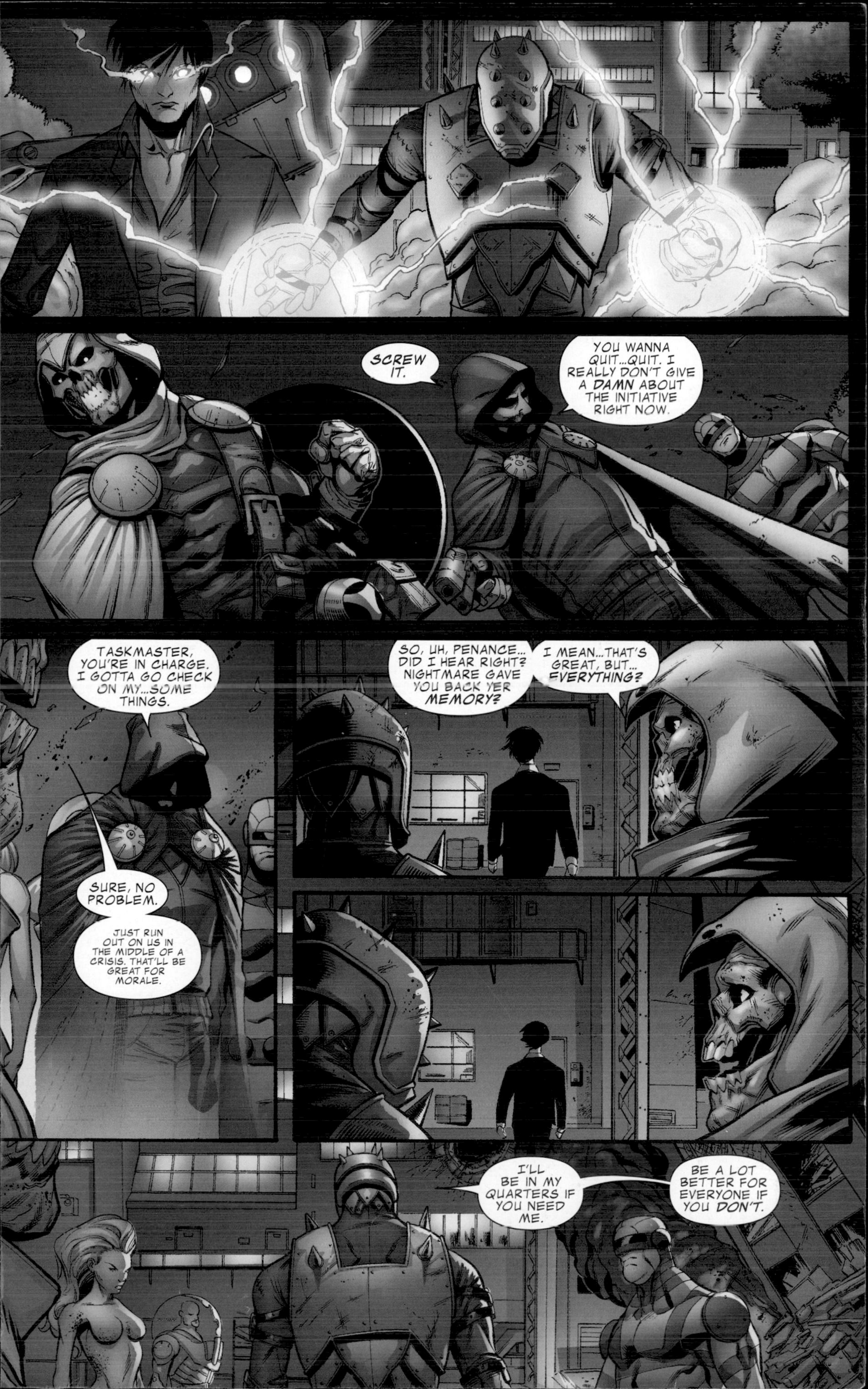
SCREW IT.
YOU WANNA QUIT...QUIT. I REALLY DON'T GIVE A DAMN ABOUT THE INITIATIVE RIGHT NOW.
TASKMASTER, YOU'RE IN CHARGE. I GOTTA GO CHECK ON MY...SOME THINGS.
SURE, NO PROBLEM.
JUST RUN OUT ON US IN THE MIDDLE OF A CRISIS. THAT'LL BE GREAT FOR MORALE.
SO, UH, PENANCE... DID I HEAR RIGHT? NIGHTMARE GAVE YOU BACK YER MEMORY?
I MEAN...THAT'S GREAT, BUT... EVERYTHING?
I'LL BE IN MY QUARTERS IF YOU NEED ME.
BE A LOT BETTER FOR EVERYONE IF YOU DON'T.

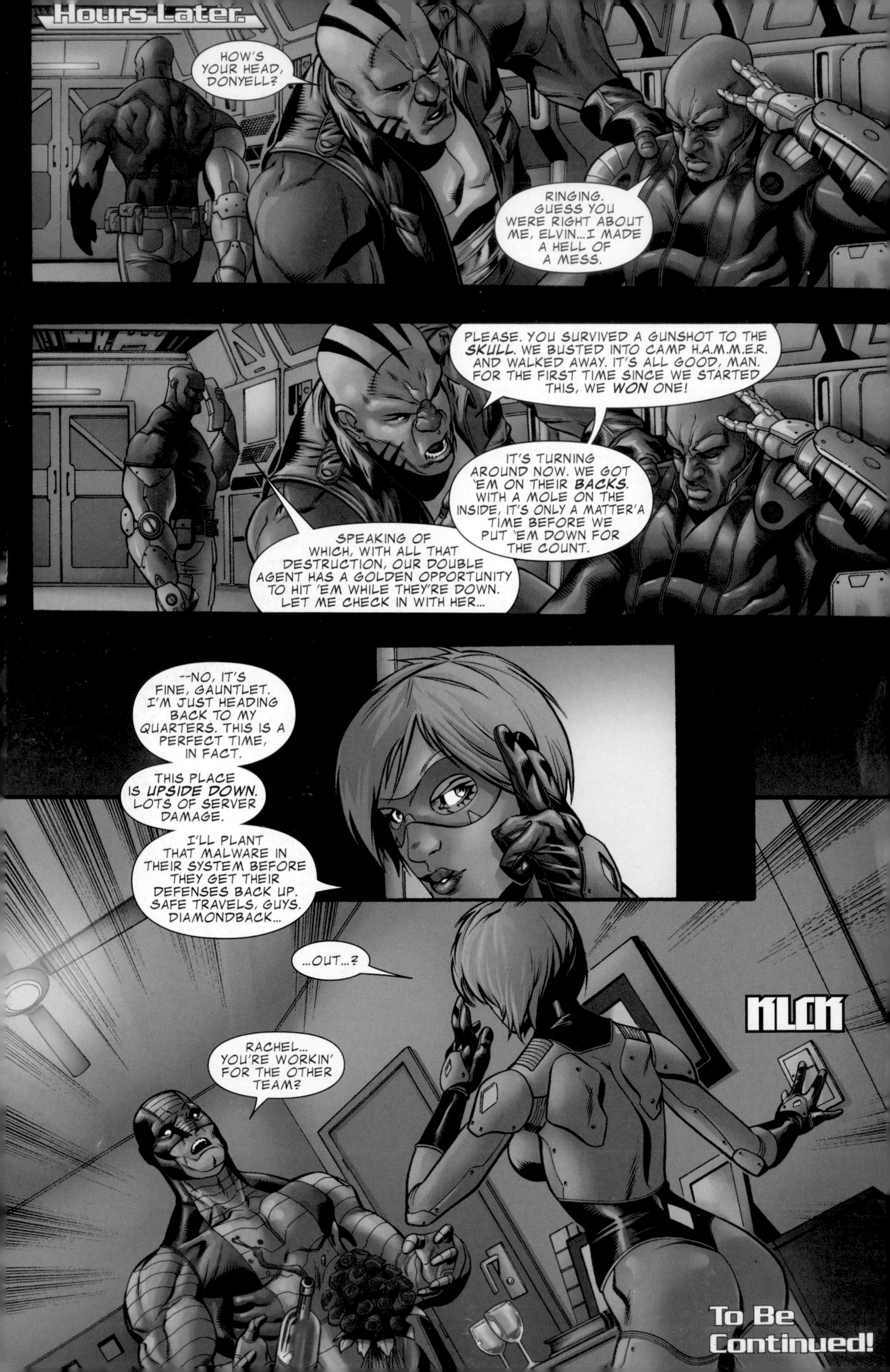
Hours Later
HOW'S YOUR HEAD, DONYELL?
RINGING. GUESS YOU WERE RIGHT ABOUT ME, ELVIN...I MADE A HELL OF A MESS.
PLEASE. YOU SURVIVED A GUNSHOT TO THE SKULL. WE BUSTED INTO CAMP H.A.M.M.E.R. AND WALKED AWAY. IT'S ALL GOOD, MAN. FOR THE FIRST TIME SINCE WE STARTED THIS, WE WON ONE!
IT'S TURNING AROUND NOW. WE GOT 'EM ON THEIR BACKS. WITH A MOLE ON THE INSIDE, IT'S ONLY A MATTER'A TIME BEFORE WE PUT 'EM DOWN FOR THE COUNT.
SPEAKING OF WHICH, WITH ALL THAT DESTRUCTION, OUR DOUBLE AGENT HAS A GOLDEN OPPORTUNITY TO HIT 'EM WHILE THEY'RE DOWN. LET ME CHECK IN WITH HER...
--NO, IT'S FINE, GAUNTLET. I'M JUST HEADING BACK TO MY QUARTERS. THIS IS A PERFECT TIME, IN FACT.
THIS PLACE IS UPSIDE DOWN. LOTS OF SERVER DAMAGE.
I'LL PLANT THAT MALWARE IN THEIR SYSTEM BEFORE THEY GET THEIR DEFENSES BACK UP. SAFE TRAVELS, GUYS. DIAMONDBACK...
...OUT...?
KLCK
RACHEL... YOU'RE WORKIN' FOR THE OTHER TEAM?
To Be Continued!